DEVELOPMENTS IN ENVIRONMENTAL ECONOMICS

VOLUME 1

Economics of Environmental Conservation:

Economics for Environmental & Ecological Management

DEVELOPMENTS IN ENVIRONMENTAL ECONOMICS

VOLUME 1

Economics of Environmental Conservation

Economics for Environmental & Ecological Management

by

Clement A. Tisdell

Department of Economics
University of Queensland
Queensland 4072
Australia

ELSEVIER
Amsterdam · London · New York · Tokyo

First edition 1991
Second printing 1993

ISBN: 0-444-89075-0

HD 75.6
T 563
1991

Published by:
Elsevier Science Publishers BV
P.O. Box 211
1000 AE Amsterdam
The Netherlands

Printed in The Netherlands on acid-free paper

Contents

10. Tourism, outdoor recreation and the natural environment

11. Sustainable development and conservation

12. Population, development and prospects for environmental sustainability: a concluding perspective

Preface

Study of the relationship between economic systems and ecological and environmental ones is important for managing and conserving the Biosphere on which all life, including that of humans, ultimately depends. Fortunately, the importance of combining economic, ecological and environmental studies is now increasingly recognised in policy circles worldwide as, for example, is evident from the report of the United Nations' World Commission on Environment and Development, *Our Common Future*, Oxford University Press, New York, 1987, and from subsequent international fora dealing with these matters. One might expect these relationships to be a central focus at the Second United Nations Conference on the Environment and Development to be held in Brasilia in 1992.

But the more relationships between economics, ecology and the environment are studied, the more acutely one becomes aware of the fact that our knowledge is imperfect, that many gaps remain to be filled and that we need to convince more people to join in exploration and discovery in this area because of the magnitude and importance of the task.

Of course, recognition is only the first step in dealing practically with an issue or problem. The second step is to study, observe and analyse it and develop relevant principles and from these, formulate an appropriate plan of action. The final step, from a practical point of view, is to put the plan of action or strategy into effect. In large, complex societies, such as modern ones, in which individuals are highly specialised in their social functions and activities, this requires co-operation or co-ordination between all groups in society, and given the global nature of many environmental and ecological effects of economic activity, it calls for international co-operation.

This book on environmental economics concentrates on the ecological dimensions of the subject. It concentrates on living or biological resources and their life-support systems. It considers the way in which economic development and change affects these and the way in which these resources can be better managed, or conserved to meet human objectives or aspirations. But it does not ignore the possibility of non-anthropocentric objectives. It also considers, in an economic context, the likelihood of Mankind being able to respond effectively to ecological and environmental crises and problems.

I hope that this book will be of interest, not just to economists, but to all those interested in ecological and environmental issues. To that end, I have written the book in a non-technical manner, preferring to concentrate on basic issues, some of which raise awkward philosophical questions. A deliberate attempt has been made to keep 'economic jargon' to a minimum and to explain economic terms used so as to make this material available to a wider audience.

Most of the material in this book has been exposed in one form or another to a wide range of audiences as part of lectures or seminars given in Australia, China, Hungary, New Zealand, South Africa, United Kingdom and the United States. I am grateful for the opportunities which have been available to me in all these countries to develop and express my ideas. Presentations have been given to both graduate and postgraduate students, to government bodies, in academic seminars and at international conferences. The number of individuals and organisations who should be mentioned is large so I shall not catalogue them here. My thanks to all who have helped in some way, no matter how small. However, I am especially grateful to David Pearce and Peter Jackson for their encouragement when I first floated with them the idea of a book along these lines (with an ecological focus) during a visit to the United Kingdom several years ago, and to Dr. John Gowdy of Rensselaer Polytechnic Institute, Troy, New York State for regularly urging me to complete the manuscript. Nicholas Polunin has encouraged my interest in environmental conservation in many ways and I value the support which has given me through his journal, *Environmental Conservation*. I am grateful to Brian Wilson, Vice-Chancellor of the University of Queensland, for thoughtfully supplying me on his return from Helsinki with a copy of the WIDER paper mentioned in Chapter 12. I also benefited greatly from the comments of anonymous reviewers (appointed by the publishers) on my introductory chapters. It has also been valuable to be able to 'try out' some of the material used in this book in lectures to environmental economics students at the Universities of Newcastle and Queensland, as well as elsewhere. Some of the material in Chapter 10, for example, was covered in lectures to tourism management students at the Nankai University, China, and MBA students at Queensland University.

While some of the research for this book was completed at the University of Newcastle, New South Wales, with the financial assistance of a small grant under the Australian Research Grants Scheme, practically the whole of the manuscript was completed at the University of Queensland. I am grateful to both institutions for their support. I wish to thank Jenny Hargrave from the University of Newcastle for typing the first draft of the initial chapters, and Deborah Ford of the University of Queensland for typing the entire final manuscript, in the format required by Elsevier Science Publishers. I would like to acknowledge the kind and efficient assistance of the staff of Elsevier in Amsterdam. Finally, but not least, I thank my wife Mariel, and children, Anne-Marie and Christopher, for being supportive once again.

Clem Tisdell,
Brisbane, Australia.

List of Tables

List of Figures

Chapter 1

Economics and the living environment

1.1 Introduction

Man's welfare and continuing existence depends upon the living environment because, apart from anything else, other species are biologically essential for Man's
existence, for example, via the food chain (Owen, 1975). The presence of other
living things influence human welfare, sometimes to Mankind's benefit but at
other times to his detriment, as with pests. We depend on nature for continuing
economic productivity, welfare and ultimately existence. Biological resources
should be taken into account in socio-economic planning and evaluation of economic systems. Conversely, economic analysis can be of value in helping to determine whether to conserve or utilise living resources.

This is not to say that Man's welfare depends only on biological resources but
rather that it depends significantly upon these resources. Furthermore, they may
become of greater importance to Mankind in the future as non-renewable resources such as fossil fuels are depleted. As the number of species in existence declines
and the human population increases, the value of remaining species to Man is
likely to rise substantially.

This book is principally concerned with the economics of conservation, utilisation and management of natural biological resources. It deals with economic factors that should be considered in devising policies for the conservation, utilisation
and management of biological resources. Such factors become increasingly important as our biological resources become scarcer from an economic point of
view. As stressed in the World Conservation Strategy (IUCN, 1980) and more recently in the Brundtland Report, *Our Common Future* (World Commission on Environment and Development, 1987), a strong case exists for biological conserva-

tion, even on economic grounds alone. Economics is an important consideration in biologically based activities such as wildlife conservation and use, pest control, agriculture, forestry, fisheries and living marine resources, the preservation and use of natural areas such as national parks and tourism based on natural resources. In turn these activities have further environmental consequences for Mankind. For example, forests and tree cover influence water quality, soil erosion and air quality. Indeed, economics is relevant to the whole Biosphere that is 'The integrated living and life-supporting system comprising the peripheral envelope of Plant Earth together with its surrounding atmosphere so far down, and up, as any form of life exists naturally' (Polunin, 1985).

1.2 Welfare economics, environment and the biosphere

Economics is the science which studies the allocation of scarce resources in society as a means to the satisfaction of human wants or desires. In order to deal with the essential problem of economics, one has to take account of available resources and methods of production of commodities, their exchange and the way in which income is distributed. Economics, as it has evolved, is essentially an anthropocentric (man-centred) subject. Nevertheless, this does not mean that economics cannot be supportive of the conservation of the environment and in particular the biosphere. Framers of the World Conservation Strategy (IUCN, 1980) and the World Commission on Environment and Development (1987) were correct in believing that economics can provide significant arguments in favour of conservation of biological resources. Conservation of environmental and biological resources is frequently required as a means of maximising human welfare (or at least, avoiding inferior welfare outcomes) in a world of limited resource availability. Let us therefore broadly consider the relevance of alternative types of welfare economics to biological conservation.

The major portion of the dominant theory of welfare economics is based upon the view that the wants of *individuals* are to be satisfied to the maximum extent possible by the allocation of resources. It is based, at least in the West, upon the view that individual preferences are to count and that human welfare is to be maximised subject either to existing property rights of individuals or to an ideal distribution of property rights.

The foundations of Western welfare economics were laid by the Utilitarian School. The Utilitarian School of economic thought believed that each individual obtains utility or measurable satisfaction from his or her consumption of commodities. It was argued that the use of society's resources should be such as to maximise the sum of utility obtained by individuals. Therefore, given this view, since components of the biosphere itself are used as inputs to produce commodities or to provide utility directly to individuals, it follows that management of the biosphere should be subject to the strategy of maximising the grand total of utility in society. Apart from other difficulties, the Utilitarian approach has foundered because utility has not proven to be measurable objectively and comparably between individuals.

This led to the substantial replacement of the Utilitarian approach to welfare economics by an alternative approach, sometimes called New Welfare Economics or Paretian Welfare economics after is chief proponent Vilfredo Pareto (Little, 1957). This is also an individualistic approach reliant on individual preferences but avoids interpersonal comparisons of utility. It is based upon the view that an economic system or a system for utilising resources should be efficient in satisfying human wants. Its basic tenet is that welfare cannot be at a maximum if it is possible to make any individual better off without making another worse off. Hence, a *necessary* condition for a maximum of human welfare is that it be impossible to alter the way in which society uses its resources to make any individual better off without making another worse off. No matter what is the distribution of property rights in society, the use of society's resources including the biosphere should be so organised (in the light of the production or transformation possibilities open to Mankind) that the welfare of no person can be increased without reducing that of another person. Many neo-classical economists argued that a system of perfect market competition would, with a few minor exceptions, achieve this social ideal. However, as discussed in later chapters, market mechanisms may fail significantly as means for ensuring a Paretian optimal use of resources, especially of those resources contained in the biosphere.

A rule closely related to Paretian optimality, is the notion of a Paretian improvement. A Paretian improvement is said to occur when as a result of a change in the use of resources some individuals are made better off without anyone being made worse off. It is usually contended that any change in resource-use which brings about a Paretian improvement is socially desirable. In practice, however, few possible changes may have this quality. It is more frequent for changes in resource-use to make some individuals worse off and others better off. For example, the acquisition of private land for a natural park or restrictions on private land-use for environmental reasons may damage the original landholders but benefit other groups.

The notion of *potential* Paretian improvement (sometimes called the *Kaldor-Hicks criterion*) was suggested as a means of dealing with this problem. It suggests that if the gainers from a change in resource use *could* compensate the losers from it and remain better off than before the change, the change should be regarded as an improvement. Note that actual compensation need not be paid to the losers. If compensation is paid then of course this criterion reduces to the Paretian criterion. The criterion of a *potential* Pareto improvement underlies much of social cost-benefit analysis which itself has been applied to decision-making involving the environment (Hufschmidt et al., 1983).

A difficulty with the Kaldor-Hicks criterion is that it may sanction a change in resource-use which seriously worsens the distribution of income. Cases have for example occurred in which land has been acquired for national parks without compensation or adequate compensation to the traditional users of the land who have sometimes been quite poor. In view of the income distribution question, Little (1957) has proposed that a potential Paretian improvement should only be unequivocally regarded as a social gain if it does not worsen the distribution of income. If a potential Pareto improvement is associated with a worsening of the distribution of income, one has to consider whether this is sufficient to offset the net benefits otherwise obtained.

While the above criteria (which can, for instance, be applied to piecemeal decision-making involving the environment) have an individualistic basis, the role of economising is not confined to social orderings having a individualistic basis. As Bergson (1938) has pointed out, a variety of different types of social welfare functions or social orderings are conceivable. They could for example reflect the values of *particular* individuals. Nevertheless, if one is to engage in economising one needs at least some preference ordering of the resource-use possibilities of society. Such an ordering need not be complete but if it is complete and transitive, it will allow an 'optimum' allocation of resources to be determined.

By way of introduction, consider how economics can help us conceptualise some *general* problems in the allocation of resources involving the biosphere and the environment. Conceptually, the natural environment or biosphere itself is able directly to produce goods, e.g., recreational opportunities, maintenance of a genetic stock of species, clean air and water. But in addition, Man draws upon the resources of the biosphere (uses these as inputs) to produce goods of his own creation, 'man-made' goods. There *may* therefore be a trade-off between the production of environmental natural goods and man-made goods. The production possibility frontier involving man-made goods and environmental natural goods might be of the type indicated by curve ABCD in Fig. 1.1. This indicates that the provision of natural environmental goods up to a level of x* is complementary to the production of man-made goods. Such complementarity might come about for example, because the retention of natural tree cover reduces flooding and erosion and helps maintain agricultural output. Given all the techniques available, the production possibility set might consist of the set bounded by OABD. Some techniques of production may for instance be such that the combination at point J results. Given that both more natural environmental goods and more man-made goods are desired, J is an inferior economic position. If welfare is to be maximised, society must adopt a pattern of resource-use that results in its being on its production possibility frontier in the efficiency segment BCD. Not only are combinations below the production possibility frontier socially inferior but in view of the complementarity relationship so too are combinations on the segment AHB.

In both these cases it is possible to produce more of all the types of desired goods by reorganising resource use.

It seems that a complementary production relationship does exist up to a point (a segment like AHB) between the production of man-made goods and goods provided by the natural environment and this on its own would provide an argument for conservation of biological resources. However, in addition humans directly value many goods produced by the natural environment. When this is taken into account, there is an additional economic reason to be concerned with the conservation and management of natural biological resources. Given the preference indicated by the indifference or iso-welfare curves marked W_1W_1, W_2W_2 and W_3W_3 in Fig. 1.1 (and assuming that these curves have the usual properties associated with indifference curves e.g., each indicates combinations giving an equal level of human welfare and higher curves are associated with greater welfare) (Tisdell, 1972), the combination at position C is socially optimal. This involves the production of y^{**} of man-made goods and x^{**} of environmental goods. Consequently it is optimal to forgo some man-made production for additional goods produced by the natural environment.

A position below the production possibility frontier such as J may come about because of the use of inferior technologies or because of a poor allocation of resources between man-made production and natural production e.g., some land areas comparatively suited to natural production may be allocated to man-made production and vice versa (cf. Tisdell, 1979, Ch. 1). A position such as H may be reached because of ignorance or because of common access to natural resources or in general due to deficiencies of societal mechanisms for managing resource-use. Specific reasons for such failures will be outlined in later chapters.

In some circumstances, social objectives may be expressed differently to that

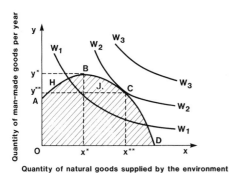

Figure 1.1. Choice and trade-off between supply of man-made goods and those provided by the natural environment.

6

just considered. A minimum 'standard' or target may be set for the production of natural goods of the environment. Economic considerations then need to be taken into account in an attempt to meet this standard if it is not already being achieved. The objective may be one of maximising some welfare function subject to the target. For example the objective may be to maximise man-made production subject to a target level of production of goods by the natural environment. The last rule can be illustrated by Fig. 1.2 which has the same interpretation as Fig. 1.1. If the target level of production of environmental goods is a level of not less than x** per year, this constraint can be represented by the line KLM. Position L involving the production of y** of man-made goods and x** of goods from the natural environment is the optimal Should however, the environmental constraint be below x* (which corresponds to point B) it will be optimal to achieve point B. For example, if the constraint is for production of goods of the natural environment of at least x' as represented by the constraining line M′K′, it is optimal to achieve point B because of the complementarity relationship. A similar set of considerations will apply if the objective is one of maximising the production of goods from the natural environment subject to a minimum level of production of man-made goods. It is also easy to illustrate the case where a preference function of the type indicated in Fig. 1.1 by indifference curves is to be maximised subject to constraints of the type just mentioned.

Cases can arise in which simultaneous constraints are placed on man-made production and production from the natural environment. Minimum levels may be set for both types of production. The basic decision-making problem then becomes one of determining whether it is possible given available transformation possibilities for resources to meet these constraints simultaneously. Economic factors need to be taken into account to determine this.

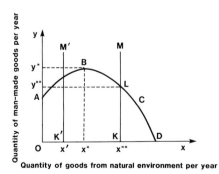

Figure 1.2. Choosing between goods provided by the natural environment and man-made goods subject to constraints or minimum 'standards'.

1.3 Ethics, values and environmental economics: alternative views

In considering any of the above matters, ethical assumptions cannot be avoided. Questions about ethics are important because all prescriptions about what society *ought* to do in managing the environment and natural resources are ultimately based on normative considerations and therefore involve value judgments. The review given in the previous section of the application of economics to the environment accords with mainstream economic thought as, for instance, outlined by Kneese and Schultze (1985) even though they use slightly different terminology. They refer to utilitarianism as classical utilitarianism and Paretian welfare economics as neoclassical utilitarianism or the Libertarian approach and point out that both approaches are anthropocentric, that is, man is the measure of all things. The value of natural environment is determined solely by the value placed on it by human beings and so in contrast to the naturalistic approach, nonhuman objects have no intrinsic values (Cf. Kneese and Schultze, 1985, p. 211).

Classical utilitarianism requires that human actions be chosen from an available set of alternative actions so as to maximise the good (utility) of the whole society taking account of all individuals including future generations. It may require an individual to take an action injurious to himself or herself for the good of the whole society. By contrast, neoclassical utilitarianism (the Paretian criterion) sanctions no actions which make any individual worse off, given an agreed system of property rights. Kneese and Schulze (1985, p. 211), point out that classical utilitarianism *may* sanction projects involving nuclear waste storage because the probable damages to future generations are much less than the present gains whereas the Paretian criterion may not sanction such storage assuming that future generations have a right to a risk-free nuclear environment. Similarly, the elimination of natural resources or environments and species of living things to provide a benefit to Mankind now but creating a net disbenefit to future generations may be sanctioned by classical utilitarianism but not by the Paretian criterion, it being assumed that future generations have (property) rights in existing natural environments.

The Kaldor-Hicks criterion of social choice (or criterion of a *potential* Paretian improvement) forms the basis for most social cost-benefit analysis and is also anthropocentric. It can give different indications to the utilitarian and Paretian criteria about desirability of social actions. For example, the Kaldor-Hicks criterion favours the destruction of a natural environment or species if gains to the current generation are more than sufficient to compensate future generations for any losses, whether or not compensation is made available. However, given that future generations have rights in present natural environments, the Paretian criterion does not support such action in the absence of compensation for these losses. The prescription of the classical utilitarian criterion depends upon the size of utility gains of beneficiaries compared to utility reductions suffered by future generations. It may not sanction a destructive action even when the Kaldor-Hicks criterion favours it.

All the above 'economic' criteria apart from being man-centred, assume at least implicitly that rational choices can be made by society. Mainstream economics is consequentialist focusing on the outcome of decisions. It contrasts with 'the historical view that the prevailing institutional structures that set the social framework between persons lie beyond any process of rational, deliberative evaluation and choice' (McLennen, 1983, p. 335). However, as discussed later, those economists rejecting the historicist view differ in their opinions about the extent to which existing social institutions limit rational choices by society.

The above overview does not capture the full diversity of choice-theoretic models used by economists, since a detailed study of choice – theoretic models would be misplaced in this context. A more detailed review, however, is given by McLennen (1983). In particular it is clear from Harsanyi (1977) and Sen and Williams (1982) that conceptions of utilitarianism show greater philosophical variation than can be portrayed in the above introductory review.

In the current context the contention by Cooter and Rappaport (1984) that modern economists have misinterpreted classical utilitarianism needs consideration. They claim that economists associated with classical utilitarianism (Bentham, Mill, Pigou and others) restricted economic considerations to material goods and saw economics as the science of 'material welfare'. They imagined that goods could be arranged in a hierarchical order with purely economic or material goods at one end and the purely non-economic or non-material ones at the other end. Purely economic needs definitely include necessities such as food, clothing and shelter but as one moves along the hierarchy to consider such items as comfort and leisure their material content is less certain and it is less clear that they are subjects for economics. Cooter and Rappaport (1984) claim that economists advocating classical utilitarianism restricted its application to material goods required for human welfare and this has not been realised by many modern economists (ordinalists). Cooter and Rappaport argue that if the restrictive application of classical utilitarianism is taken into account, interpersonal comparisons are supportable.

The modern view of economics is wider than that of the 'material welfare' approach. Economics, in accordance with the view expressed by Robbins (1937), is now generally seen to be science concerned with the social administration or management of scarce resources in order to satisfy to the maximum possible extent human desires for commodities, whether necessities or not. Robbins' approach to economics extended the list of goods of equally legitimate concern to economists. Provided someone does not have as much of a good as he/she desires, it is a subject for economics.

These two different interpretations of economics imply differences in its applicability to environmental conservation. The material welfare–utility approach suggests that economists (as economists) should only be concerned about environmental conservation to the extent that it affects material wealth or the supply of material goods, especially basic necessities. On the other hand, the Robbins' scarcity approach sees environmental conservation of relevance to economics provided that it uses scarce resources and affects human satisfaction. For example, the preservation of a species or a cultivar which could affect future food production, shelter or health would be a concern for economists given either approach. However, the preservation of a species having no consequence for material welfare would be excluded from economic concern given the material utility approach as outlined by Cooter and Rappaport (1984) but would be included on the basis of the more modern view if the presence of the species affected human satisfaction. A species valued solely by individuals for its existence (existence-value) is a subject for economic analysis on the basis of the modern view but not if the material utility approach is adopted. The material welfare approach since it concentrates on basic material needs seems more appropriate to a society in a general state of poverty (a less developed one) than to a more affluent one.

The influence of the materialistic school remains strong in that economic growth and increases in production of material goods as measured by GDP are often taken as indicators of rising economic welfare. As demonstrated by a number of writers (Pearce, et al., 1989; Barkley and Seckler, 1972; Boulding, 1970; Mishan, 1967) rises in Gross Domestic Production (GDP) and in the gross output of material goods and marketed goods, are sometimes associated with a decrease in welfare rather than an increase in welfare. For instance, GDP might rise and the state of the environment can decline to such an extent that welfare actually falls.

An important issue for the applicability of traditional economics to environmental issues and other matters is the extent to which goals and preferences of individuals are moulded by institutions. Traditional welfare economics respects the preferences of individuals. But to the extent that pre-existing institutions determine goals and preferences, individual preferences do not have independent status, and choice and strategies are indirectly constrained by such institutions. Kelso (1977) argues that for the last 400 years our institutions have moulded our preferences towards greater consumption, production and economic growth. He suggests that institutions and educational processes need to be altered so that preservation rather than consumption is seen as an important goal in itself. This theme is also reflected in the writings of Boulding (1966), Ciriacy-Wantrup (1963), Daly (1980) and Georgescu-Roegen (1971). While these approaches are not entirely man-centred, those of Daly and of Georgescu-Roegen emphasise the importance of natural resource conservation as a means of ensuring the longest possible period of survival for the human species. Thus to this extent, they remain man-centred.

The idea, however, that man has ethical responsibilities towards nature, apart from his own self-interest has gained ground in Western Culture despite the anthropocentric nature of Christianity in its Western form (White, 1969; Passmore, 1974; Kneese and Schulze, 1985). Several writers claim that Man has a responsibility to act as a steward for nature and in particular, to conserve species even in the absence of utilitarian or pragmatic benefits to Man. For instance, Aldo Leopold (1933, 1966) argues that Man is a holistic part of an organic community, of a web of life, and has no special right to exterminate parts of it, even species of predators. In this community one must live in harmony with the whole of nature or land. As Worcester (1985) points out, Leopold's views about conservation were intended to contrast strongly with the utilitarian efficiency, man-centred approach to the use and management of nature. Leopold believed that his 'land ethic' involving respect for nature as a community was a way out of the narrow economic attitude toward nature management that had come to dominate ecology (Worcester, 1985, p. 289).

As pointed out in the previous section, it is possible to incorporate constraints on man-centred actions into rational or choice-theoretic policy models. Such choice models can be modified or varied in several ways to accommodate naturalistic ethics. However, in many cases the rights of non-human objects and naturalistic ethics are insufficiently defined for this purpose by proponents of naturalistic ethics. Furthermore in some instances, proponents of naturalistic ethics reject the application of choice-theoretic models to public policy, some preferring to take a more romantic view of the world or to stress the limits of rationality. Conflicts about ethics tend to become sharper when resource allocation over time is at stake. Let us turn to this matter.

1.4 Economic growth, dynamics, uncertainty and the environment: differing views

Opinions differ considerably about the consequences of economic growth for the natural environment and about the extent to which continuing economic growth is sustainable and desirable. A long standing question for Mankind has been what are the limits to economic growth given that natural resources are an important, indeed an essential input for economic production and are limited in availability. Since at least the late 1700s a number of prominent social philosophers, including economists, have seen natural resources as the basic constraint to continuing unlimited economic growth. While the actual basis of the argument has altered somewhat and has been extended, most arguments concerning ultimate limits to economic growth are based upon the view that natural resources (such as soil, water, minerals, forests, air) either as inputs for production or receptors for human wastes, constitute the main limits to the continued expansion of economic production. In this respect, it might be noted that classical and neoclassical economists used the term 'land' to include all natural resources (or gifts of God).

Early arguments about such limits were based on the law of diminishing marginal productivity of land used for production. This is implicit in the thesis of Malthus (1798) that human population tends to increase in geometrical progression whereas economic production expands only in arithmetic progression. Assuming that human population tends to increase when incomes per head are above subsistence level, Malthus was led to the gloomy view that incomes per head above subsistence level would not be sustainable in the long run unless individuals consciously controlled their reproductive activity. For instance, he suggested late marriages as one possibility.

David Ricardo (1817) developed the Malthusian model more explicitly and extended it specifically by taking account of the law of diminishing marginal productivity. With increasing population, individuals would be forced to cultivate more marginal lands, utilise less productive forest areas and fishing grounds, open less productive mines and so on. Consequently, though production might increase, it would increase at a decreasing rate in the absence of technological progress because production would *extend* to use natural resources of decreasing additional productive value. At the same time, intensified use of already employed natural resources would occur, again with diminishing marginal contributions to production.

The Ricardian view of limits to growth posed by natural resource scarcity can be illustrated by Fig. 1.3. Imagine that the state of technological knowledge in society is such that curve OEBF (representing production function $Y = f_1(P)$) indicates the overall level of production achievable at alternative population levels remembering that population provides labour for productive effort. Production is shown to increase with population increases but at a diminishing rate because of the operation of the law of diminishing returns. The line OD represents the total

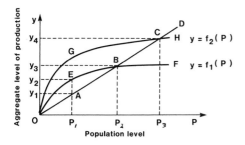

Figure 1.3. Ricardian model of limits to economic growth emphasising importance of population levels and of technological change.

level of production necessary to sustain each level of population at subsistence level. (Its slope is equivalent to the subsistence level of income per capita.)

In this model, given that population tends to increase when income per head is above subsistence level, equilibrium is achieved when population has reached a level resulting in just enough total production to support the level of population at the subsistence level. This corresponds in Fig. 1.3 with the intersection point, B, of the production function with line OD and implies an equilibrium level of population of P_2 and an equilibrium level of total output of Y_3 given the conditions previously described. For example, if the population level is initially at P_1, income per head, Y_2/P_1, is greater than the subsistence level, Y_1/P_1, and population increases. As it does so, income per head falls and eventually falls to subsistence levels when a population level of P_2 is reached.

Ricardo, however, was aware that expansion in scientific and technological knowledge could stave off a reduction in per capita income even given population growth. This it could do in effect by shifting the production function upwards over time. As illustrated in Fig. 1.3, the production curve might shift up with the passage of time to become curve OGCH which corresponds to production function, $Y = f_2 (P)$ and is higher than OEBF.

Note that this model has an optimistic implication: If population growth can be limited and technological progress can be maintained, income per capita can rise continually. Even in the absence of technological progress, it suggests that relatively high per capita incomes are sustainable *provided that* population growth can be contained.

The Ricardian model is important in highlighting the crucial importance of human population growth as an element in the sustainability of per capita incomes, even though it neglects a number of other important considerations. The Ricardian model also brings attention to the fundamental importance of growing scientific and technological knowledge as a means of overcoming the production limitations posed by natural resources. Indeed, some technological optimists dismiss concerns about population growth and deteriorating environmental conditions believing that scientific and technological progress can be relied on to overcome such possibilities. The technological optimists include amongst their numbers, Engels, Karl Marx's friend and benefactor, who rejects Malthus' fear of overpopulation and view that production increases by an arithmetic progression, claiming that

'..... Science increases at least as much as population. The latter increases in proportion to the size of the previous generation, science advances in proportion to the knowledge bequeathed to it by the previous generation, and thus under the most ordinary conditions also in geometrical progression. And what is impossible to science?' (Engels, 1955 [1844], p. 204).

In more recent times this optimistic view has been presented forcefully by Julian

Simon (1981). He basically argues that the larger is the world's population, the more minds there are and the greater is growth in knowledge. In his view this expansion of knowledge will overcome resource-constraints to population growth. This rather simplistic view is considered in the next section.

Following Ricardo, some prominent economists continued to be concerned about the prospects for sustainable economic growth. These included John Stuart Mill (1964, reprint) who saw some virtue in having a stationary economic state, that is one in which population growth and economic production is stationary. Jevons (1972–1977) expressed his concern about the depletion of non-renewable natural resources as a result of economic growth, in particular mineral deposits especially coal. Nevertheless, by the end of the Nineteenth Century an optimistic view of prospects for continuing economic growth prevailed. Few economists paid much attention to natural resources as a limitation on economic growth until the late 1960s. Problems of full employment (not surprisingly in the light of the Great Economic Depression of the 1930s), inflation, market structure and competition and formal welfare economics preoccupied most economists. After World War II, the main emphasis of policies was on the need to achieve continuing economic growth so as to maintain full employment and to improve living standards. Economic growth was viewed as desirable on both grounds. By the late 1960s, however, new and renewed concerns about environmental and natural-resource limitations to economic growth began to be expressed.

These concerns include the following:

(1) Wastes and pollution are end-products of economic production and consumption. These end-products were ignored in earlier economic theories. With economic growth, waste emissions can be expected to rise and pollutants are likely to build up in the environment and threaten production, human health and welfare.

(2) Economic growth is attained to a considerable extent by drawing on the *stock* of non-renewable natural resources. Stocks of some important resources used in modern production, such as oil, may become exhausted or depleted in the near future and this may impede future production.

(3) Living resources unless subjected to extreme conditions are normally renewable but economic growth is unfortunately subjecting an ever increasing range of living resources to extreme conditions and rendering them non-renewable. Amongst other things, this loss of genetic diversity may hamper future economic production and make current economic growth unsustainable.

(4) Economic growth by reducing environmental quality can depress the quality of human existence. Let us consider each of these concerns in more detail:

(1) *Wastes and pollution as end-products of economic activity*

Economic production and human activity produce wastes. Many of these wastes are returned to the environment and cause pollution. In the past, economists usually ignored the problem of wastes in modelling economic activity. However, continuing economic growth can lead to growing environmental pollution with adverse consequences for economic production and human health. In more and more instances, the ability of the natural environment to assimilate wastes (and in essence recycle these or render them innocuous) are likely to be exceeded as a result of rising economic production. There are also *global* dangers from pollution to consider such as the 'greenhouse effect', the possible warming of the atmosphere, as a result of such factors as rising carbon dioxide levels due to the combustion of fossil fuels and the destruction of forests. Local climatic conditions might be altered by the 'greenhouse effect' and it could trigger melting of the ice-caps and so result in considerable rises in sea levels. Or to take another example, nuclear production of electricity does not appear to add to the 'greenhouse effect' but accidents at power stations or in nuclear waste storage can involve wide-spread, even global, radiation risks.

(2) *Depletion of non-renewable resources*

Beginning in the 1960s, renewed concern was expressed about the possible depletion of non-renewable natural resources, especially fossil fuels such as oil and coal, as a result of economic growth. The substantial rises in oil prices in the 1970s [even though mainly a result of a cartel agreement by OPEC (Organisation of Petroleum Exporting Countries) to restrict supplies] seemed to add to the urgency of the problem. Even the National Academy of Sciences in the USA published reports predicting imminent shortages of renewable resources. One of its reports estimated that world crude oil production would peak by 1990 and that all but 10 per cent of world reserves would be exhausted by 2032. It further predicted that if petroleum products (crude oil, natural gas, natural-gas liquids, tar-sand, oil) continue to supply the bulk of the world's energy requirements only 10 per cent of these reserves are likely to remain after 2070 (National Academy of Sciences, 1969). The influential report for the Club of Rome, *Limits to Growth* prepared by Meadows et al., (1972) also stressed imminent shortages of minerals and metals as a result of economic growth.

(3) *Loss of genetic diversity*

Society has in recent years become more keenly aware of the possible and actual dangers of economic growth to the abundance, existence and diversity of living resources and their life-support systems. The dangers to living species include (a) rising levels of wastes and pollutants from agriculture (pesticides, artificial fertilisers for example), from industry such as emissions of sulphuric acids associated with acid rains, and from human consumption of products; (b) loss of space and habitat by non-human species because of its appropriation by humans for their use; (c) increased competition of humans with other species for common food sources and (d) more efficient and larger-scale direct destruction of non-human species either as pests or for utilisation by Man. Some of these issues are addressed for example by Hardin (1960) and Myers (1979). The *World Conservation Strategy* (IUCN, 1980; IUCN-UNEP-WWF, 1990) specifies conservation policies believed to be necessary to secure sustainable economic development and benefit Man. Trends in the disappearance of living resources are not only worrying from the point of view of naturalistic ethics but also because in the long-term the loss of genetic diversity may endanger the economic welfare of Man (Brown and Shaw, 1982).

(4) *Economic production and the quality of life*

Economists, sociologists and others have become increasingly aware of several ways in which materialistic economic growth, especially as measured by increases in GDP (Gross Domestic Product) can reduce the quality of life and human welfare. Economic growth can lead to a more polluted and less diversified environment, crowding and increased time being spent in travelling to work, reduced control by individuals and local communities over their environment, their economic fortunes, and so on. Views of this type can be found for example, in Mishan (1967). Substantial agreement exists that GDP and GDP per capita are a very imperfect measures of welfare (Barkley and Seckler, 1972; Mishan, 1967), and attempts have been made to construct more suitable indices (Nordhaus and Tobin, 1970).

Widely divergent opinions exist about the extent of possible disbenefits from and limits to economic growth. [Compare for example the views of Beckermann (1973) and Simon (1981) with those of Mishan (1967) and of Daly (1980).] Disbenefits or costs of economic growth do not always outweigh benefits – in some circumstances economic growth improves environmental quality, judged from a human perspective. For example, in the last 150 years expected length of life in Western countries has increased partly as a result of improvements in public health, for instance as a result of better sanitation, quality of community drinking water and immunisation (Culyer, 1980, p. 209). Economic growth can, but need not, lead to a reduction in environmental quality. Nevertheless, some social philosophers believe that continuing economic growth is fundamentally unsustainable. For instance, Daly (1980) suggests if the human species is to survive for as long as possible that the appropriate policy is to promote zero population growth (ZPG) and reduce levels of the capita consumption in developed countries, that is, adopt a steady-state economic approach in which consumption resource use is restrained. Georgescu-Roegen (1971) expresses a similar viewpoint.

Considerable uncertainty exists about the likely future environmental effects of economic growth. Because we do not fully know the future value of resources, such as species, but will learn more about their value as time passes, it can be rational (from an economic point of view) to conserve resources that otherwise might be irreversibly utilised or altered now (Arrow and Fisher, 1974). This is so even when individuals are not risk-avoiders. The argument for conservation may be strengthened even further if individuals are risk-avoiders. In practice, considerable conflict exists between individuals in society about the extent to which we should avoid collective risks, for example, from nuclear wastes or species extinction. It is essential to take account of uncertainty in most decisions involving the use of natural resources and the environment.

1.5 Environmental quality and resource availability trends: broad estimates and projections

Several studies have been completed since 1970 estimating environmental and resource trends (that is, trends in the quality of the environment, resource-use and availability) and making predictions about future patterns. An early, well-known and influential report was that prepared for the Club of Rome (Meadows et al., 1972). Here attention will be focused on *The Global 2000 Report to the President of the U.S.* (Barney, 1980) because it gives greater attention to biological resources. The issues raised in this report will continue to be important at least into the next Century and continue to be raised in more recent reports such as the Brundtland Report (World Commission on Environment and Development, 1987) and in *Caring for the World* (IUCN-UNEP-WWF, 1990). Projections into the next century (see Chapter 12) confirm the trends highlighted in *The Global 2000 Report*.

    The Global 2000 Report suggests that rising global levels of human population and growing levels of per capita consumption may create severe natural resource shortages and pollution problems by the early part of the next Century.

Its predictions can be summarised as follows:

(1) *Population.* By the end of this Century (by 2000), the world's population is expected to increase by 50 per cent to 6.35 billion. It is anticipated that 90 per cent of this growth will be in the world's poorest countries. While the rate of world population growth is expected to decline, the anticipated fall from 1.8% per year to 1.7% is marginal.

(2) *Food and Agriculture.* Although food production is expected to rise by 90%, most of the increase in per capita consumption is predicted to occur in developed countries and in fact, per capita food consumption in less developed countries is expected to remain static. The scope for raising the amount of arable land under cultivation is small (4% increase projected by 2000) so most of the increase in food production will have to be met by more intensive cultivation of land already cropped. This may require greater use of non-renewable and potentially polluting inputs such as artificial fertilisers, pesticides and fuel.

(3) *Energy*. Energy resources are predicted to remain in short supply and to be a continuing source of pollution.

(4) *Water*. Regional water shortages are forecasted to become more severe as population rises, and standards of living increase in some regions. In half the world, population growth will double water requirements even if old standards are maintained. In many less developed countries (LDCs), water supplies will become more erratic as a result of intensive deforestation.

(5) *Forests*. Considerable declines in the world's forests are anticipated. These forests are now disappearing at the rate of 20 million hectares per year (about half the area of California) mainly to supply forest products and firewood. Most of these losses are occurring in the humid tropical forests of Africa, Asia and South America. It is estimated that about half of the remaining forest cover in LDCs will be lost by 2000 with serious consequences for the extinction of species, the environment and economic production.

(6) *Soils*. Serious deterioration of agricultural soils is occurring worldwide due to erosion, loss of organic matter, desertification, salinization, alkalinization and waterlogging. Losses are expected to continue.

(7) *Extinction of Species*. Given current trends, extinctions of plant and animal species are expected to increase dramatically. Half to two million species (15–20 per cent of estimated numbers of species present now) could be lost by 2000. A large proportion of this loss will be due to reduction in areas of tropical forests and their disturbance, but other factors such as physical alterations in the landscape and pollution resulting from Man's activities will play a role.

(8) *Fisheries*. Sustainable yields obtained by traditional fisheries are not likely to increase or to increase significantly. Overfishing is already a problem in a number of countries and in many cases yields are already falling.

(9) *Low-Probability, High-Risk Events Affecting All Environments*. In recent times, the world has become more susceptible to low-probability high-risk events. These include the possibility of widespread disruption of food production due to increased fluctuations in climatic conditions, the possible 'greenhouse effects', potential barriers to maintaining the yield from modern crops and animals given

the disappearance of wild progenitors needed for breeding purposes to provide resistance to pests and pathogens, global nuclear risks and so on. Risks of this nature and the range of phenomena involving potentially disastrous events, are expected to increase rather than decrease.

While projections in the Global 2000 study, may overestimate demands on natural resources and their irreversible decline, it does highlight resource issues of widespread concern requiring continuing attention. It is very difficult, for instance, to estimate future growth of gross world product. It is *possible*, as indicated in the Report, that estimates used by the study for 2000 are too high by 15–20 per cent (Barney, 1980, p. 45) so demands on natural resources and environmental consequences of economic growth could be less that projected in the study. Nevertheless, the extreme optimism projected by writers such as Simon (1981) also appears misplaced.

Simon (1981) suggests that we are not 'entering an age of scarcity'. He argues that in fact natural resources have actually fallen in price and are becoming less scarce, on average there is less pollution as reflected in greater human longevity, and increasing population is not a problem since the additional persons normally produce more than they consume and add to the accumulation of knowledge and so productivity. As he points out, however, 'you can see anything you like in a crystal ball' (Simon, 1981, p. 3). Furthermore, he does not address the issue of the threat to other living species and its possible consequences.

Whatever one predicts about *future* natural resource scarcity and the likely condition of the environment, many natural-resource and environmental problems are with us now. *The Global 2000 Report* and more recently *Our Common Future* (World Commission on Environment and Development, 1987) highlight these problems.

1.6 Conclusion

Man has substantially altered the natural environment and is likely to change it further with the passage of time and economic growth. (For further evidence on this see, for example, World Resources Institute and International Institute for Environment and Development, 1986.) These variations can have important consequences for economic welfare and development, society and the quality of life. It is naive to believe that all such changes are bound to be beneficial to Mankind although many may be.

Especially taking into account irreversibilities in resource-use, it is necessary to consider natural resource trends and make projections even though these are based on assumptions and are subject to considerable uncertainty. Economic and resource predictions need to be made and taken into account for such projections.

In that respect, economics has a role to play. Furthermore, economics has *a part* to play in the more immediate management of the natural environment, especially in the evaluation of alternative uses of available resources.

Economic evaluations are based on *particular* sets of ethical assumptions. The contributions of economics therefore remain qualified. Nevertheless, in a holistic approach to environmental management and prediction, economics cannot be ignored. Economics provides useful tools *to assist* in environmental decision-making even though it cannot supplant the final judgment of the decision-maker. The economics discipline can make and has made a worthwhile contribution to environmental policy discussions and decisions. This book aims to illustrate this particularly for the management of natural biological resources.

References

Arrow, K.J. and Fisher, A.C., 1974. Environmental preservation, uncertainty and irreversibility. Quarterly Journal of Economics, 88:313–319.

Barkley, P.W. and Seckler, D.W., 1972. Economic Growth and Environmental Decay: The Solution Becomes the Problem. Harcourt, Brace and Jovanovich, New York.

Barney, G.O., 1980. The Global 2000 Report to the President of the U.S. Entering the 21st Century. Pergamon, New York.

Bergson, A., 1938. A reformulation of certain aspects of welfare economics. Quarterly Journal of Economics, 52:310–334.

Boulding, K.E., 1970. Fun and games with Gross National Product – role of misleading indicators in social policy. In: H.W. Helfrisch Jr. (Editor), The Environmental Crisis: Man's Struggle to Live with Himself. Yale University Press, New Haven.

Boulding, K.E., 1966. The economics of the coming spaceship Earth. In: H. Jarrett (Editor), Environmental Quality in a Growing Economy. John Hopkins University Press, Baltimore, pp. 3–14.

Brown, L.R. and Shaw, P., 1982. Six Steps to a Sustainable Society. Worldwatch Institute, Washington.

Cooter, R. and Rappaport, P., 1984. Were the ordinalists wrong about welfare economics? Journal of Economic Literature, 22:507–530.

Culyer, A.J., 1980. The Political Economy of Social Policy. Martin Robertson, Oxford.

Daly, H.E., 1980, Economics, Ecology, Ethics. Freeman, San Francisco.

Engels, F., 1959. Outlines of a critique of political economy in: K. Marx, Economic and Philosophic Manuscripts of 1844. Foreign Languages Publishing House, Moscow.

Georgescu-Roegen, N., 1971. The Entropy Law and the Economic Process. Harvard University Press, Harvard, Cambridge, Mass.

Hardin, G., 1960. Nature and Man's Fate. Cape, London.

Harsanyi, J., 1977. Rational Behaviour in Bargaining Equilibrium in Games and Social Situations. Cambridge University Press, New York.

Hufschmidt, M.M., James, D.E., Meister, A.D., Bower, B.T. and Dixon, J.A., 1983. Environment, Natural Systems and Development. Johns Hopkins University Press, Baltimore.

IUCN, 1980. The World Conservation Strategy: Living Resource Conservation for Sustainable Development. International Union for the Conservation of Nature and Natural Resources, Glands, Switzerland.

IUCN-UNEP-WWF, 1990. Caring for the World: A Strategy for Sustainability. Second draft, World Conservation Union, Glands, Switzerland.

Jevons, W.S., 1972–1977. Papers and Correspondence of William Stanley Jevons. R.D.C. Black and R. Konekemp (Editors). Macmillan, London.

Kelso, M.M., 1977. Natural resource economics the upsetting discipline. American Journal of Agricultural Economics, 59:814–823.

Kneese, A. and Shulze, W.D., 1985. Ethics and environmental economics. In: A.V. Kneese and J.L. Sweeney (Editors), Handbook of Natural Resource and Energy Economics. Elsevier Science Publishers, Amsterdam, 1:191–220.

Leopold, A., 1933. Game Management. Scribner, New York.

Leopold, A., 1966. A Sand Country Almanac: with Other Essays on Conservation from Round River. Oxford University Press, New York.

Little, I.M.D., 1957. A Critique of Welfare Economics. 2nd. Edn., Oxford University Press, London.

Malthus, T.R., 1798. An Essay on the Principle of Population as it Affects the future improvements of Mankind. Reprint 1976, Norton, New York.

Meadows, D.H., Ronders, J. and Behrens, W., 1972. The limits of Growth: A Report for the Club of Rome's Project on the Predicament of Mankind. Universe Books, New York.

Mill, J.S., 1964. Principles of Political Economy with Some of Their Applications to Social Philosophy. Kelley, New York.

Mishan, E.J., 1967. Costs of Economic Growth. Staples, London.

Myers, N., 1979. The Sinking Ark: A New Look at the Problem of Disappearing Species. Pergamon Press, Oxford.

McLennen, E.F., 1983. Rational choice and public policy: A critical survey. Social Theory and Practice, 9:335–379.

National Academy of Sciences, 1969. Resources and Man: A Study and Recommendations. Freeman, San Francisco.

Nordhaus, W. and Tobin, J., 1979. Is Growth Obsolete? Cowles Foundation Discussion Paper No. 319, December. Yale University, New Haven.

Owen, O.S., 1975. Natural Resource Conservation, 2nd Edn. Macmillan, New York.

Passmore, J.A., 1974. Man's Responsibility for Nature: Ecological Problems and Western Traditions. Duckworth, London.

Pearce, D., Markandya, A., and Barbier, E.B., 1989. Blueprint for a Green Economy. Earthscan Publications, London.

Ricardo, D., 1817. The Principles of Political Economy and Taxation. Reprint 1955, Dent, London.

Robbins, L., 1937. An Essay on the Nature and Significance of Economic Science, Macmillan, London.

Sen, A.K. and Williams, B., 1982. Utilitarianism and Beyond. Cambridge University Press, Cambridge.

Simon, J.L., 1981. The Ultimate Resource. Princeton University Press, Princeton.

Tisdell, C.A., 1972. Microeconomics: The Theory of Economic Allocation. John Wiley, Sydney.

Tisdell, C.A., 1979. Economics in our Society. Jacaranda Press, Brisbane.

White, L., 1967. The historical roots of our ecological crisis. Science, 155:1203–1207.

Worcester, D., 1985. Nature's Economy: A History of Ecological Ideas. Cambridge University Press, Cambridge.

World Commission on Environment and Development, 1987. Our Common Future. Oxford University Press, Oxford.

World Resources Institute and International Institute for Environment and Development, 1986. World Resources 1986. Basic Books, New York.

Chapter 2

Strategies for world conservation: an economic assessment

2.1 Introduction

Severe pressures are being placed by Man on the Earth's living resources. As pointed out in the previous Chapter, these are mainly a result of human population growth, the spatial extension of human activities and their impact on the environment as well as the growth in the sheer volume of man-made goods as mainly measured by GDP (Gross Domestic Product). These pressures could increase in the future and most likely will do so especially in less developed countries. If past trends continue unabated, they are likely to cause severe and permanent deterioration of the environment considered as a whole, lead to adverse global events, such as polar ice-melts resulting in large rises in sea levels, and cause considerable reduction in and have catastrophic effects on the level of economic production.

While the possibility of irreversible environmental catastrophe *underlines* the need for Man to consider adequate environmental management measures, one does not need to appeal to a Doomsday philosophy to appreciate the importance of taking into account the impact of economic activity on the environment. Improved conservation policies can raise human welfare and economic development projects can be more soundly, securely and sustainably based if adequate attention is given to their ecological and environmental implications. Even in the absence of economic growth and the possibility of doom for Mankind, scope exists for improving environmental conservation strategies so as to raise human welfare by paying attention to economic principles.

If one takes a less anthropocentric approach and gives greater weight to naturalistic ethics, the 'land-ethic' and 'ecocentrosism', the need for emphasising the 'human-doom' thesis as a basis for action concerning environmental conservation is even less relevant. Indeed, present threats to other species, the extinction of many, the severe population reductions of others and erosion of their life-supports plus the demise of many natural biosystems must currently be of great concern and a spur to action on the part of individuals who put some weight on naturalistic ethics in their value system.

On the basis of a wide range of ethics or goals, it seems that 'Panglossian' views about world conservation are unjustified. Both on grounds of human self-interest and on naturalistic grounds, complacency about conservation of the world's living resources is misplaced. Given the major impact of the activities of Man on the natural world and his dependence upon it, he needs to weigh up his actions rationally and adopt policies for resource use, management and conservation consistent with his long-term goals. Thus for many reasons, it is rational to give serious consideration to strategies for conserving and appropriately utilising the world's living resources.

In this chapter, prime attention will be given to the World Conservation Strategy (IUCN, 1980), in particular to assessing it from an economic perspective. This strategy raises most issues of current concern for living resource conservation. Although this strategy is in the process of being updated, indications are that its essential features will remain unchanged and that greater emphasis can be expected on methods of implementing the strategy including the use of economic incentives and instruments (IUCN-UNEP-WWF, 1990). However, before considering the World Conservation Strategy, it will be useful to classify proposed conservation policies.

2.2 A classification of conservation policies

One can classify conservation policies in many different ways. One approach is to divide these into three sets:

(1) Those policies emphasising macro-variable, aggregative or 'broad-brush' strategies;

(2) Those emphasising micro-adjustment, *relative* balancing of forces and management controls and attention to detail; and

(3) Policies proposing a mixture of these aspects.

Category (1) has most in common with macroeconomic policy-making whereas category (2) has most in common with microeconomic approaches to policy.

Policies emphasising the importance of reducing aggregate growth in economic production, lowering consumption levels per head in high income countries and of diminishing population growth rates as conservation measures tend to fall into category (1) above.

Policies favouring steady-state economies (SSEs) involving zero economic growth, zero population growth (ZPG) and limited per capita levels of consumption, as for example proposed by Daly (1980) and other writers, such as Brown and Shaw (1982) belong to category (1). The World Conservation Strategy (IUCN, 1980) while giving considerable attention to macro-variables such as population growth also gives much attention to the diversity of natural environments and their relative balancing in conservation. It, therefore, seems to be most appropriately placed in category (3), the mixed group. This is even more so for the IUCN-UNEP-WWF (1990) follow-up document. The Brundtland Report (World Commission on Environment and Development, 1987) tends to take a macro-overview but not entirely.

Many economists who have analysed conservation issues and alternatives have done so by applying social cost benefit analysis based on partial approach. Their approach therefore falls into category (2). This, for example, is true of case studies reviewed by Krutilla and Fisher (1975) involving development and environmental preservation alternatives for Hells Canyon, The White Cloud Peaks, Mineral King Valley, prairie wetlands and the Trans-Alaska pipeline.

Doeleman (1980) warns that a microenvironmental approach based on cost-benefit analysis can lead to creeping compromise in the sense that resource conservation may be steadily adjusted over time so as to obtain the best or socially optimal pattern of use of preservation of resources but absolute costs may be ignored. For example, due to population growth, technological change and increasing demand for consumption, it *may* be rational to slowly reduce the area allocated for conservation or wilderness after examining *relative* costs and benefits of land-use. But by concentrating on the *balancing* of net benefits, there is a danger of ignoring basic long-term environmental influences such as population growth and economic growth which might be restricting or lowering absolute net benefits or welfare for all or most alternative uses of resources.

Figure 2.1 can be used to illustrate the point. Suppose that the Earth's area can be allocated between the area used for economic development and that reserved for wilderness preservation. A 45-degree line like ABCD represents the trade-off possibilities for land-use. In a particular initial period of time, preferences might be as indicated by the set of iso-value curves (equal value or iso-welfare curves) indicated by W_1W_1 and W_2W_2. These are assumed to have similar properties to indifference curves. Initially, considering the *comparative* value of land-use for alternative purposes, it is optimal to reserve an area of x_2 for wilderness and and area of y_1 for development or commercial activity. At a later period the iso-value curves may alter so that the set represented for example, by $W_1'W_1'$ and $W_2'W_2'$ applies. This set now implies that the relative allocation corresponding to point B

24

is 'socially' optimal from a comparative point of view. Hence, a smaller area is reserved for wilderness and a greater area is used for economic development. However, the absolute value of, or welfare flowing from the second situation could well be much less than in the previous situation and this fact should not be lost sight of.

In fact, any overall realistic strategy for conservation of the world's living resources, needs to give consideration both to relative *balancing* of demands on such resources against alternative uses as well as the level of *absolute* demand for them. The problem is somewhat analogous to that of driving a motor vehicle safely, that is without an accident occurring. To concentrate on directing the vehicle while ignoring its speed is likely to be irrational, especially if the vehicle is accelerating. But to consider only the speed of the vehicle without paying attention to its direction is also irrational. Both aspects need to be simultaneously considered.

This is not to suggest that it is irrational to undertake partial cost-benefit analyses, that is, assume that certain variables are beyond the analysis and must therefore, be taken as 'givens'. But preoccupation with partial cost-benefit analysis can blind the analyst and others to basic forces altering valuations and result in inadequate policy responses. By paying attention to both macro-variables and the balancing of relative demands on resource use, the World Conservation Strategy, (IUCN, 1980) provides a comparatively balanced outlook on conservation and economic development.

Before considering the World Conservation Strategy (WCS) in some detail, it might be noted that conservation policies can also be classified by characteristics other than those mentioned above. For instance, they can be categorised by the nature of values, ethics or objectives assumed. The World Conservation Strategy, the assessment in *Our Common Future* (World Commission on Environment and Development, 1987), and most conservation policies proposed by economists, are

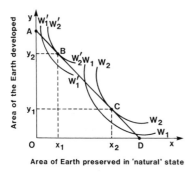

Figure 2.1. Difference in constrained optimum for welfare maximisation (in relation to conservation and development) which pay no attention to differences in absolute welfare.

based on anthropocentric or homocentric values. Ecocentric or naturalistic values, as implied by Leopold's land ethic (Leopold, 1966) underlie some other approaches to conservation. For example, G.C. Ray in developing policies for the establishment of marine parks and reserves states that 'socio-economic issues should be secondary to ecocentric ones in the decision-making process. The nature of ecosystems is our paramount concern, not to be diluted by overriding concern for monetary value, non-conforming social custom, or 'needs' and desires which may result in deleterious environmental impact' Ray, 1976, p. 34).

2.3 The World Conservation Strategy: its origins, aims and basic principles

The World Conservation Strategy (WCS) (IUCN, 1980; IUCN-UNEP-WWF, 1990) and *Our Common Future* (World Commission on Environment and Development, 1987) express concern about the irreversible damage that Man is doing to the biosphere. They suggest that if this damage continues at recent rates, the economic welfare of Mankind will be undermined. Standards of living in developed countries may eventually deteriorate and development in more impoverished countries could be short lived. The rapid disappearance of species, the major loss of forests especially rainforests, soil deterioration and denudation of terrain and loss of many natural or (otherwise stable) ecosystems all provide reasons for concern on a global scale. Such issues have been highlighted for example by Myers (1979), Allen (1980), the *Global 2000 Report* (Barney, 1980) and *Our Common Future* (World Commission on Environment and Development, 1987). The *Global 2000 Report* for instance indicated that half a million to two million species could be extinguished in two decades. (See previous Chapter)

In response to such matters, the World Conservation Strategy (IUCN, 1980) was drawn up. The United Nations Environment Programme (UNEP) commissioned that project which was financed jointly by it and the World Wildlife Fund (WWF). The document itself was prepared by the International Union for Conservation of Nature and Natural Resources (IUCN), now renamed the World Conservation Union, in consultation with UNEP, WWF, the United Nations Educational, Scientific and cultural Organisation (UNESCO). Government agencies, conservation organisations and individuals in more than 100 countries were consulted before completion of the final document. This 'compromise' document was endorsed by the Ecosystem Conservation Group (UNEP, FAO, UNESCO and IUCN) and launched in March, 1980 with a view to making the Third Development Decade the decade of sustainable development.

It is being followed up by a new document for the 1990s (IUCN-UNEP-WWF, 1990).

The main aim of the World Conservation Strategy is in its own words to foster 'sustainable development through the conservation of living resources'. In drawing up this strategy, it was recognised that its success would depend to a considerable extent upon convincing commercial developers and influential economic pressure groups of its value. This is echoed in the statement of Allen that

'To be effective, conservationists need radically to change the public perception of their attitude to development. Too often conservationists have allowed themselves to be seen as resisting all development, although often they have been forced into that posture because they have not been invited to participate in the development process early enough.' (Allen, 1980, p. 148).

Allen goes on to argue that conservationists need to be willing to compromise and to distinguish between environmental alteration that is worth the biological cost and that which is not. Thus cost-benefit, trade-off and evaluation becomes important and provides scope for an input from a number of perspectives including the economic one.

Possibly realising the political necessity of appealing to the predominant current values of human beings, anthropocentric or homocentric aims or objectives dominate WCS. Basically, it is argued that greater attention to conservation will raise *human* welfare, especially Man's economic well-being. The man-centred focus is clear from the following statement in WCS.

'Conservation is defined here as the management of human use of [the Biosphere] so that it may yield the greatest sustainable benefit to present generations while maintaining its potential to meet the needs and aspirations of future generations' (IUCN, 1980, sec. 1.4)

This focus is made even clearer later when it is stated that 'conservation like development is for people' (IUCN, 1980, sec. 1.5). Naturalistic ethics such as the land ethic of Leopold (see previous Chapter) play little apparent role in the formulation of the Strategy, even though some mention is made of such ethics in relation to genetic diversity. Nevertheless, it is quite possible that a naturalistic ethic has strongly motivated many of those proposing the Strategy. While emphasising this might have been counterproductive for conservation from a practical political point of view, with changing community attitudes towards nature, greater mention of naturalistic ethics may not have been misplaced. Somewhat greater emphasis on naturalistic ethics is likely to be present in the updated WCS (IUCN-UNEP-WWF, 1990).

Even if it is agreed that Man's welfare or benefit is to be the central purpose of a world conservation strategy, it is difficult to obtain agreement about the objectives that Man wishes to pursue or should pursue in his own self-interest. Conflicts between the objectives of different people are common and there is no straightforward way of resolving these conflicts, even though, as pointed out in the previous Chapter, economists have suggested criteria for at least *partially* dealing with these problems. Thus it is not clear from the WCS how the benefit (welfare) of present generations let alone future generations is to be determined. Furthermore there may be conflict between conserving sufficient resources 'to meet the needs and aspirations of future generations', and maximising sustainable benefits to present generations. If such problems did not exist, optimising from a social viewpoint would be easy, but there is no point in ignoring the existence of such problems except maybe for purposes of political propaganda. We must face up to these problems.

This has led to the suggestion that we must begin from basic priorities in considering human goals. Georgescu-Roegen (1975) and Daly (1980) have suggested that our first priority should be the survival of the human species. Survival of the species rather than the individual is an ultimate end. Once this priority is assured, attention can be given to other goals. Daly (1980) believes that we should aim firstly to ensure economic and environmental conditions that maximise the possibility of the human race existing for the longest possible time. He sees the creation of a steady-state economy (SSE), that is one in which there is zero population growth and per caput material consumption is restrained, as the optimal strategy for achieving the objective. He suggests that the Benthamite or Utilitarian principle of 'the greatest good for the greatest number' be replaced by the principle of 'sufficient per caput product for the greatest number over time'.

However, this principle does not give clear guidance. Will, in fact, a steady-state economy at current population-levels ensure survival of the human species for as long as is possible? Georgescu-Roegen (1975) argues not and suggests that human population should be lowered gradually to a level that can be fed only by organic agriculture. Will SSE result in the greatest number of people living at sufficient per caput income for the longest period of time possible for survival of the human species? Can these two objectives be in conflict? Can the strategy required to ensure that the greatest number of humans live result in some shortening of the period of survival of the human race? If so, how do we choose (Tisdell, 1983, p. 45; Tisdell, 1988)? Daly (1980, pp. 370–371) states that

...'The SSE is simply a strategy of good stewardship for taking care of God's creation for however long his will is to last. In taking care of that creation special, but not exclusive, attention must be given to humanity, including not only the present but future generations...'

He goes on to say that in some appropriate degree this concern should extend to subhuman life. Thus the man-centred approach is to be modified to some (unspecified) extent.

The World Conservation Strategy while bringing attention to 'the predicament caused by growing numbers of people demanding scarcer resources [and pointing out that this] is exacerbated by the disproportionately high consumption rates of developed countries' (IUCN, 1980, p. 2) does not advocate a world steady-state economy. It is not as such an anti-economic growth document. Rather it is aimed at trying to ensure that economic growth strategies are not self-defeating or un-sustainable because of their failure to take account of ecological, environmental and related considerations. The WCS document argues that if development is to be sustainable particular care should be taken:

(1) to maintain essential ecological processes and life-support systems;

(2) to preserve genetic diversity; and

(3) to ensure the sustainable utilisation of species and ecosystems.

Essential ecological processes and life-support systems include agricultural sys-tems, forests and coastal freshwater systems. These, together with the mainte-nance of genetic diversity and sustainable levels of utilisation of species and eco-systems, have an important economic role to play in maintaining human welfare. Let us consider the above three objectives as detailed in WCS (IUCN, 1980).

2.4 Ecological processes and life-support systems: agriculture, forests, coastal and freshwater systems

The World Conservation Strategy states that special attention should be given to supporting ecosystems on which human life depends. The WCS document iden-tifies (1) agricultural systems, (2) forests, and (3) coastal and freshwater systems as the most important and threatened life support systems, and makes policy re-commendations for each of these. Consider each of these systems and the policies recommended.

The WCS document points out in Section 2 that only about 11% of the world's land area (excluding Antarctica) is reasonably suited to agriculture. But in many countries large amounts of agricultural land are being lost due to the urban sprawl and man-made constructions such as roads. In addition, it suggests that due to land degradation (soil-erosion, increased flooding, waterlogging, salinity, destructured soils, alkalinity and so on) a large proportion of the world's arable land (close to one-third) could be destroyed in two decades. It recommends that measures be taken to prevent soil degradation and restore degraded land and that ecologically sound practices be adopted to maintain the productivity of cropland and grazing land. However, it does not examine specifically the cost and benefits of adopting such measures and practices. Among the measures which it recom-mends are less reliance on chemical fertilisers and pesticides and greater use of or-ganic fertilisers and of biological control of pests including integrated pest man-agement making use of natural checks and balances. Some of the specific issues involved are taken up in later chapters of this book, such as the one dealing with agriculture, and are given coverage in *Our Common Future* (World Commission on Environment and Development, 1987).

A major priority for maintaining essential ecological processes and life-support systems is said to be to reserve prime quality cropland for crops. (IUCN, 1980, secs. 5.1, 5.2). WCS suggests that the reservation of such quality land for agriculture should take priority as a rule over its use for buildings and man-made constructions such as roads. Even land of great conservational value for preserving genetic diversity but of prime quality for agriculture also should be reserved for agriculture according to WCS. The main purpose of such an approach appears to be to maximise food production for the land area used and to 'reduce the pressure on ecologically fragile marginal lands which tend to degrade rapidly if exploited beyond their production capabilities' (IUCN, 1980, sec. 5.1).

This is a worthy objective. However, there are at least two important factors that have been overlooked: (1) Food is not produced by land alone and therefore the greatest quantity of food may not be obtained by reserving prime crop land exclusively for crops. (2) Furthermore, the *relative* or *comparative* productivity of land in producing food compared to alternative production or conservational possibilities forgone is more important than its absolute productivity in determining the *most efficient* or productive *use of land*. This will dictate in certain circumstances that land which is of prime quality for agriculture but comparatively or relatively more productive than other land in contributing to conservational objectives be set aside for nature conservation rather than agricultural production. Consider each of these aspects in turn.

Suppose that an existing city is surrounded by adjacent prime quality cropland and is expanding in population and economic activity. If it is not permitted to expand on to good cropland, a satellite urban area may have to be built a considerable distance away on low quality cropland. The cost of commuting, extra transport costs and added costs of industrial production (e.g., farm machinery production) *may* when such a locational arrangement is enforced mean that it is less economic in terms of food production than permitting the city to expand on to good quality cropland and obtaining extra food production from more marginal land or by more intensively cultivating better quality cropland. This possibility must be recognised while at the same time realising that natural market, social and political mechanisms may fail to promote the optimal pattern of growth of cities and urban areas and the 'best' location of urban settlements from a productive viewpoint (Tisdell 1975, 1982, Ch. 15). Neither uncontrolled urban growth nor the mechanical application of the rule of reserving prime quality cropland for crops is the most efficient way to realise production objectives, including food production objectives.

Take another case: The location of all dwellings on land useless for crops may add greatly to transport costs, and net food production could be lower than if the dwellings were located on good cropland. Cultivators may lose time in travelling to their fields and costs of transporting inputs and the harvest costs may be raised. Thus for example, location of some dwellings and some storage facilities on good cropland may result in a 10% reduction food production compared with its theoretical maximum possible level but a 20% reduction may come about when the prime quality cropland is reserved exclusively for crops (Tisdell, 1983, pp. 46–47). Nevertheless, loss of good cropland is a matter requiring attention since current allocation systems do not direct land use in an optimal way.

Turn now to the second aspect, namely lack of attention by WCS to the *relative* productivity of land for alternative uses. In order to maximise the production of material goods such as food and environmental or conservational services, land allocation should basically be in accordance with the relative or comparative productivity of different types of land for alternative uses not its absolute productivity for any particular use, such as food production. This accords with the economic law of comparative advantage or comparative costs which requires this condition to be satisfied in order to maximise production (Tisdell, 1982, pp. 584–588). If this rule is not satisfied, that is if land is not allocated to the use for which it is comparatively more productive, the output of at least one commodity, e.g., environmental service can be raised without lowering the output of other commodities e.g., food. This can be illustrated by a simple hypothetical arithmetic case.

Suppose that there are two grades of land consisting of 10 hectares of prime agricultural land and 20 hectares of marginal agricultural land. Suppose further that each hectare of good agricultural land is capable of producing 2 units of wheat (agricultural output) or if left in its natural state 4 units of 'natural' output (conservational or environmental services). Hence 4 units of natural output must be forgone on this land for 2 units of wheat. The opportunity cost of wheat production is $4/2 = 2$.

On the marginal agricultural land suppose that a hectare can produce 1 unit of natural output if left in its natural state or if developed 1 unit of wheat. The opportunity cost of wheat in terms of natural output forgone is 1.

Assume further that the problem is to maximise wheat production subject to the requirement that 20 units of 'natural' (environmental) output is obtained. This could be achieved by leaving the 20 hectares of marginal agricultural land in a natural state and thereby producing 20 units of natural (environmental) output and using the 10 hectares of prime land for wheat thereby producing 20 units of wheat. This allocation would accord with the WCS recommendation. But it is not optimal because the allocation is not in accordance with comparative costs.

The optimal allocation is to use 5 hectares of the prime quality land for natural (environmental) production thereby achieving 20 units of natural (environmental) output. The remainder of this prime land should be used for agriculture and will yield 10 units of wheat. In addition, the marginal land should be used for agriculture and this will supply 20 units of wheat. Thus 30 units of wheat are produced.

TABLE 2.1

Production of combinations of 'natural' (environmental) output and wheat on two grades of land for two alternative allocations of land: an example of comparative advantage.

Alternatives	Units of 'natural' (environmental) output	Units of wheat output
Alternative I		
20 ha. of marginal land conserved	20	0
10 ha. of prime land used for wheat	0	20
Total:	20	20
Alternative II		
5 ha. of prime land conserved	20	
5 ha. of prime land used for wheat		10
20 ha. of marginal land used for wheat		20
Total:	20	30

Hence, the strategy adopted in this case results in *no less* natural (environmental) production than the previous strategy but provides 10 more units of wheat. This strategy is superior to the WCS. The alternatives are highlighted in Table 2.1.

Now this is not to say that prime quality agricultural land should always be used first to meet nature conservation goals. Sometimes, the *comparative* cost of doing this will be greater than using marginal agricultural land for this purpose. We have to consider specific cases. If in practice the comparative cost of using low quality agricultural land for conservation is low compared to that use of prime quality agricultural land the WCS (IUCN, 1980) recommendation is correct (even if argued on the wrong logical grounds). However, we must be aware of cases where it is optimal to reserve some prime cropland for nature conservation, even though political opposition to this from farming groups could be intense.

Naturally, real world problems are much more complicated than can be captured by the above example. For instance, non-linear trade-off production possibilities may occur. However, these can be allowed for by allocating land-use so as to equalise rates of product transformation or rates of trade-off in appropriate cases (Cf. Tisdell, 1982, Ch. 13, pp. 584–588). In addition, measurement problems and interdependencies in production have not been considered. Nevertheless, the basic observation is valid. It requires modification to the WCS formulated in 1980.

In relation to preservation of forests, WCS suggests that watershed forests and pastures be managed mainly with the objective of protecting watersheds (IUCN, 1980, sec. 5.6). In several parts of the world, deforestation and the encroachment of agriculture on to hilly slopes is having serious environmental consequences resulting in economic loss in watersheds considered as a whole. Poor watershed management, including overgrazing deforestation and precarious cultivation, can result in erosion and flooding which destroys farmland and villages, flash flooding followed by reduced water flows in dry seasons, silting of irrigation channels and reservoirs and of ports and harbours, loss of clean water supply or of water for hydro-electricity generation, damage to fisheries and in some cases destruction of off-shore corals. From an economic point of view, significant adverse environmental externalities or spillovers can arise from clearing of forests in a watershed or environmentally destructive individualistic farming or land-use practices, especially in the headwaters of river systems. Such externalities are, as discussed in the next Chapter, a possible source of market failure or of individualistic resource-use failure and often call for government or collective intervention in order to increase social welfare. WCS also suggests that particular attention be given to conserving tropical forests. Externality or spillover arguments can also be used to support this recommendation as well as other arguments, e.g., the benefits from clearing of tropical forests for agriculture are frequently overestimated. These matters will be taken up in detail in a later chapter dealing with forests and the conservation of trees.

Coastal and freshwater systems are the third set of life support systems given special emphasis in WCS. Many of these systems are under threat as a result of urban and industrial expansion in coastal areas and shoreline economic development and some species in these environments, such as molluscs, are especially receptive to man-released toxic substances. Once again spillovers and externalities from economic activity are important. These areas often play a critical role in the breeding of fish and other marine species such as prawns or shrimps. It seems appropriate for them to be given special attention in environmental planning. WCS suggests that the main goals in managing such areas and marine areas should be the maintenance of fisheries at sustainable levels. WCS goes so far as to maintain that 'other uses of these ecosystems should not impair their capacity to provide food and critical habitat for economically and culturally important marine species' (IUCN, 1980, sec. 5.7). While this overstates the claims of fisheries on these environments (because comparative costs need to be considered), it is important to realise the great importance of these environments in maintaining the productivity of marine and aquatic life, for instance the important role of estuarine environments in the life-cycle of many sea going fish and crustaceans.

2.5 Preservation of genetic diversity

Due to the activities of man, species and varieties of species are rapidly disappearing. Habitat destruction has mostly been responsible for man-induced extinction of wild species but other factors have also played a role such as overharvesting. About 25,000 plant species and a thousand vertebrate species or subspecies are estimated to be threatened with extinction (IUCN, 1980, sec. 3.11). When all species including invertebrates are taken into account, the possibility of half to a million species becoming extinct within two decades must be seriously considered (IUCN, 1980, sec. 3.11; see also Ch. 1 of this book).

Not only is the gene bank of wild animals and plants being reduced, but the varieties of those animals kept in domestication and the available varieties of domesticated plants is declining rapidly. For example, it has been estimated that the number of wild cultivars in the Greek wheat crop has fallen dramatically in the last 50 years (IUCN, 1980, sec. 3.4). This has also happened elsewhere, and I shall return to this matter again.

Why should we be concerned with such events from an economic viewpoint? Reserves of genetic diversity are important:

(1) for improving, increasing and sustaining current production and industries such as agricultural industries dependent on biological material;

(2) for providing basic resources for new commodities of value to man: in medicine, industry, for food and fibre and so on; and

(3) to guard against permanent collapse in production of industries supporting man, for instance cereal production.

They are a source of productivity increase, a source of innovation and new discoveries and an insurance against disaster or catastrophe in production. Examples of these attributes are to be found in Myers (1979), IUCN (1980) and in Oldfield (1989) and will be considered in more detail later in this book. The WCS document points out that

> 'The genetic material contained in the domesticated varieties of crop plants, trees, livestock, aquatic animals and micro-organisms – as well as their wild relatives – is essential for the breeding programmes in which continued improvements in yields, nutritional quality, flavour, durability, pest and disease resistance, responsiveness to different soils and climates, and other quantities are achieved' (IUCN, 1980, sec. 3.3).

These characteristics are rarely permanent. For instance, pests and diseases develop new strains which overcome the resistance of these domestic varieties. Because of such factors, the average lifetime of wheat and other cereal varieties in Europe and North America is only 5-15 years (IUCN, 1980, sec. 3.3).

When this impermanence in the economic value of cultured varieties or strains of living organisms is combined with the trend to reduced number of domestic varieties (only 4 varieties of wheat are said to account for 75% of Canadian wheat production) and a severe decline in the number of strains of their wild relatives, flexibility for breeding and cross-breeding to overcome reduced environmental resistance or to introduce more resistant varieties is lost. Consequently considerable economic benefit may be forgone and it may be impossible to prevent a collapse in production of affected domestic species.

Given the above considerations as well as uncertainty about the future economic value of individual species, varieties and strains, an economic case in favour of conservation exists even when only *expected* economic or utility gains are considered (Arrow and Fisher, 1974). This case however, is further strengthened if risk-aversion is given more weight than in the expected utility approach as has been advocated by those economists favouring a safe minimum standard of conservation of species (Ciriacy-Wantrup, 1968; Bishop, 1978, 1979; Chisholm, 1988; Tisdell, 1988, 1989).

In arguing for the preservation of genetic diversity, the WCS document apart from mentioning the self-interest of Man also introduces naturalistic ethics even though they are not emphasised in the document as a whole. It states:

'The issue of moral principle relates particularly to species extinction, and may be stated as follows: Human beings have become a major evolutionary force. While lacking the knowledge to control the bioshpere, we have the power to change it radically. We are morally obliged – to our descendants and other creatures – to act prudently' (IUCN, 1980, sec. 3.2).

An agenda for the preservation of genetic diversity is drawn up in the WCS document. Basically it suggests that priority should be given to saving the rarest species, especially where they are the only member of a family or genus or the difference between this species and the nearest family or genesis is very great. In a sense, the more unique and endangered is a species the greater is the priority accorded to saving it. But the grounds for this are not given. An endangered species could have little economic or other value for Man (Cf. Tisdell, 1983, 1990). Indeed, meeting this objective could conflict with another injunction of WCS, namely

'Preserve as many varieties as possible of crop plants, forage plants, timber trees, livestock, animals for aquaculture, microbes and other domesticated organisms and their wild relatives' (IUCN, 1980, sec. 6.4).

A role is seen for both on-site preservation, e.g., in national parks, and for off-site preservation e.g., in zoos. WCS recommends that priority for on-site preservation be given

(1) to the protection of the wild relatives of economically valuable and other useful plants and animals and their habitats;

(2) to the maintenance of the habitats of threatened and unique species and

(3) unique ecosystems; and

(4) representative samples of ecosystem types.

Various desirable patterns for protected areas are suggested. In general, larger sized and non-fragmented protection areas appear to be preferred. While one can make out an argument for these patterns and a minimum-sized area for reserves, some scattering may also reduce risks for example, of disease transmission in endangered animals.

The non-optimal disappearance of species from an economic viewpoint may take place because of ignorance, individual attitudes to risk-bearing and more importantly externalities or spillovers. Any individual conserving a unique natural species which becomes of considerable economic value in the future is only able to appropriate a small fraction of that value because once genetic material is released it can be rapidly reproduced and the preserver would find it difficult to obtain payment for the spread in use and expansion in the population of the species which he or she has preserved.

2.6 Sustainable utilisation of species and ecosystems

Sustainable economic development is a central goal for WCS and the sustainable utilisation of species and of ecosystems is important for the achievement of this goal. However, Western economists have not as a rule seen any particular virtue in sustainability but have argued that it may very well be in the economic interest of a society to exploit some species to extinction and to destroy or degrade existing ecosystems at the expense of reduced production in the future (Tisdell, 1989). Clark (1976) points out that if the net value of a species grows in time at a rate less than the rate of interest, economic gain is maximised by harvesting it now and as a result wiping out the species. Thus, a species of tree that grows slowly and increases slowly in net value say by 2% per year would yield greatest economic return by harvest now if the rate of interest is 10%. Owners by realising the value of their trees can earn 10% per year on their capital, whereas if they do not harvest them, 2% per year will be earned. Similarly, arguments may be put forward to 'justify' the degradation of 'mining' of soils. These arguments do not take account of reduced genetic diversity or environmental spillovers. But even when account is taken of these, it may still pay Man to extinguish a species or to degrade an ecosystem in his own selfish interest. Nevertheless, unsustainable utilisation frequently occurs when it is not in the self-interest of Man, and attention needs to be brought to such cases as well as the environmental dangers involved in unsustainable utilisation generally.

The importance of sustainable production may vary with the nature and economic situation of societies. In societies heavily dependent for their subsistence on living natural resources such as agriculture, fisheries or forests, having little labour mobility and few alternatives for subsistence or employment, sustainability of production may be extremely important. This appears to be the case in many less developed countries. Sustainability is likely to become of growing importance in more developed countries as the range of available alternatives for production are reduced due to the disappearance of species and environmental degradation. A later chapter concentrates entirely on sustainability issues.

The WCS document highlights various unsustainable or potentially unsustainable resource-use practices. These involve:

(1) overfishing,

(2) overharvesting of terrestrial plants and animals,

(3) overutilisation of forests and woodlands, and

(4) overstocking of grazing lands.

Overfishing may result in the loss of aquatic species or to a level of catch lower than is sustainable or to a level of catch smaller than the one giving the maximum sustainable economic yield. In many instances, common-access or open-access to fishing resources has been the cause of unsustainable fishing practices. Technological progress has often exacerbated the situation.

A similar but more complicated situation exists or has existed in relation to terrestrial wild plants and animals, including forests and woodlands. As mentioned previously, various externality or spillover benefits may be obtained from conservation of these resources. Apart from concern about the clearing of forests, especially tropical forests for commercial use, the WCS document expresses concern about the heavy reliance of developing countries on forests and woodlands for fuel and for shifting cultivation. Indeed, the heaviest demand on forests and woodlands in developing countries is said to be for these purposes (IUCN, 1980, sec. 4.11). With rising population levels, tree and shrub cover is being reduced to provide fuel and the stock of forest and woodland is shrinking. Furthermore, the length of the cycle involved in shifting agriculture is being reduced and in some cases, due to population pressure on available land, cultivators are forced to engage in permanent agriculture which does not allow for forest regeneration.

Overstocking especially in arid areas and in mountainous areas is likely to result in a reduction of tree and grass cover. Consequently, erosion can accelerate. Deserts may spread in arid areas and hilly areas may be denuded of soil and subject to gullying due to erosion.

The WCS document recommends a number of strategies for achieving sustainable utilisation of living resources. First, species exploited for economic use by Man should not be reduced to unsustainable population-levels, that is to levels from which the population cannot recover. The document also suggests that some margin of safety needs to be allowed in this regard given variability in environmental conditions and that account be taken of other factors such as habitat modification by Man which may require a higher minimum population of a species to ensure its survival. In all these matters, there should be an allowance 'for error, ignorance and uncertainty' (IUCN, 1980, sec. 7.2).

For a species at the top of the food chain such as a fish species, the WCS document recommends that they be harvested at a rate which maximises their annual sustainable yield. But from an economic point of view this is mostly too high a rate of exploitation. Taking into account the cost of harvesting the species, it is usually most economic to exploit a species sustainably at a rate less than the maximum sustainable biological or physical rate possible. As the WCS document correctly points out, the optimal policy may require measures to limit access by harvesters to the resource or to restrict their rate of harvest. This is so even from an economic viewpoint.

The WCS document points out correctly that where a species is not at the top of a food chain account needs to be taken of the impact of its exploitation on dependent species. It states that a species below the top of the food chain should not be exploited to such an extent that populations of other species dependent on it are significantly reduced. While there may be an economic case for such restriction when dependent species are of considerable economic value, there is no economic case for this if the dependent species are of little or no economic value or are a pest. The matter is much more complicated than appears at first sight, even though from an economic point of view it is irrational to ignore the interdependence of species.

There is the further problem that some species of animals at the top of the food chain can be in competition with one another to some extent for food. So one cannot simultaneously obtain the maximum sustainable yield from them all – trade-off is required (See Tisdell, 1983, p. 48).

The WCS document suggests that measures should be taken to reduce incidental take (the accidental taking of non-target species such as sea turtles, which may be protected, during harvesting operations); that subsistence communities be assisted to utilise resources sustainably, for instance, to adopt changed conservation measures which may become necessary because of new technology; and that the habitats of resource species be maintained bearing in mind that the productivity of industries dependent on such species relies on the population level of the species and their vigour which in turn are functions of their available habitats. The WCS document also supports regulation of international trade in endangered wild plants and animals so as to reduce economic incentives for their exploitation. In particular, it supports the Convention on International Trade in Endangered Species of Wild Fauna and Flora (CITES). The signatories to this Convention limit international trade (exports and imports) of endangered species.

In addition, suggestions are made for improved management of forest concessions including replanting of logged areas, for increasing the supply of firewood and reducing the demand on timber for firewood consumption, for limiting the stocking of grazing land to sustainable levels and for utilising indigenous wild herbivores alone or in combination with domestic stock where this may retard land degradation. Nomadism and transhumance, may as is pointed out, have sustainability advantages in comparison to confined grazing of domestic livestock as may the ranching of native animals. These recommendations are worthy of closer examination and economic evaluation.

2.7 International conservation concerns and priorities

The WCS document (IUCN, 1980) presents a number of conservation subjects requiring international attention. International attention, co-operation and action is needed because many living resources are (1) shared by more than one country or (2) occur temporarily in one nation, as in the case of migrating or mobile species, or (3) exist permanently beyond national jurisdictions, e.g. in international waters, or (4) because living resources in one state are affected by activities carried out in other nations, for example through environmental spillovers such as have been experienced in the case of acid rains.

Co-operation by several nations and/or assistance to poorer nations from more developed ones may be needed and international laws and conventions affecting conservation may require additions or strengthening. Matters seen to be especially in need of international action (that is requiring action beyond those of individual states) are

(1) tropical forests and drylands;

(2) the establishment of protected areas for the conservation of genetic resources;

(3)   the global commons, resources shared by all, such as the open ocean, the atmosphere and Antarctica; and

(4)   international river basins and seas – these involve natural resources shared by several nations.

Apart from anything else, the preservation of tropical forests is important for maintaining genetic diversity. As one moves from the Poles to the Equator, the number of species and varieties of living species present per unit of area rises steeply and these are particularly numerous in tropical countries, countries currently subject to considerable economic and population pressures.

The importance from an economic viewpoint of preserving genetic diversity was commented on earlier. WCS suggests that areas should be protected where there are

(1)   concentrations of wild and weedy relatives of species of economic and useful value;

(2)   or of threatened species regardless of their economic values or usefulness;

(3)   or which contain ecosystems of exceptional diversity;

and

(4)   in addition, adequate reserves of representative areas of the main ecosystems are recommended.

Common property, shared resources and externalities or spillovers make international co-operation in conservation important. All involve some type of property-right problem. In that respect, it might be noted that the assignment of property rights to a particular nation, such as has been brought about by the declaration of 200 mile Exclusive Economic Zones (EEZs) around the coastal borders of national states, does not automatically lead to the optimal management and harvesting of species which move across national boundaries. This will be discussed in a later chapter along with similar cases of transboundary or transfrontier resource management problems.

2.8 Organisational and social aspects of conservation

The framers of WCS recognised the importance for successful world conservation of having a workable organisational framework for its implementation and the need to have adequate social support for conservation. They therefore suggested steps that countries could take to draw up and implement their own national conservation strategies. Many countries have now proceeded to draw up national conservation strategies.

In drawing up national conservation strategies, the framers of suggest that development and conservation management be *integrated*, that particular care be taken to retain flexibility in resource use, that is, to keep *options* open, that there should be a judicious mixing of conservation measures aimed at cure or restoration and prevention, and attention should be given to basic causes of environmental degradation rather than immediate causes.

Environmental planning and attention to rational resource allocation is needed, and this requires appropriate legislation and organisation. The WCS document favours a system of ecosystem evaluation to determine rational resource use (IUCN, 1980, sec. 10). The WCS document states that 'environmental assessments should be an integral part of the planning of all major actions (both public and private) requiring government authorisation' (IUCN, 1980, sec. 10.7).

The WCS document claims that training and research are important ingredients in policies to manage and conserve resources and that efforts be made to encourage public participation and support of conservation programmes especially by local communities. Environmental education campaigns and programmes are seen as especially important means of gaining public support and the support of particular interest groups in society. Many of the measures needed for living resource conservation or the implementation of these will depend on rural communities. It is important that rural communities see the benefits of these and/or be compensated for any substantial sacrifices made for the purpose of attaining conservation goals. Otherwise, there may be little or no rural support for conservation projects which can be jeopardised by lack of support and in some cases sabotage (Mishra, 1982; Western, 1982). With a little forethought, local people can often be provided with direct benefits from conservation projects such as the creation of protected nature areas, e.g., some local employment may be possible in their management, limited hunting or gathering rights may be granted to local communities and so on.

2.9 Concluding comments

The WCS document (IUCN, 1980) highlights issues that affect us all. It is a relevant and relatively comprehensive document. The issues addressed are of consequence for us, for future generations and for all other species. From the above discussion economics clearly has a role to play along with other disciplines in suggesting answers to conservation questions such as those raised by IUCN (1980) and followed up in IUCN-UNEP-WWF (1990).

The WCS document indicates that there are inadequacies in existing social mechanisms such as market and political mechanisms which determine current resource use. Because of market and political failures in relation to conservation of living resources and their support systems, Man is failing to act in his own self interest. Mechanisms for government and community intervention in resource-use need to be improved and in general greater government action is recommended by the World Conservation Strategy (IUCN, 1980) even though it seems possible that in the proposed update of WCS there will be less emphasis on direct government intervention (IUCN-UNEP-WWF, 1990). Therefore, we need to consider arguments for and against government intervention in conservation and will do so in the next chapter.

References

Allen, R., 1980. How to Save the World: Strategy for World Conservation. Kogan Page, London.

Arrow, K.J. and Fisher, A.D. 1974. Environmental preservation, uncertainty and irreversibility. Quarterly Journal of Economics, 52:310–334.

Barney, G.O., 1980. The Global 2000 Report to the President: Entering the Twenty-first Century. Pergamon, New York.

Bishop, R.C., 1978. Endangered species and uncertainty. The economics of a safe minimum standard. American Journal of Agricultural Economics, 60: 10–18.

Bishop, R.C., 1979. Endangered species, irreversibility and uncertainty: a reply. American Journal of Agricultural Economics, 61:376–379.

Brown, L.R. and Shaw, P., 1982. Six Steps to a Sustainable Society. Worldwatch Institute, Washington.

Chisholm, A., 1988. Sustainable resource use and development: uncertainty, irreversibility and rational choice, In: C.A. Tisdell and P. Maitra (Editors) Technological Change, Development and the Environment: Socio-Economic Perspective. Routledge, London, pp. 188–216.

Ciriacy-Wantrup, S.V., 1968. Resource Conservation: Economics and Policies, 3rd Ed. University of California, Division of Agriculture Science, Berkeley.

Clark, C.W., 1976. Mathematical Bioeconomics: The Optimal Management of Renewable Resources. John Wiley, New York.

Daly, H., 1980. Economics, Ecology and Ethics. Freeman, San Francisco.

Doeleman, J.A., 1980. On the social rate of discount: the case for macroenvironmental policy. Environmental Ethics, 2:45–58.

Georgescu-Roegen, N., 1975. Energy and economic myths. Southern Economic Journal, 41:347–381.

IUCN, 1980. The World Conservation Strategy: Living Resource Conservation for Sustainable Development. International Union for the Conservation of Nature and Natural Resources, Glands, Switzerland.

IUCN-UNEP-WWF, 1990. Caring for the World: A Strategy for Sustainability. Second draft, World Conservation Union, Glands, Switzerland.

Krutilla, J.V. and Fisher, A.C., 1975. The Economics of Natural Environments: Studies in the Valuation of Commodity and Amenity Resources. Johns Hopkins University Press, Baltimore, for Resources for the Future.

Mishra, H.R., 1982. Balancing human needs and conservation in Nepal's Royal Chitwan National Park. Ambio, 11:246–251.

42

Myers, N., 1979. The Sinking Ark: A New Look at the Problem of Disappearing Species. Pergamon, Oxford.

Oldfield, M.S., 1989. Value of Conserving Genetic Resources. Sinauer Associates, Sunderland, Mass.

Ray, G.C., 1976. Critical marine habitats: definition, description and guidelines for identification and management, pp. 15–59 in Proceedings of an International Conference on Marine Parks and Reserves. International Union for the Conservation of Nature and Natural Resources, Morges, Switzerland.

Tisdell, C.A., 1975. The theory of optimal city-sizes: some elementary considerations. Urban Studies, 12:61–70.

Tisdell, C.A., 1982. Microeconomics of Markets. John Wiley, Brisbane.

Tisdell, C.A., 1988. Sustainable development: differing perspectives of ecologists and economists, and relevance to LDCs. World Development, 16: 373–384.

Tisdell, C.A., 1989. Environmental conservation: economics, ecology and ethics. Environmental Conservation, 16:107–112, 162.

Tisdell, C.A., 1990. Economics and the debate about preservation of species, crop varieties and genetic diversity. Ecological Economics, 2:77–90.

Western, D., 1982. Amboseli National Park: enlisting landowners to conserve migratory wildlife. Ambio, 11:302–309.

Chapter 3

Government intervention in environmental conservation: rationale and methods

3.1 Introduction

Governments may interfere or be encouraged to interfere in economic processes affecting the conservation of living resources for a variety of reasons. These include improvements in economic efficiency, income distribution, risk, sustainability and other reasons. Many recommended strategies for conservation including the World Conservation Strategy (IUCN, 1980) rely heavily on public intervention including intervention by international public bodies. While the draft update of the World Conservation Strategy (IUCN-UNEP-WWF, 1990) still calls for government intervention, it places much greater emphasis on the use of economic mechanisms and incentives rather than direct intervention by governments.

Government intervention can sometimes increase conservation of resources and the level of economic production compared to a situation where individuals pursue only their own self-interest. More generally public conservation measures can sometimes lead to a social economic benefit in the Kaldor-Hicks' sense. This occurs if gainers could compensate losers from the intervention and be better off than without it. This is essentially a community-wide economic efficiency test of whether the intervention is justified. But governments intervene on grounds other than economic efficiency. They may do so because lack of conservation of resources will have adverse income distributional consequences for existing members of the community or for future generations. For example, if logging of a forest will provide considerable economic benefit to a few wealthy 'developers' but is at the expense of subsistence hunters and gatherers dependent on the forest, the 'development' may be prevented by a government because of its adverse income distributional effects.

There are also other reasons for intervention. Lack of attention to conservation of resources or environmental consequences of economic activity by individuals may subject the community collectively to risks, dangers or uncertainties greater than the community as a whole finds desirable. This may supply grounds for government intervention (Tisdell, 1983).

Merit good considerations may provide a motive for government interference in favour of conservation of resources. For example, the government may see greater merit in preserving a unique natural feature than the public places on its preservation. So the preference of a few individuals would dominate those of the remainder in such a case.

Because in the case of merit goods the preferences of all individuals are not respected equally, this raises the general issue of what respect should be given to the preferences of individuals. A value judgment is required about the extent to which the preferences of individuals and 'desires' of other sentient creatures are to be respected. In practice, even in liberal/democratic societies the preferences of all individuals do not count equally. For example, those of criminals, the insane and minors are given little weight. Furthermore, the *effective* weight given to the preferences of individuals in resource-use can depend upon their wealth or income (which determines their spending power and thus resource-use) and on their political, administrative or social power.

Even in societies where respect for individual preferences is the norm, a policy problem exists if individuals are not well informed about possible (environmental) consequences of human actions. Social decision-making which respects preferences based on faulty information can be disastrous, especially if extremely adverse spillovers or externalities arise from the decisions made. On the other hand, 'experts' and particular individuals have no monopoly on knowledge and no privileged claim to the truth.

Due to environmental change, individuals can collectively suffer increased instability or variability of income or of living standards. For example, deforestation in the headwaters of a river system can result in more variable water flows downstream with attendant consequences such as greater frequency of flooding. Such 'spillover' variability may provide grounds for government intervention. In addition, as mentioned in the previous chapter, the government may need to intervene to ensure greater sustainability of eonomic production and development. On the whole, this suggests that *existing* market and other mechanisms display deficiencies in ensuring sustainability. This is the import of the World Conservation Strategy (IUCN 1980), of its proposed update (IUCN-UNEP-WWF, 1990) and of *Our Common Future* (World Commission on Environment and Development, 1987).

This chapter considers reasons why market systems can fail to ensure perfect economic efficiency in the use and management of living resources. While highlighting circumstances favouring government intervention and bringing attention to factors which ought to be taken into account in valuing resources, it does not ignore government policy-failures either.

When markets fail to ensure complete economic efficiency, market failure is said to exist. Complete economic efficiency is achieved socially (using the standard economic test) when resources are allocated to uses (in space and in time) such that no reallocation can make anybody better off without making another worse off. In other words, complete economic efficiency prevails when *Paretian optimality* is achieved. Conversely, economic inefficiency exists when someone can be made better off without making another worse off by reallocating resources. But failure to achieve economic efficiency is not peculiar to market systems. Government, political, administrative and other institutional determinants of resource-use can also result in economic inefficiency. Some circumstances are highlighted where this is so.

Many economists supporting government intervention in the conservation of living resources believe that market failure is important in living resource utilisation and conservation. Those who argue against such intervention stress the shortcomings of administrative and political mechanisms of government. This group often favours reforms to strengthen market mechanisms rather than *supplant* ineffective market forces by government controls. The views of this group have influenced the proposed update (IUCN-UNEP-WWF, 1990) of the World Conservation Strategy (IUCN, 1980) to some extent.

Important sources of market failure in nature conservation include: (1) the presence of externalities or spillovers, (2) the existence of public good characteristics, (3) socially inappropriate allowances made by individuals for irreversibility of resource-use and uncertainty, and (4) the use by individuals of an excessively high rate of interest or discount of the future from a social point of view. Other sources of market failure in the utilisation of natural resources include (5) the presence of monopoly rights and (6) the existence of common-property. Let us consider each of these matters in turn and then examine possible sources of government and institutional failure in relation to nature conservation.

3.2 Externalities or spillovers

Activities (economic or otherwise) of individuals or groups may provide benefits to or impose costs not only on those engaging in the activities but on others. When costs are imposed on others without their being fully compensated or when benefits are received by others for which these beneficiaries do not make full payment, an economic *externality*, *spillover* or *side-effect* exists. These are a frequent cause of market failure especially as far as activities affecting the environment are concerned.

In a world in which individuals act in accordance with their own self-interest, spillovers are liable to lead to economic inefficiency in resource-use from a social viewpoint. But the mere existence of an (environmental) externality, as defined above, is not sufficient for market failure for it can be a Paretian irrelevant externality (Tisdell, 1970; Walsh and Tisdell, 1973; Burrows, 1986). Often, but not always, an externality is Paretian relevant when it exerts effects at the margin of existing levels of activity. When no externality- effect from a spillover exists at the margin of economic activity (the spillover is then either infra-marginal or supra-marginal), the spillover is likely to be Paretian irrelevant and hence not a cause of market failure. Nevertheless, on some occasions, even a non-marginal externality can be Paretian relevant. Actual cases must be specifically evaluated to determine whether they are a source of economic inefficiency in resource-use from a social viewpoint, that is, lead to less satisfaction of human desires than is possible given the limited resources available.

The social losses arising from externalities can be illustrated by a simplified example. Suppose that a landholder intends to remove trees or shrubs from his/her grazing property. This results in greater pasture cover on his/her property due to less competition from trees and shrubs for sunlight, water and nutrients and so on. Hence, more livestock can be carried and the property-owner may earn more profit for his/her enterprise after deducting the costs of running the extra livestock. The cost of clearing the trees or shrubs must be deducted, however, from any private gains made in order to determine private net benefits. In order to maximise his/her private net benefits, the landholder should proceed with land clearing up to the point where the additional cost of removing trees or shrubs equals his/her additional net revenue from increased livestock production from grazing. Or, in usual economics terminology, the private gains of the landholder are maximised when his/her marginal net revenue from tree clearing equals his/her marginal cost of doing so. In practice, costs and benefits should be discounted using the interest rate to determine the appropriate discount factor. So strictly we should be referring to discounted private costs and discounted private benefits.

The essence of the conflict between private choice and social optimality when spillovers occur is illustrated by Figure 3.1. Let the line identified by PMC represent the private marginal cost of tree clearing and let line DJ represent the net marginal revenue to be obtained by the landholder from land clearing. At point G, the private net marginal revenue from tree clearing equals marginal cost and the landholder adds the equivalent of the area of triangle BDG to his/her profit by clearing x_2 hectares of land. But if externalities, spillovers or side-effects are present from clearing, this amount of tree removal may not be socially optimal.

If an unfavourable externality is present overall, too much land will be cleared from a social perspective whereas if a favourable spillover dominates, insufficient clearing of tree-cover will occur from a social point of view. For instance, if tree clearing occurs in the headwaters of a river system and adds to erosion downstream, each hectare cleared might result in external costs of $BC so that the total social marginal cost of clearing is as indicated by the line identified by SMCU in Figure 3.1. If this is so, the socially optimal amount of land to clear (using the Kaldor-Hicks criterion) is x_1, not x_2. At point E the social marginal cost of land clearing equals its addition to marginal net revenue. A social loss (sometimes described as a deadweight social loss) equivalent to the area of the hatched triangle occurs when private self-interest is followed.

On the other hand if those trees or shrubs cleared have the status of pests and their clearing is instrumental in reducing their propagation on other properties, a favourable spillover could occur on balance. If this is so, the relevant social marginal cost curve might be as indicated by the line identified by SMCF. This indicates that spillover benefits of $AB per hectare cleared are obtained. Private self-interest results in only x_2 hectares being cleared whereas the clearing of x_3 hectares is socially optimal. A private decision results in the equivalent of the area of the flecked triangle being forgone in social gains. While actual situations are much more complicated than this, this example is sufficient to illustrate the nature of the externality problem.

Various policy measures can theoretically be adopted to eliminate social losses arising from spillovers or externalities. For example, in the case shown in Figure 3.1 a tax of $BC could be imposed on each hectare of land cleared if an unfavourable externality exists, whereas in the case where a favourable externality occurs a subsidy of $AB per hectare could be paid for land clearing. These policies would have the effect of bringing private and social marginal costs of land clearing into equality. However, other policies are possible and a number of complicating factors need to be considered.

For example, if the social marginal cost curve of land clearing happens to be as indicated by the curve KLG and private marginal costs are as indicated by curve

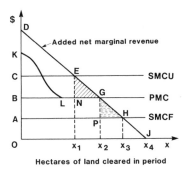

Figure 3.1. Illustration of divergence between social and private marginal cost due to externalities or spillovers and consequent social 'deadweight' losses.

BLG, the unfavourable externality is inframarginal. The marginal spillover costs are already zero by the time that point G corresponding to the clearing of x_2 hectares is reached. Thus in this neighbourhood, social marginal cost and private marginal cost coincide. In this case both private and social economic optimality are achieved by clearing x_2 hectares. However, if the spillover costs arising from tree-clearing of an area less than the marginal amount, x_2, happens to be extremely high (so that for instance, the social marginal cost curve is at first well above the net marginal revenue productivity curve before falling back to become equal to the private marginal cost curve), social economic optimality may be achieved by no clearing of trees. If this is so a corner-point social maximum (no tree clearing) occurs rather than an interior one (Tisdell, 1972). Although an inframarginal externality exists, and so there is no externality at the margin, the externality is still Paretian relevant.

Whether private self-interest results in a social maximum of net benefit depends on whether the absolute maximum of the *private* net function occurs for the same value of the controlled variable (in this case, the number of hectares cleared of trees) as does the absolute maximum of the *social* net benefit function. When these values of the controlled variable coincide, private action leads to a social optimum. Figure 3.2 illustrates the point. Suppose that curve OAB represents the landholder's private total net benefit from tree-clearing. This is at a maximum when x_2 hectares are cleared. Suppose that due to negative externalities the social net benefit from this activity is as indicated by curve OCD. In this case the clearing of x_2 hectares (the private optimum) maximises social net benefits despite the presence of negative externalities. However, if the curve of social net benefit from this activity is like that indicated by OFG or by OHJ, x_2, does not maximise social benefit. In the first instance, the maximum of the social benefit function occurs for the clearing of x_1 hectares whereas in the latter case it occurs when no land is cleared, that is, it occurs at a corner-point. In both cases, private actions

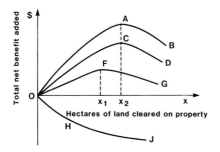

Figure 3.2. Private net benefit added by land clearing compared with various social net benefit curves with differing implications for the optimality of the extent of private land clearing.

fail to achieve a social optimum. While additional complications regarding maxima could be discussed (e.g. multiple relative maxima) enough has been said to indicate that in order to determine whether social optimality is being achieved it can be important to take account of total or absolute spillover effects rather than only marginal variations in these.

The retention of forested areas or areas of natural vegetation can have a number of external benefits. These include:

(1) A less variable supply of water downstream.

(2) Less erosion than otherwise and less siltation of dams, harbours and other installations.

(3) Better quality (potable) water with less treatment required for domestic use and less chance of disease transmission.

(4) In some areas, removal of deep-rooted vegetation raises the underground water table causing top soils to become salty and thereby raising salinity levels of water downstream. The salting of soils renders these unsuitable for many crops and water in streams may become so saline that it is useless for most purposes, e.g., for drinking or irrigation. Fish stocks are also killed.

(5) The removal of natural cover may result in the increased turbidity of streams. This can have an unfavourable impact on fish stocks.

(6) The retention of natural vegetation cover may maintain organic matter in run-off water and be favourable to fish and crustacean growth downstream.

(7) The retention of trees and other vegetation may add to the stock of wildlife of various kinds. To the extent that wildlife moves out of an area and is enjoyed by those seeing or hearing it, this is an external benefit.

(8) The area may be a breeding ground for migratory commercial species.

(9) The area may be a beneficial degrader of wastes.

(10) The visual impact of a natural area may be superior if trees or other vegetation cover is retained.

When favourable external effects such as the above exist for naturally vegetated land, the market value of land for commercial use or development is often less than its social value for conservation purposes. The market value of land usually only reflects the present discounted value of the net benefits that can be *appropriated* by its owners. The problem then is that land with favourable externalities may be developed for commercial use by individuals acting in their own self-interest when it is in the social interest to leave the area in an underdeveloped or less developed state. This can be illustrated diagrammatically by Figure 3.3.

In Figure 3.3, the supply of available land with natural vegetation cover is supposed to be OB. Its supply curve is as indicated by line BS. The net present discounted benefits of such land for commercial (private) use is assumed to be as indicated by curve DED. Consequently, the market value of this land will be OP per unit and all of it will be developed commercially at this price. However, suppose that unfavourable spillover or external marginal costs are associated with the development of this land and are as indicated by line KEG. Then it is only socially optimal to develop OA of the available land supply and to leave AV of the supply with natural vegetation cover. *The market fails* because it leads to development of all of the available land.

Consider a hypothetical illustrative example involving the use of wetlands (Cf. Dohan, 1977): If a wetland area at present unutilised for intensive economic activity is filled to provide a construction-site, its present private net discounted value (after deducting filling cost) is $10,000. If the wetland is retained for ecological and related benefits, the owner can obtain a net present value of $4,000 from fishing and collecting of produce on the wetland and $5,000 for its recreational use (a total of $9,000) but can appropriate no other benefits. Hence, his/her private interest dictates that it be filled and used for construction since by doing so he/she can make a gain of $1,000 in net present value.

Retained in its natural state, the wetland may add to the productivity of fishing industries (finfish, crustaceans and shellfish) external to the wetland. It may do this as a source of food for fish external to the area and by providing a hatchery habi-

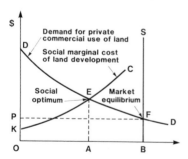

Figure 3.3. Pursuance of private gain may result in too much natural vegetated land being developed for commercial purposes. This is so if favourable externalities arise from natural vegetation cover and a social viewpoint is adopted.

tat for fish. It may also provide benefits by way of clean water management, air cleansing and supply of a storm barrier. Assume that together the net present value of such benefits amounts to $11,000. Thus the social net benefit of retaining the wetland for ecological and related benefits is at least $20,000. Dohan (1977) suggests that extra allowances should also be made for the value of the wetland as a habitat for transient wildlife (it may be in a flyway), its visual amenity and 'open space value', its contribution to preservation of endangered species and its importance in retaining options. Hence, the social value of retaining the wetland for its ecological and related benefits far exceeds that for its use as a construction-site, despite the fact that the owner's private interest dictates construction on the land.

However, unfavourable externalities can also arise from keeping land in its natural state. Unfavourable externalities can include:

(1) greater risks of fires spreading to adjoining properties; and

(2) the possibility of such areas acting as havens for pests (Cf. Timberlake, 1985, pp. 122–123). In some countries, for example, elephants, tigers and other large animals roaming from national parks and forests inflict considerable damage on nearby agriculturalists and pastoralists. Weeds growing in national parks or forested areas may be the source of seeds causing outbreaks of weed infestation on adjoining properties.

If we take the situation depicted in Figure 3.3, the government has a number of policy options open to it to counteract unfavourable externalities. It could, for example, place a tax of AE on each unit of land developed, or provide a subsidy of AE on each unit retained in its natural state, or prohibit the development of AB of the land or purchase AB of it for a national park. Other policy options are also available. Each option has various advantages and drawbacks. Let us consider in some depth possible policies available to governments to correct for environmental externalities.

3.3 Government policies 'to correct' for externalities

Externalities may result in a socially suboptimal situation, that is, a situation in which a potential Paretian improvement or a Kaldor-Hicks gain is theoretically possible. By adopting appropriate policies, a government may be able to bring about such an improvement. But if government intervention is contemplated, the following questions should be answered in turn

(1) Is the externality Paretian relevant? If not, interference is not justified on economic efficiency grounds.

(2) If yes, will the cost of intervention such as costs of collecting taxes if taxes are involved (more generally the agency, monitoring, enforcement and transaction costs associated with policy) exceed the benefits otherwise obtained? If yes, intervention cannot be justified on economic grounds but otherwise it may be justified.

(3) If a number of alternative policies are available to correct for an externality, which *one* is likely to be most effective from an economic viewpoint?

(4) When there is a choice of different policy measures is one to be preferred to the other on grounds of equity or justice? For example, would taxation or a subsidy be preferred on income distribution grounds as a means of responding to the externality?

Means which governments may use to counteract externalities include (1) taxes, (2) subsidies, (3) fiat, prohibition or regulation, (4) auctioning of rights to engage in externality-producing activities, (5) state ownership and control of property, (6) facilitation of private negotiation and agreement, (7) strengthening of property rights, (8) internalisation of externalities by extension of ownership, even the creation of monopolies and (9) in certain cases, provision of information (Cf. McNeely, 1990; Tisdell, 1982; Tisdell, 1983b). At this stage let us consider the features of each of these possible policy measures by reference to the example of an unfavourable environmental externality illustrated in Figure 3.1 supposing that the line CE represents the social marginal cost of tree-clearing.

(1) *Taxes.* A tax of BC may be imposed on each hectare of land cleared thereby bringing the private marginal cost of land clearing into equality with social marginal cost. Assuming that the price of commodities are unaffected, this tax reduces the income of the landholder by an amount equivalent to the area of quadrilateral BCEG. If the tax is a widespread tax on many landholders who produce the same product on their land, the aggregate supply of the product may be significantly affected and so the market price of the product may change. This can be allowed for in the analysis.

(2) *Subsidies.* A subsidy of BC for each hectare of land not cleared could alternatively be paid to the landholder. By clearing land, the landholder foregoes this subsidy. When this subsidy foregone is added to the actual private cost of land-clearing, the marginal cost of land-clearing is raised to the social marginal cost. If the landholder has x_4 hectares of uncleared land, x_1 hectares will be cleared and x_4-x_1 will be left uncleared in order to maximise private gain. This policy, compared to non-intervention, raises the income of the landholder by an amount equal to $(x_4$-$x_1)$ BC less the area of triangle NEG. This, however, is a higher income transfer than is necessary to achieve the result required. If for example, the subsidy is paid *only* on the area in excess of x_4-x_1 cleared, this reduces the total amount of subsidy paid by $BC(x_4$-$x_1)$ but the effect on the amount of tree-clearing is the same.

Whether or not subsidisation rather than taxation is preferred by a government may depend upon income distribution considerations. If the landholders involved are relatively poor, the subsidisation approach may be preferred. Note that subsidisation assumes a permissive attitude to land-clearing (a 'right' to do it) and the taxation approach supposes a non-permissive attitude to land-use. Views about justice or equity, which may vary from society to society, will influence how rights to use property are determined and in turn influence whether compensation should or should not be paid to a landholder for a change in land-use (Cf. Mishan, 1981, pp 403–404, 473–474). The advantage of taxation is that 'the polluter pays' and/or the purchaser of the products causing the pollution, depending on the incidence of the tax. Furthermore, the tax enables a net contribution to state finances if *agency* costs do not exceed the revenue generated. This surplus could, if the government wished, be used for government funded conservation projects (IUCN-UNEP-WWF, 1990).

(3) *Fiat, prohibition and regulation.* The clearing of more than x_1 hectares of land may be prohibited. The effectiveness of prohibition will depend on the penalties imposed for non-compliance, the probability of detection of a violation and the likelihood of successful prosecution. It has analogies with the taxation approach but unlike the taxation approach, the only revenue which it would generate for the government is via fines for violations, if these are the penalty for non-compliance. As for all the policies considered so far, government monitoring and transaction costs are involved in prohibition and direct regulation and need to be offset against the benefits otherwise obtained.

(4) *Auctioning of rights.* Rights to engage in creation of environmental spillovers can be auctioned. For instance, certificates can be printed permitting the holder to engage in a particular level of activity such as clearing a specified quantity of land. Having, say, determined the total quantity of land to be cleared in a region, certificates to this value may be auctioned by the government to landholders. In some circumstances this method is efficient but, if the degree of externality created by the activity in question varies by location, it is less than perfectly efficient (Tisdell, 1983a). Not all markets for pollution rights or environmental degradation rights can be 'made' to operate perfectly because in some cases the number of participants is small and this reduces competition for rights and knowledge is imperfect. Once again monitoring, agency and transaction costs are involved in the government's implementation of the policy and need to be taken into account.

(5) *State ownership and control of property.* A possible way of ensuring that the desired portion of the property considered in Figure 3.1 is not cleared is to make it state property, for example, dedicate the required number of uncleared hectares as a national park or wilderness area. However, the *mere* creation of state property does not ensure social optimality. For instance, if the complete land-holding is state property, say used for forestry or farming, no less clearing may occur than under private ownership. The state organisation in control of the property may have a narrow productive goal and indeed, it is conceivable that its managers may be rewarded on the basis of the level of material production of the landholding. Hence they may have little or no incentive to take account of environmental spillovers as, for example, can be observed in a number of socialist countries e.g. China.

(6) *Facilitation of private negotiation and agreement.* In a world of no transaction costs, individuals adversely affected by externalities would be willing to negotiate with parties causing these to limit their unfavourable externalities. Those damaged might be prepared to pay for such limitation. But the costs of reaching agreement, communicating, monitoring compliance and enforcing it where necessary (that is, transaction costs) may not be trivial and can stand in the way of voluntary agreement to eliminate a Paretian relevant externality. In some cases, the government by intervening can reduce these costs, for instance by convening a meeting of parties and by providing legal support for any agreement reached. Nevertheless, impediments to private negotiation and agreement cannot always be eliminated economically by government intervention.

(7) *Strengthening of property rights.* Sometimes lack of property rights or clearly defined rights may add to negotiation costs or make it more difficult socially to control externalities. If for instance, a clear legal right exists to create an unfavourable externality, those wishing for its control have to compensate those causing the externality. On the other hand, if those affected by the unfavourable externality have a clear legal right to be free of such effects, then those wishing to create the externality must compensate those affected. Clear definition of property rights makes it easier to reach voluntary agreement. However, it does not overcome all difficulties or costs involved in reaching voluntary agreement. If an agreement is violated, difficulties still remain because those adversely affected have the burden and cost of proving that a violation has occurred and identifying the party or parties responsible. Resolution of legal disputes is not straightforward and costless especially where the spillover effect is indirect and diffused and arises from the action of several parties. Sometimes, as discussed in the next chapter, common access to natural resources can be a cause of insufficient conservation and excessive environmental deterioration. In *some* cases, this pattern can be corrected by creating private property, state property or community (collective) property.

(8) *Internalisation of externalities.* Extension of ownership of resources can mean that effects previously external to the owner become internalised. For example, extension of land ownership by an individual to include a larger area may mean that some effects of tree-clearing which were originally external to the property-owner are now internalised. Thus the property-holder would then take the previous externalities into account in pursuing his/her self-interest.

In some cases, externalities may be most effectively internalised when a monopoly is created. However, extension of ownership is not always an efficient way to correct for externalities. Diseconomies of size may arise and while increasing size may result in previous externalities being taken into account by the relevant decision-maker, extra costs of production arising from greater size may more than negate the advantages achieved otherwise. In addition, the extension of ownership can have unwelcome income distributional consequences e.g. the owner may increase his/her income substantially relative to the rest of the community and in particular cases engage in monopoly pricing.

(9) *Provision of information.* Individuals may have a misleading view of their private benefits from actions which have external effects. For example, landholders may overestimate their private net benefits from land-clearing and clear a greater amount of land than maximises their net benefit. By correcting these misconceptions, a private gain can be made and an external benefit obtained (Tisdell, 1985a). In circumstances such as this, a Kaldor-Hicks' economic efficiency ground exists for some government provision of information. The costs, however, of this provision have to be compared with the benefits. Once again, intervention is not costless.

The above sketch of policy measures available to government to correct for unfavourable environmental externalities indicates that none are perfect and costless. In every case one has to consider whether there is in fact a net benefit from intervention. While net benefits are possible, and in some cases they may be substantial, it cannot be assumed just because a Paretian relevant externality exists that government intervention designed to correct an externality will lead to a socially superior situation (Cf. Tisdell, 1985b).

3.4 Public or collective good characteristics associated with the conservation of nature

Living natural resources may be pure public or pure collective goods or may possess some characteristics associated with such goods. A pure public or collective good (a) can be consumed or enjoyed without its available supply being diminished and (b) it is impossible or uneconomic to exclude individuals from consuming it or enjoying it once it is supplied (Brown and Jackson, 1986). Consequently, individuals who fail to pay for a pure public good cannot be stopped from consuming it. These two main characteristics of a pure public good are sometimes described as non-rivalry and non-exclusion. Because of the non-exclusion attribute, a pure collective good cannot be marketed. It may, therefore, not be supplied or if it is supplied, it may be undersupplied in the sense that a potential Paretian improvement or a Kaldor-Hicks' gain could be made by greater supply. Commodities which have extremely large externalities are near pure public goods. As will be discussed in the chapter dealing with wildlife, some goods are mixed private and public goods. A private good is characterised by both rivalry and exclusion and can be marketed.

As an example of a pure public good, consider the *existence value* of a species. Some species of wildlife have little or no value from an economic viewpoint except their existence value. In Australia, the hairy-nosed wombat and the Lord Howe Island woodhen are examples of species which have little or no utilitarian or use-value but have existence value as witnessed by public donations to help save their populations. Many other species such as the giant panda, the symbol of WWF, previously World Wildlife Fund but now called Worldwide Fund for Nature, seem to fall into this category also. The optimal supply of a pure public good, failure of optimal supply and the scope for government intervention, can be illustrated by taking a species which solely has existence value as an example.

To ensure economic efficiency in satisfying wants, a pure public good must be supplied in a quantity which equates to the *collective* demand for it with the marginal cost of supplying it. Otherwise some individuals can be made better off without making others worse off. The collective demand for a pure public good is found by adding the separate demands of individuals for the commodity. Thus if 10 individuals each place a one dollar value on the supply of an additional unit of a pure public good, their collective demand for it is $10. Non-rivalry in consumption justifies this addition. This means that demand curves of individuals for a pure public good are added 'vertically', to obtain the collective demand curve for the good, whereas for a private good such curves are added 'horizontally' to obtain the aggregate demand curve.

In Figure 3.4, the line marked DD represents the collective demand for levels of population of a species (for instance, of hairy-nosed wombats or giant pandas) on the basis of their existence value alone. Given that the line identified by MC_1 is the marginal cost of conserving the various possible levels of population of the species, the socially optimal level of conservation of the species from an economic viewpoint is x_2. At this population level, the marginal cost of conserving the species just equals the additional collective demand for it.

At levels less than x_2 of the population of the species, the extra collective value from greater conservation of the population exceeds its extra cost, whereas for population levels exceeding x_2 the extra collective value from adding to the population exceeds its extra cost.

Without government intervention, the supply of a pure public good (in this case the level of the population of a species conserved) is likely to be sub-optimal. This can be appreciated from Figure 3.4. Suppose that the line marked d_ad_a is the demand curve of the individual or economic entity with the greatest demand for conservation of the species. In this case, in the absence of government intervention, the individual is willing to conserve a population of x_1 of the species. This is a greater population than other individuals individually would be prepared to conserve because their demand curves are lower. Thus the other individuals will free ride on the individual with the greatest demand for the pure public good and only x_1 of it will be supplied.

If the demand of no individual exceeds the marginal cost of conservation of the species then no individual has an incentive to conserve it. Its population falls to zero under laissez-faire even though the socially optimal population or supply is x_2 given the aggregate demand curve indicated in Figure 3.4. Thus there is market or individualistic failure to ensure a social optimum. Government intervention to conserve the species may increase economic efficiency in satisfying human desires in this case. It will do so if the costs of government intervention do not exceed the benefits otherwise obtainable.

However, there is not an economic case per se for supplying *every* good with public good characteristics or for conserving *every* species with existence value. For example, if in Figure 3.4 the marginal cost of conserving the species is as identified by MC_2 rather than MC_1, it would not be economically efficient to conserve the species – the cost of preserving the species exceeds the collective eco-

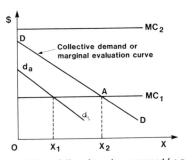

Figure 3.4. The optimal level of conservation of the population of a species considered as a pure public good on the basis of its existence values.

nomic value of doing so. Nevertheless, one should not be too dogmatic when an apparent case of this nature is identified in practice.

First, one must remember that demand curves are anthropocentric. Secondly, individuals may be poorly informed about the characteristics of the species and so their evaluations may be based on faulty knowledge. Thirdly, attitudes towards the existence-value of species change over time and the attitudes of future generations cannot be known with certainty. This together with learning possibilities and irreversibility considerations may make it rational to err more in favour of conservation than might be suggested by a simplified approach indicated above (See Chapter 5, Bishop, 1978). Let us consider reasons for this briefly.

3.5 Option demands, transaction costs, more on existence values, bequest, irreversibility and uncertainty

In a world where preferences may change or the material conditions of individuals may alter with some uncertainty, society or individuals may place a premium on keeping their options open, that is on retaining considerable flexibility. Conservation of resources can help to keep options open but the value of keeping these open may be imperfectly reflected by the market system or by the current use or value placed on resources.

For example, the willingness of visitors to pay to visit a national park or site or to see an animal in its natural surroundings, may apart from any offsite allowance for existence value (Krutilla, 1967) have an additional offsite *option value* (Weisbrod, 1964). Individuals who do not visit the site, may nevertheless be prepared to pay a sum to keep the option open of visiting it in the future. Those conserving the attraction are not as a rule able to appropriate this option-value.

While the owners of a natural site or attraction could conceivably request donations from non-visitors wanting to retain the option (and even from current users who want to keep their option of coming back open), free-riding is quite likely in such a case. The receipts of the owner will suffer as a result of free-riding. Furthermore, the owner of the attraction (and subscribers or donors) will have to incur transaction costs if subscriptions are to be collected to help 'save' the attraction and these will further reduce contributions to cover option-values.

Dolan (1969) suggests that the need for government involvement in resource-conservation because of option-values being unrecorded or inadequately so has been exaggerated. He suggests that those wishing to preserve a natural resource such as a natural area could form a *club* or a company to acquire it. Their subscriptions to shares in the company would be a reflection of their option-values and may also reflect existence values. But, this overlooks the transaction costs involved in forming a company or club for this purpose. Furthermore, a number of favourable externalities as well as existence values are likely to be enjoyed by non-club members so market failure can still be expected to some extent.

Transaction costs can be an important source of market failure. These are costs involved in establishing property rights, enforcing these and in marketing products. Transaction costs cannot always be safely ignored, but sometimes government intervention in resource-use can eliminate or reduce such costs.

While option-values and existence values are conceptually different, it is not always easy to distinguish them in practice. Certainly if one asks an individual the maximum amount he or she is willing to pay for the preservation of a site or a species, this value is likely to include a mixture of pure existence value, of option value, and of bequest value.

Bequest value represents the demand to conserve resources for the benefit of future generations (Krutilla, 1967). Especially when the resources involved are pure public goods, bequest conservation may be subject to market failure because of the free-riding problem. The combination of option, existence and bequest demands have been described by Walsh et al. (1984, p. 14) as representing *preservation values*. They are non-use or non-consumptive values flowing from the existence of a natural resource. They are non-marketable public goods because their consumption is nonrival and nonexclusive (Walsh et al., 1984, p. 15).

Public or collective goods characteristics of conservation are important and this raises the issue of how best to evaluate the demand for such goods by empirical means. Some of the alternative available methods such as contingent valuation methods (Bradford, 1970; Brookshire et al., 1980) are outlined in Hufschmidt et al., (1983) and are discussed in Chapter 7 (see also Bennett, 1982).

The above indicates that market failure can occur when option-values are important and the development or utilisation of a natural resource results in the irreversible loss of the resource. Because of transaction costs and other market imperfections, those wishing to keep their options open may not be able to or be prepared to record an effective monetary 'vote' in favour of conservation of an asset which gives them option-value.

Apart from this, those conserving natural resources may face greater risks than those proceeding with development. The demand for a natural resource and the economic gains that one can appropriate from it in the future may be more uncertain than if one develops it and obtains immediate economic gains. There may also be a greater chance of an underdeveloped (natural) site being resumed by government for development purposes and being resumed at a low rate of compensation to the owner. In cases of resumption of developed sites, greater compensation usually needs to be paid by the government and a greater number of individuals (voters) are normally *on the site* or directly affected to a considerable extent by resumption. This group may therefore take vocal political action, whereas those with an interest in the natural site may not do so because actual owners may be few, and those with an indirect interest may be scattered and, although large in numbers, the benefit of each from conservation of the area may be so small that they do not find it individually worthwhile to take political action, even though aggregate welfare may be reduced by the development. The economics of politics therefore, suggests a preference for the resumption of less developed sites even when this is not in the collective interest.

Arrow (1965) has argued that when individuals are risk-averse they are more reluctant to commit resources to risky or uncertain projects than is socially optimal. To the extent that conservation projects are risky compared to developmental ones, the latter are favoured by private individuals to a greater degree than is socially optimal.

3.6 Discount rates as grounds for government intervention

A sum of money available in the future is generally regarded as being worth less than the same sum of money available now because if the future sum were available now it could be invested at the going rate of interest to ensure its return *plus* accumulated income from interest on it at the later date. The sum of money which if invested now will accumulate to a future sum after addition of interest is the net present value or discounted present value of the future sum. Clearly the net present value of a future sum of money is lower the higher is the rate of interest and the more distant in time is the availability of the future sum.

Individuals trying to maximise their present net worth or wealth should make investment choices which maximise their net present value at interest rates available to them. If these interest rates (market rates of interest) are too high from a social point of view, this results in individuals investing in projects which are not socially optimal. Projects giving quick returns will be excessively favoured in comparison to those providing more distant returns in time.

A number of writers have argued that market rates of interest are too high from a social point of view. The main arguments are summarised by Brown and Jackson (1986, pp. 200–203) They are also discussed, for example, by Perrings (1987), Howe, (1979) and Dasgupta and Pearce, (1972). The relevant factors include the following: Pigou's view that individuals are myopic about their future, the existence of unfavourable externalities for future generations resulting from development now, Sen's isolation paradox (involving a circumstance in which individuals are willing to save more for future generations but only if they can be sure that all others or many others like themselves also save more), high rates of interest in the private sector due to monopoly-elements in the capital market and an excessive risk premium or allowance for risk reflected in the private rate of interest. Let us not debate the merit of these arguments here but rather observe that given these views individuals can be expected to show a socially excessive pref-

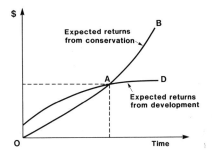

Figure 3.5. In the above case, the higher is the rate of interest used for discounting the more likely development is to be preferred to conservation of a natural resource.

erence for present gains over future ones. This can favour development relative to conservation.

For example, take the case illustrated in Figure 3.5. Suppose that an individual owns a natural resource which can either be conserved or developed. His/her stream of expected returns from developing it is indicated by curve CAD and from conserving it by curve OAB. The higher the rate of interest applied by the individual the more likely the development alternative is to be preferred. If these curves are relatively typical of alternatives, development tends to be privately preferred over conservation, even though socially this choice may not be optimal. V. Kerry-Smith (1974) has argued that natural conserved resources are likely to increase more rapidly in value in the future than developed resources so the type of relationship indicated in Figure 3.5 may not be atypical.

Note also that when the government is using social cost-benefit analysis to choose between alternatives, use of the market rate of interest as a discounting device may be inappropriate. If the market rate is excessive from a social viewpoint, the government by using it for cost-benefit analysis may, in cases such as those illustrated by Figure 3.5, be led to choose development whereas conservation is socially optimal. This is, of course assuming that reconversion of developed resources to a natural state is impossible or extremely costly.

3.7 Monopolies and conservation

Monopolists are sometimes said to be a conservationist's best friend. This is based upon the observation that monopolists tend to restrict supply of products in order to maximise their profit and not 'spoil the market'. In consequence, monopolists are believed to use less natural resources than would be used in a competitive market. However, such an argument overlooks a number of important considerations. Briefly these are:

(1) In order to maximise profit, a monopolist may, from a social viewpoint, excessively restrict use of a resource.

(2) For the product in which the monopolist has a monopoly, he/she may restrict use of a resource but may use the resource for other production not involving his/her monopoly so no net conservation occurs.

(3) In cases where conservation groups wish a particular resource conserved but a monopolist wishes to use it to some extent, the monopolist may prove politically more powerful than would a large group of small businesses.

(4) By promoting demand for and new uses for resources (that is by fostering economic growth) large monopolies and corporations may add to resource-use even though they act at any point of time in a monopoly-like fashion.

Consider each of these points.

Take the first possibility. Assume that a firm has sole ownership of a natural landscape which may contain a unique feature and which has economic value for recreational visits. Let curve AD in Figure 3.6 represent the demand for visits to the natural area and suppose that the marginal cost of visits to the natural site is zero. The benefits to society of the natural site are maximised when entry to it is free and in such a case there will be OD visits per year. But in order to maximise his/her gain a monopolist will charge $OF per visit and earn a monopoly profit equivalent to the area of the rectangle OBCF. The monopolist's price-level for entry is the one which equates his/her marginal revenue to his/her marginal cost, in this case zero. At the monopoly price, only OB visits per year occur and a deadweight social loss equivalent to area of triangle BDC eventuates. In such a case, state ownership of the site combined with free entry can lead to a social gain.

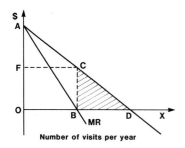

Figure 3.6. Monopoly in this case has no conservation advantages and results in a deadweight social loss.

A monopolist may conserve less of a resource than a socially optimal level because only a portion is retained for the monopolised market. He/she may preserve a smaller area of a unique or special site than is socially optimal and use the remainder for development, for instance for grazing enterprises or for housing estates (Tisdell, 1972). Politically a monopolist may also prove to be a powerful antagonist. The monopolist is able to appropriate gains from political action which would be diffused in the case where there are many firms. Furthermore, a monopolist does not have the problem of organising large numbers of individuals for political action. On the other hand, a monopolist may prefer a 'quiet life' and may not wish to create an unfavourable public image by confrontation with conservation groups.

Schumpeter (1942) extolled the powers of monopolies and oligopolies to generate economic growth through their innovative and demand expanding ability. To the extent that such firms are generators of economic growth, this will make for more rapid use of resources than otherwise. By continually developing new products using a natural resource and by advertising these products, total demands on the resource may be considerably raised by imperfectly competitive firms even though prices are maintained above levels which would prevail under perfect competition. Hence, it is far from clear that monopolists (and ologopolists) are a conservationist's best friends.

3.8 Common property and intervention

Common-property resources are those to which there is common access. Exclusion, while it may be possible, does not take place but at the same time rival or competitive use of the resource occurs unlike in the case of pure public goods (Brown and Jackson, 1986). When use of a resource is competitive but access is non-exclusive, inefficient use of the resource can be expected. In the case of living resources, they may be overharvested to such an extent that the species involved is extinguished even though this is not in the social interest. Common pasture land, communal woodlots and fish on the high seas provide examples. In some instances, resources are common-property de jure (such as fish in non-territorial marine areas) and all individuals have *common access* to these. In other cases, resources are common property de facto because they are fugitive resources. Such resources may stray or move from one 'property' to another and can be appropriated by any property-owner while on his or her property. Some wildlife is of this nature.

Common-property resources are likely to be overexploited from a social point of view. This and its possible remedies are discussed in Chapter 6. Common-property resources are unlikely to be optimally conserved because an individual who undertakes conservation effort now to conserve the future stock of these re-

64

sources cannot be sure of appropriating the benefits or a substantial proportion of the benefits.

3.9 Failure of political and administrative mechanisms in relation to conservation

Reasons why markets and self-interest may not lead to a social optimum have been outlined. As already pointed out, while government intervention may lead to a social improvement in such cases, government intervention is not always economic and effective because of transaction costs involved in carrying out policies and actually intervening. However, we should also be aware that political and administrative mechanisms can fail for fundamental reasons not connected with actual costs of policy implementation. While it is only possible to indicate a few of these reasons here, the sketch should be sufficient to indicate that on the whole no perfect mechanisms for social control of resource use are available. The choice is not between imperfect markets and perfect government and vice versa but between imperfect mechanisms, and the problem on each occasion is to choose the best of the imperfect mechanisms available.

Where a decision about resource-use is reached by *majority voting*, socially optimal use may not be achieved. At least this is so, if the Kaldor-Hicks criterion for a social optimum is adopted. This criterion suggests that a change is a social improvement if those benefiting from the change *can* compensate losers and remain better off than before the change. A social optimum is achieved when there is no potential for changes such that gainers could compensate losers.

The majority voting problem can be illustrated by Figure 3.7. Imagine that a natural site exists and the question is how much of it should be developed. Line DAC represents the marginal willingness of those in favour of development to pay for development whereas line OAB represents the marginal willingness of

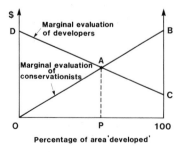

Figure 3.7. Illustration of how majority voting may lead to insufficient or too much conservation judged by the Kaldor-Hicks economic efficiency test.

those in favour of conservation of the area to pay for its conservation. At point A, the marginal willingness to pay for development equals the marginal willingness to pay to prevent it so P represents a Kaldor-Hicks optimal level of development of the site. However, if the matter is to be decided by majority vote in which both developers and conservationists have a vote, 100 per cent development will occur if developers are in the majority. On the other hand, if conservationists are in the majority, 100 per cent conservation of the site will prevail. Neither possible outcome is optimal from the Kaldor-Hicks social point of view.

In practice the area in which majority voting determines resource use may be small. Where a number of issues are coming forward, as in Parliament, there may be scope behind the scene for trades (logrolling) which may lead to modifications of bills (compromise bills) that help to promote a Kaldor-Hicks optimum (Buchanan and Tulloch, 1962).

When the benefits of conservation are spread thinly over many voters but the gains of development flow in a more concentrated fashion to a limited number of developers, the economics of politics (Downs, 1957) suggests that development interests are liable to prevail. Developers individually will set greater store by any political decision influencing development and may find it economic to try to influence it, whereas conservationists even though their overall loss from development may be greater in aggregate may individually pay little attention to it because individually they do not find it economic to organise and take political action.

In a democracy, governments often tend to be myopic in their decisions. The desire of a government or individuals to be re-elected may put a premium on short-term benefits to the detriment of the long-term interest. This can mean that development and rapid resource exploitation is favoured, at least in a democratic system in which elections come up at relatively short intervals.

Individuals within government do not have perfect information. Indeed they often have very imperfect information. Centralisation of government can lead to serious erosion of local authority and inadequate communications between government bodies located in a city and rural-dwellers. In some less developed countries, the replacement of local controls on land-use by central government control has meant the elimination of virtually all effective control in some country areas. This is reputed, for example, to have happened in Nepal (Jefferies, 1982).

Governments, of course, change and alter their view. There is always a risk that an area conserved by one government will be subsequently developed by another. In attempts to deal with the problem, conservation areas in some countries, e.g. U.S.A., are dedicated in perpetuity for conservation. All developmental activities (except some recreational facilities) are banned. This at least makes it more difficult for a future government to reverse land-use. Also, if mixed use of a natural site involving some development is allowed, some development may become the 'thin' edge of the wedge to justify further development.

In addition, it needs to be recognised that government is not a monolithic organisation but consists of many bodies and organisations with differing aims, objective, charters and measures of success. For many such bodies, achievement of economic growth objectives often narrowly defined is the measure of success. Each such body or individual within government does not necessarily pursue the maximisation of social welfare, however defined, but rather may foster the growth of the organisation and his or her own self interest within it (Downs, 1957).

In extreme cases, government may be completely ineffective in maintaining law and order and ensuring conservation. Several less developed countries are for example, shaken by civil war and in such circumstances it is not surprising that there is scant regard for wildlife conservation. Less developed countries face considerable difficulties in ensuring optimal use of their resources and desirable levels of conservation. The next chapter will concentrate on their situation.

3.10 Concluding comment

While markets cannot be relied on to conserve wildlife and natural resources optimally from a social point of view, neither can government. Nevertheless, government intervention can sometimes bring about social improvement and results in more nature conservation than would occur in its absence. There is probably no institutionally *perfect* and universal means of ensuring an optimal degree of conservation. Our existing institutional systems (and proposed ones) therefore, need to be subjected to continual scrutiny and we must search continually for ways to improve them. As pointed, out there are a number of economic instruments or mechanisms, such as pollution or environmental degradation taxes, which governments can sometimes use effectively to promote the conservation of living resources.

This chapter has concentrated on allocative aspects of environmental and conservation issues, particularly aspects of static allocative efficiency, rather than the influence of dynamic and evolutionary elements of socio-economic change. As discussed in the previous chapter, both aspects are important. In the next chapter, in discussing conservation issues in Third World countries (issues similar to those faced by more developed countries in the early stages of their development) more emphasis will be placed on the impact on conservation of socio-economic development and change, including institutional developments.

References

Arrow, K.J., 1965. Aspects of the Theory of Risk-Bearing. The Academic Bookstore, Helsinki.
Bennett, J.W., 1982. Valuing the existence of natural ecosystems. Search, 13:(9–10):232–235.

Bishop, R.C., 1978. Endangered species and uncertainty: The economics of a safe minimum standard. American Journal of Agricultural Economics.

Bradford, D.F., 1970. Benefit-cost analysis and demand curves for public goods. Kyklos, 23:775–791.

Brookshire, D.S., Randall, A. and Stoll, J., 1980. Valuing increments and decrements in natural resource service flows. American Journal of Agricultural Economics, 63: 165–177.

Brown, C.V. and Jackson, P.M., 1986. Public Sector Economics, 3rd ed. Basil Blackwell, Oxford.

Buchanan, J., and Tulloch, G., 1962. The Calculus of Consent. University of Michigan Press, Ann Arbor.

Burrows, P., 1986. Nonconvexity induced by external costs on production: theoretical curio or policy dilemma? Journal of Environmental Economics and Management, 13: 101–128.

Dasgupta, A.K. and Pearce, D.W., 1972. Cost-Benefit Analysis: Theory and Practice. Macmillan, London.

Dohan, M.R., 1977. Economic values and natural ecosystems. In: C. Hall and J.W. Day (Editors), Ecosystems Modelling in Theory and Practice, John Wiley and Sons, New York, 134–171.

Dolan, E.G., 1969. TANSTAAFL: The Economic Strategy for Environmental Crises. Holt, Rinehart and Winston, New York.

Downs, A., 1957. An Economic Theory of Democracy. Harper and Row, New York.

Howe, C.W., 1979. Natural Resource Economics. John Wiley, New York.

Hufschmidt, M.M., James, D.E., Meister, A.D., Bower, B.T. and Dixon, J.A., 1983. Environment, Natural Systems and Development: An Economic Valuation Guide. Johns Hopkins University Press, Baltimore.

IUCN, 1980. World Conservation Strategy. IUCN, Gland, Switzerland.

IUCN-UNEP-WWF, 1990. Caring for the World: A Strategy for Sustainability. Second draft, IUCN, Gland, Switzerland.

Jefferies, B.E., 1982. Sagarmatha National Park: The impact of tourism on the Himalayas. Ambio, 11(5):246–251.

Krutilla, J.V., 1967. Conservation reconsidered. American Economic Review, 57:777–786.

McNeely, J.A., 1988. Economics and Biological Diversity: Developing and Using Economic Incentives to Conserve Biological Resources. IUCN, Gland, Switzerland.

Mishan, E.J., 1981. Introduction to Normative Economics. Oxford University Press, New York.

Perrings, A.C., 1987. Economy and Environment: A Theoretical Essay on the Interdependence of Economic and Environmental Systems. Cambridge University Press, New York.

Schumpeter, J.A., 1942. Capitalism, Socialism and Democracy. Harper Brothers, New York.

Smith V. Kerry, 1974. Technical Change, Relative Prices and Environmental Resource Evaluation. Resources for the Future, Washington, D.C.

Timberlake, L., 1985. Africa in Crisis: The Causes, the Cures of Environmental Bankruptcy. International Institute for Environment and Development, London.

Tisdell, C.A., 1970. On the theory of externalities. The Economic Record, 46:14–25.

Tisdell, C.A., 1972. Provision of parks and preservation of nature. Australian Economic Papers, 11:154–164.

Tisdell, C.A., 1982. Microeconomics of Markets. Wiley, Brisbane.

Tisdell, C.A., 1983a. The law economics and risk-taking. Kyklos, 35:175–185.

Tisdell, C.A., 1983b. Pollution control: policies proposed by economists. Journal of Environmental Systems, 12:363–380.

Tisdell, C.A., 1985a. Conserving and planting trees on farms: lessons from Australian cases. Review of Agricultural and Marketing Economics, 53:185–194.

Tisdell, C.A., 1985b. Externalities and Coasian considerations in project evaluation: aspects of social CBA in LDCs. Indian Journal of Quantitative Economics, 1:33–43.

Walsh, C. and Tisdell, C.A., 1973. Non-marginal externalities: as relevant and as not. The Economic Record, 49:447–455.

Walsh, R.G., Loomis, J.B. and Gillman, R.A., 1984. Valuing option, existence and bequest demands for wilderness. Land Economics, 60:14–29.

Weisbrod, B., 1964. Collective – consumption services of individual-consumption goods. Quarterly Journal of Economics, 78:471–477.

Chapter 4

Environmental conservation in developing countries

4.1 Introduction

From an economic viewpoint, developing countries are heavily dependent on living resources and natural environments. Furthermore, developed countries benefit substantially from the conservation of such resources in developing countries. In Third World countries living resources are the main source of sustenance and in many cases are the major source of foreign income through exports of goods, such as timber, fish and agricultural produce (See for instance, McKee and Tisdell, 1990). Natural environments in such countries may also be an important source of 'invisible' trade such as international tourist trade. To a large extent, however, Third World countries appear only to appropriate a small proportion of the world's benefits from the conservation of their living resources. This, combined with their particular economic, social and demographic pressures for economic growth, means that the preservation of their living resources is threatened. Therefore the developed world needs to address itself to this matter both from the point of view of its own self-interest and with a view to aiding Third World countries.

One reason for singling out conservation in Third World countries for special attention is that by far the largest proportion of the world's species exist only in Third World countries. Most developed countries lie outside tropical and semi-tropical areas which contain the majority of the world's species (Myers, 1979). Today, by far the greatest number of the world's species are threatened by economic change in Third World countries. While many species are bound to disappear others can be saved by changed policies and by international aid or assistance (Allen, 1980; IUCN-UNEP-WWF, 1990).

The purpose of this chapter is to outline economic and social factors which make conservation in less developed countries difficult to achieve and to consider 'self-help' policies that might encourage greater conservation in these countries. The rationale for foreign aid, debt remission and more favourable international trade policies to assist less developed countries with conservation is also given some attention.

4.2 Basic conservation problems in the Third World: origin

Species are increasingly endangered or are disappearing in the Third World mainly due to the activities of man. As a result of economic and technological change, (1) the habitats of species are being increasingly destroyed by man and consequently wildlife is losing food or shelter or other means of life-support; (2) man is harvesting the population of many species at a faster rate than ever before, in many cases at unsustainable rates; (3) in some cases, even though the species itself may not be harvested nor its habitat threatened, man is competing more intensely with the species for a vital resource (such as a food-source or water) and thereby creating a shortage of the resource for the species; and (4) as a result of pollution and degradation of the Biosphere by economic activity eliminating vital elements of the life-support systems of many species.

Habitat destruction is often an insidious threat to nature but sometimes it occurs rapidly. In the Third World major habitat destruction is occurring as forests and trees are removed, as wetlands are drained, as urban and rural settlements expand, and as land areas are transformed to meet the immediate demands of man (Myers, 1979). Changes of this type had a major impact on the disappearance of species in more developed countries in their earlier stages of development (Cf. Harting, 1880).

Loss of forests and tree cover is coming about, for instance, because of logging (very often for sales of exported commercial timber to developed countries, as in the case of rainforests). In addition, tree cover is being reduced by the cutting of timber for fuel (the main source of fuel in the Third World), the clearing of land for agricultural use, and overgrazing by domestic animals, which hampers or prevents the regeneration of trees. Again, land is being more extensively and intensively used for agriculture. In areas of nomadic and shifting agriculture, permanent settlement is becoming more common. Permanent settlement often leads to rapid deterioration of the local natural environment. In the case of shifting agriculture, cycles of use are shortening so that there is less time for natural regeneration of areas to occur between shifts.

While the 'Green Revolution' has transformed traditional agriculture in many less developed countries and has been hailed as a means of raising crop yields and relieving poverty, it has not been without environmental costs and doubts have been raised about the long-term prospects of sustaining agricultural yields using 'Green Revolution' techniques (Alauddin and Tisdell, 1991; Alauddin and Tisdell, 1990; Tisdell and Alauddin, 1989). The Green Revolution has relied upon the introduction of high yielding varieties of crops in less developed countries. But in order for these to provide high yields they must be grown as a rule in artificial environments created by the use of artificial fertilisers, pesticides and irrigation. Many of the resources required for the creation of these artificial environments are non-renewable. Furthermore, Green Revolution technologies have increased the incidence of multiple cropping and the use of mechanical means of cultivation e.g. by tractors. The land is therefore more intensely cultivated to the detriment of most wildlife. Furthermore, the available time for fallowing or resting the soil is reduced, soil structure deteriorates and its fertility tends to fall, often requiring even greater applications of artificial fertiliser to maintain yields. In addition, pollution from increasing artificial fertiliser-use and pesticide-use in developing countries appears to be reducing the availability of wildlife e.g. natural stocks of fish have been adversely affected in Bangladesh (Minkin, 1988). On the whole, the process of the Green Revolution appears to be unfavourable to nature conservation, at least in the short-term.

Agriculture is also encroaching increasingly on to arid and semi-arid lands and marginal agricultural ones in some Third World countries e.g. in Africa. Such changes in land-use, apart from hastening the disappearance of species, are causing environmental changes such as desertification, erosion, siltation, hydrological disturbances and possibly weather changes. Considerable doubt has been expressed about whether economic development can be sustained in these circumstances (Allen, 1980).

These environmental problems stem from a number of socio-economic trends in Third World countries – rising human populations, heightened income aspirations, the expansion of the market system, the availability of new technology, high effective rates of interest, difficulties in enforcing conservation measures in Third World countries and, in some cases, increased centralisation of government and resource-control and the rapacious nature of some political and power structures. While most of these factors have been well canvassed, it is appropriate to emphasise their significance by considering each briefly (Cf. Tisdell, 1990, Ch.4).

4.3 Population growth and income aspirations

Important factors contributing to the deterioration in the natural environment of LDCs are the growth of human population and rising aggregate levels of consumption of goods. Even though incomes per head are not rising significantly in many LDCs, levels of population growth are such in most that even with relatively constant levels of consumption per capita, aggregate consumption and production is rising and placing mounting pressure on natural resources (Barney, 1980; World Commission on Environment and Development, 1987). The demands of developed countries for imported natural resources such as minerals, timber and fish from LDCs puts further strain on the natural environment of the Third World.

No major reversal of these influences is likely in the near future. While overall *rates* of population increase are declining in the Third World (Eberstadt, 1980; World Bank, 1990) and rates of population increase are close to zero in many developed countries, substantial absolute increases in the levels of population in the Third World can still be expected to occur and pressures for rising levels of material consumption are likely to continue throughout the world (See Chapter 12). Indeed, such pressures for economic growth may intensify in LDCs. Casual observation suggests that residents of LDCs try to emulate the consumption patterns of more developed countries when their incomes rise.

There is a strong rural to urban drift of population in LDCs (Barney, 1980; World Commission on Environment and Development, 1987). It might be thought that this drift will reduce environmental pressures in the countryside. But this may not occur. The drift to cities may encourage commercial agriculture and commercial fisheries and raise income aspirations thereby adding to pressures in the countryside. Furthermore, the link between man and nature may be weakened with possible economic costs and conservational disadvantages to society.

Urban residents and the urban educated may fail to see adequately the interdependencies which exist between man and nature, especially in rural settings. If the urban educated become public decision-makers, they may propose technocratic solutions for the economic transformation of the countryside and these may fail to take account of ecological interdependence. This can result in severe economic detriment of rural communities as has been observed in India (Sinha, 1984).

Issues about desirable levels of human population, desirable limits on human consumption and the efficacy and acceptability of possible methods to achieve these objectives, cannot be ignored by individuals interested in supporting the conservation of nature. For example, are the type of policies for zero-population growth and for steady-state economies proposed by Hermann Daly (1980) desirable and workable on a global scale? Should the developed countries be the first ones to 'pull in their belts' as suggested by Ehrlich (1970) and reduce their levels of per capita consumption? Would this be effective in influencing conservation efforts in the Third World and in moderating income aspirations there, especially amongst the wealthiest members of these communities? Some of these issues are taken up in Chapter 12.

4.4 Expansion of the market system

With the advent of relatively low cost transport and communication systems, most of the world (subject to some qualifications for socialist countries) is now integrated into a (modified) market system. In socialist countries strong calls to expand the market systems are being made. Remaining isolated pockets of the world are being increasingly drawn into the world economic system and partially integrated areas are becoming more completely integrated.

While expansion of the market system and of markets can bring economic advantages, it can also result in greater exploitation of natural resources and reduced conservation of nature, as previously isolated communities find they have markets for natural resources previously unexploited or used on a limited scale and greater access to capital and technology to exploit these resources.

As a result of expanded markets and international trade, traditional people, according to Raymond F. Dasmann as discussed by Klee (1980, Ch.1), have been transformed in outlook from 'Ecosystem people' to 'Biosphere people' depending not just on the resources of their localised ecosystem but upon the resources of the entire Biosphere. Dasmann claims that when groups are dependent for their existence on a local ecosystems, they will adopt economic practices that sustain local ecosystems, but they no longer have strong incentives to do this when their dependence on local ecosystems is reduced by the extension of markets and exchange e.g. by international trade. However, it should not be concluded from this that all traditional peoples lived in harmony with nature. Several cases exist in which traditional peoples have destroyed species (Tisdell, 1989, p.108).

The growth of the market fosters the development of impersonal relationships. For example, it encourages the growth of private self-interest in behaviour to the neglect of social considerations necessary for environmental preservation. This tendency is reinforced by an expansion in private-property rights and, in particular, greater mobility of individuals. Increased *mobility* of individuals encourages a short-term attitude towards conservation (even where conservation is within private control) because an individual always has the prospect of moving away to *other* economic possibilities once a natural resource has been exhausted or degraded in his or her present location. Localised forms of social control, e.g. social criticism, may also become relatively ineffective with greater social mobility.

As the socio-economic system changes, resources may increasingly come under the control of absentee-owners, with little or no interest in the general well-being of the community in which such resources are located (Gregory, 1981). The absentee-owners can include absentee-landlords, and large companies, including multinational companies, effectively controlled by individuals resident in distant areas. This also helps to sever the link between nature and man, that is, alienate man from his environment.

But markets are not the only 'modern' socio-economic mechanisms which do this. The growth of centralised systems of resource direction, such as have been common in socialist countries but not absent either in capitalist countries because of the growth of centralised government and large corporations, have increased the incidence of impersonal relationships between individuals and have reduced the bonds between man and Nature. These developments have increasingly alienated man from Nature, and from his/her local community. Combined with modern technologies and direction of activity often by distant technocrats, this has lead to widespread destruction of Nature and disregard for local environments. Even in those cases where centralised bodies would be receptive to the wishes of local communities, lack of knowledge about the impact of modern technology by local communities and the transaction costs involved (both for the local community and a centralised authority) in interacting may be so high as to make effective communication between the local community and the centralised authority impossible.

4.5 New technology

New technology (and sometimes capital) imported from abroad can provide means for accelerated exploitation of natural resources in the Third World. Any previous social restrictions on the use of common-property resources, such as closed seasons or areas, may prove ineffective in ensuring the preservation of living resources once, for instance, advanced hunting technology is introduced.

The rate of harvesting of a wildlife species, including of course species of fish, can be pushed beyond the rate of growth of their populations once new hunting or harvesting technology is introduced. Consequently the exploited species may be driven to extinction. Hence, if a species is common-property (or effectively so), stricter social regulations on hunting or harvesting may be needed to forestall extinction of the species when new technology is introduced. However, the necessary changes in regulations may be slow in coming. The community may be slow to perceive the danger to the continued existence of the species, to formulate alternative courses of action to deal with the danger and to obtain social support for a particular policy.

One method sometimes used in the Third World is to ban new hunting or harvesting technologies or to limit their use to specific locations or time-periods. Provision has been made for this in the wildlife management areas of Papua New Guinea (Parker, 1977; Kula, 1979; Downes, 1981). While this policy may be effective in conserving the species under threat, it does result in the cost of the actual harvest or catch being greater than necessary.

It is not only harvesting or hunting technologies that can threaten the existence of a species. Other new technologies used in economic activities may result in the habitat of endangered species being destroyed at a faster rate (Harting, 1880) or may give rise to unfavourable spillovers for a species. For instance, chemicals and metal wastes from economic activity may poison a species or adversely affect its reproduction.

The introduction of new technologies to LDCs has not only adversely affected wildlife but has created ecological and, in many cases, economic problems for the sustainability of agriculture, forestry and commercial fisheries. Techniques have sometimes been introduced which threaten the maintenance of production in the long-term. In some cases unfavourable externalities have not been taken into account in evaluating new technologies and projects.

4.6 Problems illustrated by some cases

Consider briefly some examples of species which have been threatened in LDCs by economic development. Experience with populations of dugong and giant clams are instructive. The dugong or sea cow (*Dugong dugong*) is a saltwater-dwelling mammal with a natural range confined to the Indo-Pacific region. However, the dugong has been virtually eliminated from all of its former natural range except in northern Australia and surrounding New Guinea. But it is also now endangered in areas surrounding New Guinea (Hudson, 1980, 1981).

The dugong lives in shallow bays and similar areas where it feeds on marine grasses that are not utilised to any great extent by other species (Sadleir, 1970). The meat is tasty and eagerly sought after by Papuan and aboriginal people, and the animal helps provide protein from a resource that otherwise would be virtually unutilized.

Traditionally, dugongs were hunted along the Papuan coast of New Guinea from canoes using hand-thrown harpoons, though even more limited methods relying on harpooning from platforms were used earlier (Olewale and Sedu, 1980). Although some barter trading of dugong occurred (for example, with more distant villages for sago), most dugongs were consumed by the village catching them. Harvesting pressure on the dugong have increased because of the following factors.

(1) The addition of outboard motors to traditional canoes – once a dugong is sighted it has little chance of escaping – and the use of nylon nets (Eaton and Sinclair, 1981).

(2) The increased trade in dugong meat between villages and in Daru, for example, for cash. The outboard motor has made it easier to bring dugong meat to Daru for sale.

(3) The increasing Papuan population and their rising income aspirations have added to the hunting pressures as have demands for cash to pay taxes, to provide for educational fees, and to purchase Western goods such as beer and tobacco.

The social response to the changed circumstances of the dugong have been slow. In 1976 the dugong was made a National Animal of Papua New Guinea, which meant that it could only be *legally* hunted by traditional methods for traditional purposes. Nevertheless, the take continued at a high level. In 1976, for example, the Kiwais of the Western Province of Papua New Guinea (PNG) remained opposed to any regulation of dugong hunting, even though the species is culturally most important for them (Hudson, 1983). However, in 1978, after extensive education by the Wildlife Division of PNG, the Kiwais created the Maza Wildlife Management Area for the conservation and management of dugongs and appointed their own Committee to manage it. Nevertheless, the people of the coastal villages were allowed to continue to supply meat to the market at Daru (Eaton and Sinclair, 1981). The population of dugong in the North Torres Strait continued to decline because hunting pressures remained the same. In the early 1980s the Government of PNG considered further conservation measures but was slow in gazetting them (Olewale and Sedu, 1980).

The matter has been complicated by the fact that the village people were not aware of the danger of local extinction of the species and felt neglected in central government decision-making. Two Kiwai have said:

'But if they [the village people] were consulted and involved in the various studies, their pride in dugong will grow. People will understand that it is our responsibility to protect the dugong' (Olewale and Sedu, 1980).

The dugong problem, apart from illustrating the impact of a market cash economy, new technology and consequences of centralised decision-making, illustrates various social/administrative lags in implementing conservation policies. These include a perception lag, a lag in convincing individuals of the need for collective action, a lag in devising alternative possible policies and a delay in selecting a policy from amongst the alternatives and obtaining its social acceptance.

As another example consider the fate of giant clams, species of the family Tridacnidae (Copland and Lucas, 1988; Lucas, 1988; Heslinga, 1989). Giant clams are marine bivalve molluscs which occur in the warmer waters of the Indo-Pacific region particularly in association with coral reefs. All species of this family are now considered to be endangered and have become locally extinct in many areas, mainly as a result of the activities of man. Introduced technology, access to international markets, economic growth and human population pressures have all played a part in the depletion of giant clam populations.

For example, the availability of improved and simplified diving equipment has meant that clams can be harvested at greater depth, access to motorised boats has made it possible to harvest clams in remote areas. Export and transport over long distances of clam adductor muscle e.g. to Taiwan, has been made possible by freezer units on ships. These developments all added to harvesting pressures. In some countries, such as the Philippines, giant clams have been sought for their shells which apart from being sold to foreign tourists have mainly been exported to developed countries for resale in shell shops. In some areas too, increased local human populations resulted in unsustainable harvesting of giant clams for subsistence.

Partially because of concern about the disappearance of populations of giant clams techniques have now been developed mainly by researchers from developed countries to breed and rear giant clams under controlled conditions. The recently developed mariculture of giant clams will provide a means to restock areas in less developed countries which have been depleted of natural stocks of clams and could form the basis of a new aquaculture industry (Copland and Lucas, 1988; Tisdell, 1989).

Other examples can easily be given e.g., the impact of economic developments on the green turtle *Chelonia mydas* (Tisdell, 1986). Furthermore the ecological impacts of economic change are not limited to marine wildlife. Important Biosphere changes have arisen from changed agricultural, forest, commercial fishing and industrial practices with the introduction of new technology and the extension of trade.

4.7 High effective rates of discount

Discount rates (interest rates) in less developed countries are often very high or effectively so. When rates of interest are high, as pointed out by Clark (1976), it is often profitable to liquidate slow-growing populations of marketable living resources, such as slow-growing tree species like teak. When the costs of liquidating such assets is the same, one might expect them to be realised more frequently in countries with high discount rates.

The logic of the argument can be seen from the following: Suppose that the going rate of interest is 10 per cent and a stock of living resources e.g., a stand of trees, grows in market value at 4 per cent per annum. If the stock can be harvested and sold at zero or negligible cost to the owner, the sum obtained (its market value) can be invested to earn 10 per cent interest giving a gain in economic return of 6 per cent. Therefore, from a strictly commercial point of view, the most profitable action is to liquidate the living resource.

Taking a narrow economic point of view, it is likely to be more economic to drive a species to extinction in a less developed country than in a developed one, if the rate of interest is the only material consideration. However, shortages of available capital may impede the harvesting process in LDCs (Tisdell, 1970). On the other hand, direct investment by multinational companies such as those in-volved in logging may help to overcome capital limitations in particular cases. Such companies may apply a particularly high rate of discount to their operations in LDCs to allow for political risks and to take account of insecurity of their ten-ure over resources. In addition, the management and shareholders of large cor-porations and multinational corporations not being a part of local communities, and in most instances being remote from such communities, may be relatively in-sensitive to local environmental considerations.

4.8 Difficulties in enforcing conservation measures and questions of social structure

It is one thing for central governments to pass regulations designed to encourage conservation, and another to ensure that these regulations are respected and en-forced. Sometimes stringent laws are passed limiting the hunting of wildlife in LDCs but these are not enforced – the resources for policing the regulations may not be available, there may not be a will to enforce them, and it may be easy to bribe low-paid officials (Momin Khan, 1981; Allen, 1980).

Individuals damaged by conservation measures are likely to resist them. For example, residents near national parks suffering damages from marauding animals or losing traditional rights in areas set aside for parks cannot be expected to be sympathetic to conservation of wildlife unless they are compensated in some way for their losses. Their natural reaction to marauding 'dangerous' animals from na-tional parks would be to attempt to kill them.

Even when it is known that the benefits to the poverty-stricken are likely to be short-term and their action may result in long-term deterioration of their environ-ment, a moral dilemma is involved in preventing those in dire economic circum-stances from using living resources (Mishra, 1982). For although it is clear that encroachment on to lands bordering the Sahara and their more intensive agricul-tural use will lead to environmental degradation, such encroachment is difficult to prevent when individuals have no alternative means of support. One may basi-cally have to come to grips with the problem of increasing population in order to act 'humanely' in such cases. In the longer term, programs to encourage human population control appear to be needed possibly in conjunction with expanded in-ternational aid, trade or migration opportunities (World Commission on Environ-ment and Development, 1987).

4.9 Policies for influencing and improving conservation practices in the Third World

A variety of policy approaches have been suggested for achieving greater conservation of living resources in the Third World. For example, the World Conservation Strategy document basically assumes that most men want to act in their own self-interest and claims that in many cases, greater conservation of resources would be in their self-interest (IUCN, 1980; IUCN-UNEP-WWF, 1990). This suggests that inadequate conservation may occur either because of ignorance about the value of conservation or because social or other impediments result in inadequate rewards to individuals for their conservational efforts. Consequently, given this view, appropriate strategies for influencing conservation effort in LDCs are: (a) to ensure that decision-makers in the Third World (and elsewhere) are adequately informed about the benefits to them of conservation, and (b) to promote social and economic reforms so as to ensure that relevant decision-makers are rewarded for conservational effort. In the latter case, LDCs may have as a goal obtaining an increased payment from developed countries for the benefits obtained by residents of developed countries from conservation in LDCs. LDCs may, for example, be able to appropriate larger payments from foreign tourists or obtain greater foreign aid for making a greater contribution towards conserving the gene pool.

Conservationists differ widely about the most effective social means for promoting conservation in LDCs. Some believe that greater marketing or sales (appropriation) of benefits provided by conservation will be effective (Allen, 1980) whereas others see development along market lines as contrary to the interest of most individuals in LDCs and to conservation (Plumwood and Routley, 1982; Grainger, 1980). The latter group believes that the market system, especially when reinforced by the multinational operations of business enterprises and international agencies, leads to exploitation of both human and natural resources in LDCs, partially because it encourages myopic self-seeking behaviour and the introduction of inappropriate technology. Not all members of this group agree on the ideal solution or indeed suggest one. Nevertheless, the writings of some suggest a separist (autarkic) solution – that conservational goals of LDCs might be best achieved by minimal contact of the Third World with the market system and with the socio-economic system of the developed world (Sahlins, 1974).

The *World Conservation Strategy* (IUCN, 1980) and its proposed update (IUCN-UNEP-WWF, 1990) and *Our Common Future* (World Commission on Environment and Development, 1987), in contrast to this radical view, see economic development and conservation as compatible. Indeed, conservation is seen as a prerequisite for sustainable economic development. These documents envisage increasing contact between the developed and the Third World and the developed world as playing a significant role in fostering conservation in the Third World.

The approach in the World Conservation Strategy document (IUCN, 1980) is not to attempt to change human values so that man, for example, places greater intrinsic value on forms of life other than human life (that is, to create a reverence for life in all of its forms or promote naturalistic ethics) but to take the selfish inclinations of man as given and (by means already suggested) to increase conservational effort. In practice, this involves working with and within existing socio-economic systems. To some this is the only realistic approach. To others, it involves the possibility of undue compromise on conservational issues – the possibility, for example, that by association, conservation groups will 'legitimise' conservation efforts which are only minimal or which are only window-dressing, or be 'captured' by self-interest groups in favour of economic exploitation for their own gain (O'Riordan, 1988). But it might be noted that the proposed update of the World Conservation Strategy (IUCN-UNEP-WWF, 1990) takes a less man-oriented point of view than the IUCN (1980) document.

4.10 Provision of information and education

The World Conservation Strategy (IUCN, 1980) claims: (1) 'Public participation in conservation/development decisions is seldom adequate,' and (2) 'although there has been progress, there is insufficient environmental education,' and suggests particular target groups to which educational campaigns should be directed. Great emphasis is placed on the importance of environmental education and communication.

Advice and education for the Third World needs to be soundly based. While traditional knowledge can be more helpful than introduced Western ideas, this is not always so. Furthermore, ideas need to be communicated effectively and propaganda that fails to take into account the local social and cultural context is not likely to achieve its purpose (Downes, 1981). Sometimes well-meaning Western-based conservation bodies and natural scientists are out of contact with local realities in providing aid and advice to LDCs – their own information is inadequate. Care and humility are needed in supplying information to residents of the Third World.

Note that knowledge does not ensure that individuals will act e.g., conserve living resources, in their *collective* self-interest. This is clear from the prisoners' dilemma – a case in which individuals are perfectly informed but action in accordance with their narrow self-interest leads to the welfare of all being adversely affected; that is, to a suboptimal collective outcome (Luce and Raiffa, 1955). Nevertheless, knowledge about a social problem may help to increase the social acceptability of any regulations designed to alter individual actions based on narrow self-interest.

4.11 Appropriating greater gains nationally from conservation

The willingness of LDCs (or of their governments) to undertake conservation effort is likely to be reduced if they fail to appropriate a sufficient share of world gains from their conservational activity. Sometimes, Third World countries can adopt policy measures to increase their share in world gains from their conservation efforts. But in some instances no such measures are available because an international type of public good is involved and the best that they can hope for is support from foreign aid.

An LDC may fail to appropriate benefits, to maximise its benefits or fail to obtain substantial benefits from its conservation efforts for several reasons. These include:

(1) Public good consequences such as those from preservation of a gene pool when 'gene rights' cannot be protected in the market place. The preservation of a gene pool is important for maintaining the productivity and vitality of many species of domesticated animals and cultivated plants. In relation to plants, it is uncertain which wild cultivars will be used in the future for breeding and cultivation purposes and determining a price for their sale and use outside a country involves many bargaining difficulties and uncertainties. The same applies to the preservation of species that are not yet of commercial value but could become of commercial use in the future (Tisdell, 1972).

(2) An LDC may fail to crop or harvest its conserved living resources on a sustainable maximum economic yield basis and to market the produce from these resources adequately. Note that the controlled cropping of conservation areas can be consistent with their sustainable conservation and sometimes is the most economic use of a land area. However, economists have not traditionally seen sustainability of an economic activity as a virtue in itself (See Chapter 11). Overharvesting as well as underharvesting and inadequate marketing back-up of produce can result in a reduction of national gains from conservation in LDCs.

(3) An LDC may not succeed in appropriating maximum gains from tourism (especially international tourism) generated by the existence of natural resources. The tourism option for appropriation of benefits is considered below.

(4) Even after all avenues for appropriation have been fully exhausted, residual benefits of a public good-type or favourable externalities from conservation of living resources in Third World countries will continue to exist on an international scale. These include, (a) *option benefits* – the *possible* values of being able to make use of a resource in the future if it continues to be available; (b) *existence benefits* – the value of merely knowing that a species exists or continues to do so, and (c) *global spillovers* or *transnational spillovers* of benefit – for example, the possible slowing of rises in carbon dioxide levels or of the greenhouse effect, maintenance of transboundary weather conditions, or reduced siltation of internationally-shared river systems, and so on (Myers, 1979).

Even when the most sophisticated available techniques for appropriating gains from conservational effort are adopted by LDCs (and some of these may be impractical in LDCs), residual unappropriated benefits from conservation can be expected to continue. In such cases, LDCs may engage in insufficient conservation from a global viewpoint unless foreign aid is forthcoming for supporting extra conservation effort. But of course such 'failure' is not exclusive to LDCs – developed countries also may fail to appropriate a substantial share of global benefits from their conservation efforts. This issue will be taken up later in this chapter.

4.12 Tourism as a means of appropriating gains from conservation

A number of conservationists see international tourism based on natural resources as a means of appropriating gains from conservation and encouraging it. The role of tourism in conservation is complicated because in some cases tourism destroys tourism and conserved resources as well (OECD, 1980). It can also have undesirable cultural effects. Furthermore, some would argue that international tourism in developing countries is frequently controlled by multinational companies and becomes a part of the dual economy with little benefit to the indigenous people (Britton, 1980). While international tourism brings in foreign exchange, it can impose a large drain on reserves of foreign exchange – imports are needed to varying degrees to satisfy foreign tourists (United Nations, 1982). Nevertheless, tourism still provides a means, but not a costless means, of appropriating gains nationally from conservation, and it can be an inducement for the conservation of living resources in the Third World (See Chapter 10; Tisdell, 1982). However, government policies are required to ensure that benefits from tourism are in fact married with conservation. There is no automatic link between tourism and greater conservation because the prisoners' dilemma problem seems to apply. In fact, the greater the gains from tourism the more quickly living resources are sometimes destroyed.

The scope of LDCs in encouraging foreign tourists is limited by the poor social infrastructure of many (for example, poor communication systems and inadequate utilities), health and similar risks in some countries and the distance of some LDCs from the developed countries of the world (McKee and Tisdell, 1990). Nevertheless, as the amount of wilderness in the world dwindles, the number of foreign tourists visiting LDCs can be expected to increase. In some LDCs substantial rises in the number of foreign tourists has already occurred and have posed serious management problems.

For example, difficulties have arisen in Indonesia, Thailand, Tanzania and elsewhere (Tisdell, 1983; Viryasiri and Tisdell, 1988; Elliott, 1982). In Indonesia, the development of the island of Bali for foreign tourists has resulted in environmental damage to coral reefs as has also occurred in Phuket. Thailand. In the Indonesian case, plans to contain tourism, as recommended by French advisers. within a limited area or restricted pockets, have proven to be difficult to maintain in practice. Areas not sharing in economic gains from foreign tourists have demanded foreign tourism development and over the long-term the Indonesian Government has been unable to resist such pressures (Daroesman, 1973).

Tanzania has tried to develop its wildlife resources as tourist attractions. But in recent years it has experienced difficulties because of the inadequate standard of service in hotels and lodges and the unavailability or shortage of imported supplies needed to satisfy foreign tourists. Many of the hotels and lodges are run by the state and indications are that they may not be managed efficiently. In the 1980s a loan from the World Bank was used to assist the Tanzanian tourist industry given its financial difficulties (Prestige, 1982).

These two examples indicate that foreign tourism is not universally a magic road to economic success and to enhanced conservation of nature. The role of tourism in relation to conservation and the environment will be discussed in Chapter 10.

4.13 Improving distribution of gains from conservation within LDCs

The World Conservation Strategy recommends that individuals bearing costs of conservation measures should directly share in the benefits from them. Framers of the World Conservation Strategy (IUCN, 1980) point out that it is not enough for local communities to benefit indirectly from tourism e.g., if receipts by the national treasury are spent on such services as roads, water supply and health facilities. Local commitment to a protected area can only be assured if local advantages such as increased opportunities for employment and commerce e.g., new benefits from recreation and tourism are obtained.

One can find examples where the local community has been given a substantial share in gains from conservation areas, to their own benefit and to the benefit of wildlife preservation. The case of the Masai in the Amboseli National Park in Kenya is a well-documented example (Western, 1982). In this case, the Masai have been employed in the management of the Park and in shops at the Park.

In contrast, local villages in the neighbourhood of the Royal Chitwan National Park (where wildlife conservation has also been successful) have been unable to share in the tourist benefits from the Park and have suffered loss of life, livestock and crops from marauding animals from the Park, and loss of grazing and timber-gathering areas in the Park (Mishra, 1982). Mishra points out that, tourism is a service-oriented industry but the well-paying jobs in it can only be filled by the educated. Because of low levels of educational attainment, only a few locals are employed, and then only in menial jobs. 'Tourism has not generated local jobs, despite the tourist industry's promises. Most of the well-paying jobs are taken by qualified and experienced people from outside Nepal...' (Mishra, 1982, p. 249).

Furthermore, the prices of products such as foodstuffs have increased rapidly in the Chitwan area as a result of tourism, and Mishra goes so far as to say that, 'except for a few traders and merchants, most people in the vicinity of the national park are losing instead of gaining from tourism'.

In the Sagarmatha (Mount Everest) National Park in Nepal local Sherpas have been trained to participate in management of the Park. While this has benefits, Jefferies (1982) points out, the Sherpas 'are subject to pressure for special consideration from relatives and friends in the local community'. In the Sagarmatha area, food prices and fuel prices have also risen under the pressure of tourist demand. Serious degradation of the Park is now threatened by the cutting of trees and shrubs for wood sales to expeditions and trekkers. Jefferies (1982) maintains that this is difficult to control. The selling of firewood is now probably essential to the villagers to finance the cost of high-cost foodstuffs on which they have become increasingly dependent because of the change in their lifestyle brought about by increasing tourism.

Changed structure of government has contributed to reduced conservational effort in the Sagarmatha area. In 1957, common forest and pasture lands were nationalised and in 1963 democratic government was introduced. Consequently, social decision-making became the prerogative of the central government and gravitated to Kathmandu. Previously local forest guardians had regulated the use of forest products on a village-by-village basis. When control was taken away from locals it was not replaced by *effective* control over forests from Kathmandu. Kathmandu is remote from the Sagarmatha region. Lack of social control brought about by changed structure of government has therefore contributed to deforestation.

4.14 International aid and assistance, loans and trade

As mentioned above, conservation in the Third World can yield favourable spillovers for the rest of the world, and global benefits. The principle that 'he-who-benefits should pay', could provide one reason for the rest of the world giving aid for conservation in the Third World. Pure self-interest of the rest of the world can form the basis of the subsidy or grant in this case. Altruism may form the basis of a grant where increased conservation is expected to benefit the recipients of the aid but will provide little or no benefit to the grantees.

Some aid for conservation is not motivated by anthropocentric considerations because some individuals believe that mankind's responsibility for nature should extend beyond self-interest or self-centred considerations (Ashby, 1978; Passmore, 1974). Grants to the Third World for conservation clearly can arise from a range of motives. The rest of the world can also influence conservation in the Third World through aid and financial assistance given for projects other than direct conservation projects. Environmental factors can be taken into account in providing support. As Myers (1979) points out, the World Bank and U.S. AID now undertake environmental assessments in supporting Third World projects and an increasing number of aid agencies are doing that. The World Commission for the Environment and Development (1987) points out that it is especially important that the World Bank, International Monetary Fund and regional Development Banks give particular attention to environmental factors and sustainable development in making loans and that they pay more than lip-service to these considerations: The Commission suggests that promising beginnings by the World Bank must be accompanied by a 'fundamental commitment' (World Commission on Environment and Development, 1987, p. 337).

Trade provides another means by which the rest of the world can have an impact on conservation in less developed countries. Both in the World Conservation Strategy document (IUCN, 1980) and in *Our Common Future* (World Commission on Environment and Development, 1987) the view appears to be accepted that less restrictions on international trade (less trade protection) and an increase in international trade is likely to be in the interest of less developed countries and the rest of the world both from a conservation and an economic viewpoint. The neoclassical and economic position is that the extension of free trade is as a rule in the general economic interest. However, in the past this school of economic thought paid little attention to the conservational consequences of this, particularly for ecological resources. The reality is that not *all* may gain from an extension of free trade (in some circumstances it even leads to a general economic loss) and it may be unfavourable to conservation especially if significant ignorance and market failures exist. In reality, the consequences of extended free trade are so complicated that only qualified support for it appears rationally defensible.

In some circumstances, an extension of trade will lead to greater conservation of nature but in other cases it will not. Some examples have already been given in which the extension of trade has threatened the existence of particular species. However, it is possible that extended international trade could reduce the amount of natural resources required for economic production. Fewer resources will as a rule be required to produce a given level of global production when international trade is possible. But in our present socio-economic circumstances any economic advantages coming from gains from international trade are likely to be directed to the expansion of global economic growth, that is, to increasing global production. In practice, the gains may be harnessed to expand production and/or population with deleterious nature conservation consequences in LDCs at the macro-level.

Our Common Future (World Commission on Environment and Development, 1987) argues that it is important to *revive* economic growth and especially to achieve economic growth in less developed countries (which of course may be facilitated by extension of international trade). Economic growth is seen as a means to greater conservation of nature. True this is qualified by pointing out that economic growth should be based on sustainability considerations and should take account of environmental factors. However, many LDCs may be unable given their existing socio-economic structures and power networks to take much account of the qualifications, at least for some time to come. Furthermore, there is no guarantee that economic growth will assist those most in need in the LDCs. While those in dire need will hardly be in a mood to be sympathetic to broad conservation goals, it is not clear that overall economic growth will solve the environmental problem easily or surely.

Economic growth may accelerate environmental deterioration before it improves the situation. Given existing socio-economic structures and values, it is not easy to make economic growth and conservation compatible. The economic growth component of the slogan may be put into effect but the environmental and sustainability part overlooked or considered in a perfunctory manner. The political likelihood of this should not be underrated (O'Riordan, 1988).

4.15 Global public good/externality considerations

Conservation of nature and protection of the environment in any country can have global public-good benefits and/or external or transboundary benefits for other nations. Consequently from a global point of view, insufficient conservation of nature and protection of the environment is to be expected if not only individuals but also nations act in their own self-interest. In the absence of international co-operation and in some cases aid transfers, a less than optimal global environmental situation will result.

Figure 4.1 can be used to illustrate. Let curve D_TD_T represent the marginal evaluation of a Third World nation of conservation in the country and let curve D_RD_R represent the marginal evaluation of the rest of the world of this conservation. [The example may also be recast in terms of the whole of the Third World and the rest of the world.] Following its own self-interest the Third World country would conserve an amount X_1 of resources given that line AC represents the marginal cost of conservation in the Third World country. The rest of the world, however, will perceive this as an inadequate amount of conservation from its point of view. It would indeed be prepared to pay all the extra cost of increasing the amount of conservation in the Third World country from X_1 to X_2.

However, from a global viewpoint conservation of X_3 of resources in the Third World country is optimal. This is because the marginal global benefits of conservation in the Third World country are as indicated by the line marked D_GD_G which is the vertical addition of the curves marked D_TD_T and D_RD_R, assuming no negative marginal evaluations of conservation. At the level X_3 of conservation, the marginal cost of conserving resources in the Third World country equals the global marginal evaluation of this conservation. If this optimum is to occur in practice, the rest of the world needs to provide appropriate grants or incentives to the Third World country to increase its conservation of resources beyond the level which it would choose.

In the example discussed in Figure 4.1, benefits of conservation to the rest of the world exceed that to the Third World country. While it may be common for the marginal benefits to developed countries of conservation in the Third World to exceed the marginal benefits to the Third World, the opposite pattern of relative benefits can occur. In such cases, developed countries may not immediately *perceive* the global benefits of extra conservation in the Third World. Nevertheless, provided positive spillovers exist, an economic case exists for expanding the level of conservation in the Third World until marginal cost of doing so equals the *global* marginal evaluation of this. This would still require some transfers or subsidies from the rest of the world to the Third World.

It should, however, be pointed out that conservation in the developed world e.g., in USA, can provide spillovers to the Third World. Spillover benefits are not all one way, although it seems likely that as far as conservation spillovers are concerned they are mainly to the advantage of more developed countries (Cf. Old-

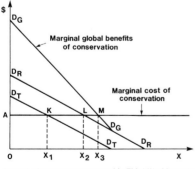

Figure 4.1. Conservation of living natural resources in a developing country to some extent provides a global public good. Hence, an optimal amount of conservation may not occur in developing countries if LDCs follow their own self-interest.

field, 1989, esp. Ch. 2). If developed countries were to follow their own narrow self-interest, they would also engage in inadequate conservation from a global viewpoint. They would need some extra incentive to increase their level of conservation to a globally optimal level. They might, for example, do this in return for some extra conservation in the Third World. After this scope for co-operation is exhausted, it seems likely that the developed world will need to subsidise less developed ones in order to bring about an optimal level and pattern of global conservation. (For some further discussion of this matter see Tisdell, 1990, Ch. 4.)

In the 1980s a number of less developed countries, especially Latin American and African countries, faced international debt crises and substantial debts remained at the beginning of the 1990s. A common suggestion was that the developed world should forgive their debts or arrange for concessionary repayment in return for greater conservation in the Third World countries involved. This can be regarded as a means of providing aid to the Third World but it should be borne in mind that a substantial proportion of the benefits from this policy is likely to accrue to the developed world, and that it may not be without cost to the Third World. Nevertheless, it is a positive suggestion.

Irrespective of motives for providing aid for conservation in Third World countries, it has to be channelled to existing communities. Existing social structures (elites, power relationships and attitudes) can interfere with the effective deployment of such aid and it is by no means clear that socio-economic arrangements in the Third World will evolve in a way which will avert the large scale disappearance of species. If we are to hold back the tide of extinction of species, we must obtain a better understanding of the socio-economic relationships involved in the Third World and combine this with appropriate aid from the developed world. Other measures such as those discussed in Chapter 11 should also be considered.

References

Alauddin, M. and Tisdell, C.A., 1991. The Green Revolution and Economic Development: The Process and Its Impact in Bangladesh. Macmillan, London.

Allen, R., 1980. How to Save the World: Strategy for World Conservation. Kogan Page, London.

Anon., 1982. Tanzania Tourist Corporation at ITB – Berlin 1982. Karibu Tanzania, No. 7: 5–8.

Ashby, E., 1978. Reconciling Man with the Environment. Oxford University Press, Oxford.

Barney, G.O., 1980. The Global 2000 Report to the President of the U.S. Vol. 1. Pergamon Press, New York.

Britton, S.G., 1980. Tourism and economic vulnerability in small Pacific island states: the case of Fiji. In: R.T. Shand (Editor), The Island States of the Pacific and Indian Oceans: Anatomy of Development. Australian National University, Canberra.

Clark, C.W., 1976. Mathematical Bioeconomics: The Optimal Management of a Renewable Resource. John Wiley, New York.

Daly, H., 1980. Economics, Ecology, Ethics. Freeman, San Francisco.

Daroesman, R., 1973. An economic survey of Bali. Bull. of Indonesian Studies, 9:(3) 28–61.

Downes, M., 1981. The development of wildlife management in Papua New Guinea. In: T. Riney (Editor) Wildlife Management in the 80s. Monash University, Clayton, pp. 63–67.

Eaton, P. and Sinclair, P., 1981. Wildlife in Papua New Guinea. Division of Wildlife, Department of Lands and Environment, Konedobu, PNG, pp. 16–17.

Eberstadt, N.N., 1980. Fertility declines in less-developed countries: components and implications. Environmental Conservation 8(3) 187–190.

Ehrlich, P.R., 1970. The Population Bomb. Ballantine Books, New York.

Elliott, C., 1982. The political economy of sewage: a case study from the Himalayas. Mazingire 6 (4) 44–46.

Grainger, A., 1980. The state of the world's tropical forests. The Ecologist 10, Nos. 1/2:6–54.

Gregory, C.A., 1981. A conceptual analysis of a non-capitalist gift economy with particular reference to Papua New Guinea. Cambridge Journal of Economics, 5:119–135.

Harting, J.E., 1880. British Animals Extinct Within Historic Times. Trubner and Co., Ludgate Hill, London.

Hudson, B.E.T., 1980. Dugong Conservation, Management and Public Education Programme. Wildlife Division, Department of Natural Resources, Konedobu, PNG.

Hudson, B.E.T., 1980. Dugong myth and management in Papua New Guinea. In: L. Morauta et al. (Editors) Traditional Conservation in New Guinea: Implications for Today. Institute of Applied Social and Economic Research, Boroka, PNG, pp 311–315.

Hudson, B.E.T., 1981. Dugongs of the northern Torres Strait: aerial surveys, observations during a tagging project, catch statistics, with recommendations for conservation and management. In: Pacific Science Association 15th Congress Abstracts, Vol. 1:108. University of Otago, Dunedin.

Hudson, B.E.T., 1983. Dugongs: can the Kiwai survive without them? Paper presented to XIth International Congress of Anthropological and Ethnological Sciences, Vancouver, B.C., Canada.

IUCN, 1980. World Conservation Strategy. IUCN, Gland, Switzerland.

IUCN-UNEP-WWF, 1990. Caring for the World: A Strategy for Sustainability. Second draft, IUCN, Gland, Switzerland.

Jefferies, B.E., 1982. Sagarmatha National Park: the impact of tourism on the Himalayas. Ambio 11, No. 5:302–308.

Karibu Tanzania, 1982. No. 7:39. Tanzania Tourist Corporation, Dar es Salaam.

Kula, G., 1979. The Siwi-Utame Wildlife Management Area. Papua New Guinea Printer, Port Moresby.

Luce, R.D. and Raiffa, H., 1955. Games and Decisions. John Wiley, New York.

McKee, D.L. and Tisdell, C.A., 1990. Developmental Issues in Small Island Economies. Praeger, New York.

Mishra, H.R., 1982. Balancing human needs and conservation in Nepal's Royal Chitwan National Park. Ambio 11(5) 246–251.

Momin Khan, K., 1981. Problems of Wildlife Management in Southeast Asia. In: T. Riney (Editor) Wildlife Management in the 80s. Monash University, Clayton.

Myers, N., 1979. The Sinking Ark: A New Look at the Problem of Disappearing Species. Pergamon Press, Oxford, pp. 21–24.

OECD Group of Experts on Environmental Tourism, 1980. The Impact of Tourism on the Environment: General Report. Organisation for Economic Co-operation and Development, Paris.

Olewale, E. and Sedu, D., 1980. Momoro (the dugong) in the Western Province. In: L. Morauta et al. (Editors) Traditional Conservation in Papua New Guinea: Implications for Today. Institute of Applied Social and Economic Research, Boroka, PNG, pp. 251–255.

O'Riordan, T., 1988. The politics of sustainability. In: R.K. Turner (Editor), Sustainable Environmental Management, pp. 29–50. Belhaven Press, London.

Parker, F., 1977. The Wildlife Management Area in Papua New Guinea. Wildlife Division, Department of Natural Resources, Konedobu, PNG, 1977.

Passmore, J., 1974. Man's Responsibility for Nature: Ecological Problems and Western Tradition. Duckworth, London.

Plumwood, V. and Routley, R., 1982. World rainforest destruction – the social factors. The Ecologist 12(1) 4–22.

Prestige, R., 1982. A shot in the arm for tourism in Tanzania. Karibu Tanzania No. 8:5–12.

Sadleir, R., 1970. Animals of Australia and New Zealand. Hamlyn, London.

Sahlins, M., 1974. Stone Age Economics. Tavistock, London.

Tisdell, C.A., 1972. Provision of parks and preservation of nature – some economic factors. Australian Economic Paper 11:154–162.

Tisdell, C.A., 1979. On the Economics of Saving Wildlife from Extinction. Research Report or Occasional Paper No. 48. Department of Economics, University of Newcastle.

Tisdell, C.A., 1982. Natural and related resources in the generation of international tourism in Australian and ASEAN countries. Report for ASEAN-Australia Joint Economic Research Project, Trade in Services Study. Roneo. Department of Economics, University of Newcastle.

Tisdell, C.A., 1983. An economist's critique of the World Conservation Strategy, with examples from Australian experience. Environmental Conservation 10(1) 43–52.

Tisdell, C.A., 1986. Conflicts about living marine-resources in Southeast Asian and Australian waters: Turtles and dugongs as cases. Marine Resource Economics, 3:89-109.

Tisdell, C.A., 1989. Giant clams in the Pacific – the socio-economic potential of a developing technology for their mariculture. In: A.D. Couper (Editor) Development and Social Change in the Pacific Islands, pp. 74–88. Routledge, London and New York.

Tisdell, C.A., 1990. Natural Resources, Growth, and Development: Economics, Ecology and Resource-Scarcity. Praeger, New York, 1990.

United Nations, 1982. Transnational Corporations in International Tourism. United Nations, New York.

United Republic of Tanzania, 1969. The Tourists Agents (Licensing) Act, 1969. Government Printer, Dar es Salaam.

United Republic of Tanzania, 1974. Wildlife Conservation Act, 1974. Government Printer, Dar es Salaam.

Viryasiri, S. and Tisdell, C.A., 1988. Tourism and the state of the marine environment in Thailand: A case study of marine pollution in Phuket. In: C.A. Tisdell, C.J. Aislabie and P.J. Stanton (Editors) Economics of Tourism: Case Study and Analysis. Institute of Industrial Economics, University of Newcastle, N.S.W., 2308, Australia, pp. 275–286.

Western, D., 1982. Amboseli National Park: enlisting landowners to conserve migratory wildlife. Ambio 11(5) 302-308.

World Bank, 1990. World Bank Report 1990. Oxford University Press, New York.

World Commission on Environment and Development, 1987. Our Common Future. Oxford University Press, New York.

Chapter 5

Preservation of wildlife and genetic diversity

5.1 Introduction

In its broadest sense 'wildlife' refers to all undomesticated living things and includes both plants and animals as well as primitive forms of life. In the recent past, the economic value of this biodiversity has not been fully appreciated and the possible disastrous economic consequences of loss of genetic diversity (loss of species and their varieties) appears to have been poorly comprehended (Plucknett et al., 1986). Possibly this is still the case on the whole if the views of all of humanity are considered. This may be because the ability of man to dominate and to manipulate nature has grown so much in recent times and because the adverse consequences of destruction of nature are not always immediately obvious. Indeed, environmental trends can be deceptive - yields and economic returns may rise as nature is destroyed and historical results may provide little forewarning of an eventual irreversible collapse of economic production due to the destruction of nature (Cf. Tisdell and Alauddin, 1989; Tisdell, 1990a).

From an economic point of view, wildlife can have value both because of its tangible and intangible characteristics (Cf. McNeely, 1988; McNeely et al., 1990). Depending upon the species or combination of species in some cases, wildlife can provide physical commodities of value such as meat, fur, feathers and medicinal products, and can be a means for enjoying outdoor recreation (for example, amateur hunting, fishing, photography and sightseeing) and therefore stimulating tourism. In addition, biodiversity can provide means for improving or maintaining the productivity of biological resources used in agriculture, aquaculture and forestry. The preservation of nature, at least up to a point, tends to keep open future economic options and this has economic value (Pearce, Markandya, Barbier,

1989). It is useful to keep options open not only to maintain economic productivity but also to cater for uncertainty about future human preferences (Bishop, 1978).

Sometimes option value, existence value and the bequest value of species are grouped together as the preservation value of intangible characteristics of species (See section 3.5). The existence value of a species is the amount individuals would be willing to pay merely to know and to ensure that a species continues to exist and bequest value is the amount they would be willing to pay to ensure the preservation of a species, a resource or natural object for future generations. The value of the thing conserved in both these cases is not a consequence of its direct use by the individual. Nevertheless, these values may be influenced by the individual's direct contact with knowledge and experience with the natural objects to be preserved. The fact however that the above items are classified as intangible may be a little misleading because to some extent these values can be quantified, and

TABLE 5.1
Main sources of value of conserving wildlife with examples and explanations

Value	Examples or explanations
Tangible:	
Material use (direct)	Meat, fur, feathers, for medicine
Material use (indirect)	Environmental spillovers or externalities. Reconditioning or improving air and water quality, commercial productivity, etc.
Intangible:	
Existence	The mere existence of a species may be valued even when it has no material or recreational use and, as discussed in Chapter 3, this attribute has pure public good characteristics. The mere existence for example of a particular species of whale may be valued though it will never be seen or used by an individual.
Bequest	Sometimes individuals express the wish that their children and their children's children should have an opportunity to enjoy wildlife and nature existing now e.g., species of the largest whales. For this reason they may place an economic value on their preservation.
Options	Keeping options open for meeting changed tastes or for better meeting existing tastes. Includes options in relation to material use, recreational use, existence and bequest value. Gene banks to improve or sustain productivity of agriculture, aquaculture, forestry and industries based on living resource productivity.
Vicarious	This involves the enjoyment of photographs, movies, stories and so on, the content of which or the relevance of which is dependent upon the existence of the wildlife involved.

retention of options can have a physical effect when it influences the level of material production.

Table 5.1 sets out the main sources of economic value of conserving wildlife together with some examples (Cf. McNeely, 1988, Ch.2; Oldfield, 1989; McNeely et al., 1990, Ch.2). Observe that option value is not an independent value in itself but is a consequential value. It arises because of uncertainty *and* possible changes exist in relation to other values (Tisdell, 1968, 1970).

Table 5.1, although relatively comprehensive in coverage, may not include all human values which could possibly affect the preservation of wildlife. For example, some tribal and other groups, e.g. Australian aboriginals, at least in the past, believed that they had a special affinity to particular species. This often resulted in those species not being killed or their harvesting being restricted. Some individuals also oppose the killing of animals on ethical or sympathetic grounds and this can affect the use of animals and their conservation.

While the economic value of some species may stem solely from 'intangible' values such as existence value, many have both direct value in use as well as intangible values e.g., whales, seals, kangaroos.

5.2 Managing wildlife as a mixed good: simple analytics

Wildlife harvested to supply private goods may have economic value for other purposes, such as existence value, and this will not be taken into account by harvesters (and users of their products) because the benefits which they each might personally (individually) obtain from taking those other values into account would be minuscule. Market failure occurs at least partially and is likely to occur even if economic optimality (economic efficiency) were fully achieved in relation to the private good component. The latter, of course, is unlikely to occur if wildlife is harvested under conditions of imperfectly regulated common access to the harvesting of the resource (See Chapter 6).

In the mixed good case (the case in which the biological resource supplies both private and public good), the existence of spillover and related benefits (such as existence value) which depends on the size of the population of the species implies as a rule that the species is overharvested when it is purely exploited on a commercial basis for private goods. This is so if the Kaldor-Hicks criterion is used to judge the situation. This can be seen from Figure 5.1.

In Figure 5.1 curve DD represents the value per unit of a harvested species e.g., whales or seals, when used for private goods, e.g. meat or fur. The curve SS represents the private marginal costs of harvesting the species. It is the supply curve if the industry is *optimally* regulated in relation to its contribution of private goods. But the social marginal cost of harvesting the species may be as indicated by curve S'S'. The market equilibrium harvest of the species would correspond to

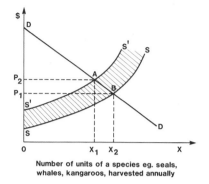

Number of units of a species eg. seals, whales, kangaroos, harvested annually

Figure 5.1. Species of wildlife sometimes provide a mixed good. In such cases, private harvesting of species to supply private goods is unlikely to maximise economic welfare because the social marginal cost of harvesting diverges from the private marginal cost of harvesting the species.

point B and the annual number of units of the species harvested would be X_2 selling at a price per unit of P_1. The socially optimal harvest level however is X_1 units annually given that the difference between curve SS and S′S′ represents the 'spillover' or externality costs of the harvest. The socially optimal harvest level may be achieved by placing a tax of $P_2 - P_1$ on each unit of the species harvested or by imposing an annual quota of X_1 on the catch or harvest. In these circumstances a new market situation corresponding to point A would prevail and the price per harvested unit of the species for private use would increase.

The difference between SS and S′S′ might represent the marginal existence value of the species or other spillover characteristics. But it might be objected that existence value and other 'spillovers' are related to the stock (population) level of the species rather than the level of the harvest. However, this is not a difficulty if

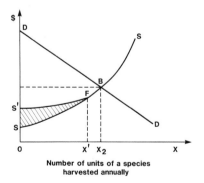

Number of units of a species harvested annually

Figure 5.2. The mere fact that the private cost of harvesting a species diverges from the social cost of harvesting it does not imply that its level of harvest is *always* socially inappropriate or suboptimal.

the level of the population of the species is negatively related in equilibrium to the rate of its harvest. As the harvest (rate of removal of the population) is reduced, it is assumed that the level of population of the species increases up to the maximum sustainable level of population of the species. This accords with standard population models for many species (Clark, 1976; Christiansen and Fenchel, 1977).

While usually the existence of favourable 'spillovers' which depend upon the level of population of a species imply for social optimality a reduced harvest compared to a situation in which these spillovers are not taken into account, the occurrence of such spillovers *may* sometimes be without welfare consequences. For example, Figure 5.2 has a similar interpretation to Figure 5.1 but in this case the social marginal cost curve is S'FS. Thus the market equilibrium at B is socially optimal in the Kaldor-Hicks sense even though the harvest imposes spillover costs equivalent in total to the cross-hatched area. In this particular case the externality is Pareto irrelevant (See section 3.2).

By contrast the social marginal and total costs of harvesting a species may be so high that no commercial harvest is optimal. Such a case is illustrated in Figure 5.3 which has the same interpretation as the previous figures. As can be seen, the social marginal cost curve S'S' is higher than the demand curve to harvest the species for use in private goods at all levels of the harvest. 'Spillover' costs amount to the hatched area. If these spillover costs are not taken into account, an annual harvest of X_2 would occur and market equilibrium would be established at point B. The externality is Pareto relevant in this case.

Whether or not whales are currently in the situation depicted in Figure 5.3 is debatable but at present (1990) a moratorium has been placed on their harvest. Because of political factors, it is possible that actual policies for the harvesting of whales are not optimal from a Kaldor-Hicks economic viewpoint.

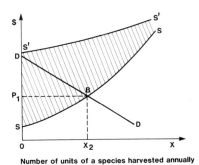

Number of units of a species harvested annually

Figure 5.3. The social marginal cost of harvesting a species may be so high that no harvesting is socially optimal. In such cases, all private harvesting is inappropriate.

Other circumstances involving wildlife can also be considered using this simple analytical approach (Tisdell, 1979). For example, sometimes a species is regarded as a pest by at least one group in society. For example, some farmers in Australia regard kangaroos and emus, especially in large numbers, as pests because they can have an adverse impact on their grazing and farming activities. Commercial harvest of the species can therefore have an external benefit for farmers if it succeeds in reducing pest populations. In the absence of any other spillovers from the presence of the species, economic optimality may require harvesting on a greater scale than would occur commercially.

This is illustrated in Figure 5.4. This diagram has the same interpretation as before except that a line identified by MM has been added. This represents the social marginal benefit of the harvest. The difference between this curve and curve DD is the marginal benefit of pest control to farmers. Let curve SS represent the social marginal cost of the harvest. In the case shown, a Kaldor-Hicks socially optimal position corresponds to point G. This could be achieved by paying a subsidy of GH per unit of the species harvested to harvesters. As a result the annual quantity harvested of the species would increase from X_2 to X_3 and the market price per unit would fall from P_1 to P_0.

A species may not be a pest until its population reaches some threshold level. In that case if the level of population of the species needed before it is considered to be a pest exceeds that population *corresponding* to an annual harvest of X_2, no intervention in commercial harvesting is called for on economic efficiency grounds.

For the harvesting of some species e.g. kangaroos and seals, it is possible for both spillover benefits and spillover costs to occur. This can be accommodated in terms of this simple analytical approach. For example, if there are spillover costs in terms say of loss of existence value by urban dwellers from the harvesting of

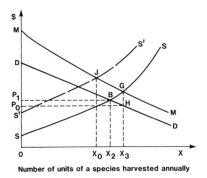

Number of units of a species harvested annually

Figure 5.4. A wildlife species may be regarded as a pest by some social groups and as an asset by others. Using the Kaldor-Hicks criterion, the level of harvesting of the species can be adjusted to take this into account.

the species this might be taken into account in Figure 5.4. Suppose that the difference between curve SS and S'S' indicates marginal spillover costs. In that case point J corresponds to the socially optimal level of the harvest. An annual harvest of X_0 is optimal but instead of a subsidy being appropriate, a tax on the harvest to restrict its level may be appropriate despite the fact that the species constitutes a pest for some members of society.

The above assumes that the main means of altering the level of population of a species is by varying its harvesting rate. But for most species their population levels can also be altered by varying their environments. Environmental (habitat) variation is a policy instrument in some circumstances e.g. provision of water supplies in national parks, regulations on the removal of vegetation cover (on private property) the conservation of which would be favourable to the conservation of species, varying the size and location of conservation areas. These aspects will be discussed when the conservation of natural areas is considered in Chapter 7.

Observe that parts of the above analysis applies not only to wild species. In certain circumstances, it may be applied to rare and endangered domesticated species and varieties such as rare cattle, sheep and goat varieties, e.g. the Highland cattle of Scotland, Longhorns in the United States (Oldfield, 1989).

5.3 Some economic consequences of interdependence between species

The above discussion did not specifically consider the interdependence of populations of species. Populations of different species may for example be in competitive or complementary relationships to one another. In such cases altering the population level of one species, A, affects the level of population of another, B, or other species. For instance, increasing the level of population of species A may result in a reduction in the level of population of species B if they are in complementary relationship. This needs to be taken into account as an additional cost

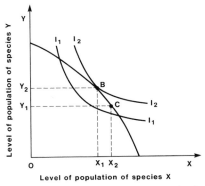

Figure 5.5. The socially optimal combination of populations of interdependent species may differ from their natural combination and encourage human intervention to change the population mix.

of varying the population of species A, if the population level of species B has value.

The situation for the competitive case can be illustrated by Figure 5.5. Curve ABCD represents relative to available resources for two species, X and Y, the competitive relationship between their population levels. Suppose that there is a social preference ordering (possibly based on a social welfare function) of the levels of the population of the species. Suppose that this preference ordering possesses the properties usually assumed in economics for rational choice – transitivity, completeness and so on. Two indifference curves based on this preference ordering are indicated by the curves marked I_2I_2 in Figure 5.5. The socially optimal levels of the populations of the species corresponds to point B given this approach. To expand the size of the population of species X from X_1 to X_2 may increase the 'utility' obtained from a greater population of X but will result in reduced 'utility' from species Y because its population will decline and overall total utility will decline. Both economic and ecological interdependence needs to be taken into account if one adopts a man-centred approach to valuation of a species and seeks a social optimum.

In Figure 5.5 the natural equilibrium between the populations of the species X and Y may be established at population levels corresponding to point C. But this is not the optimal combination given the human valuation indicated in Figure 5.5. To achieve optimality, and ignoring costs of population control or supposing it to be costless, the population level for species X needs to be reduced and that of Y increased until point B is reached. This could be achieved by 'culling' or reducing the population of species X. However, from an economic viewpoint the 'costs' of doing this should also be taken into account. In some cases the meat or other products from culled species may be sold, as in Africa, and this may more than cover the costs of culling.

In some national parks e.g. in Southern Africa, selective culling of wildlife species is undertaken 'to improve' the population-mix of species. For example, visitors (tourists) to national parks prefer to view some species rather than others. This may be taken into account by managers of national parks in altering the relative composition of species in the park. But, of course, this may not be the only consideration in culling and management programs for wildlife in nature reserves. Other reasons may include the need of park administrators to supplement their revenues by selling produce from 'cullings' or to control unfavourable externalities from particular species which roam on to neighbouring properties.

Sometimes wildlife of commercial value is present on agricultural and pastoral properties but because landowners are unable to appropriate the benefits or a significant proportion of these from conserving the wildlife and harvesting it, a smaller amount of wildlife may be conserved than is socially optimal. For instance, kangaroos have commercial value for meat and hides but because they are very mobile between properties, property owners can only appropriate a small proportion of any increase in income from increasing the kangaroo population and the level of the sustainable harvest. In this case, the number of domestic livestock is liable to be increased on properties beyond the levels which will maximise the net value of material production from the land. Thus even neglecting existence values and intangible values, a less than socially optimal composition of species is liable to emerge in this case because of the difference in relative ability of landholders to appropriate benefits from conserving the different species (Tisdell, 1973).

In some circumstances, farming of a once wild species may be a means to conserve it. However, even in that case there can be rational arguments for continuing to conserve the species in the wild. For example, animals in the wild may be regarded (valued) differently by humans to those which are domesticated. Wild stocks of the species may provide greater genetic diversity and may continue to evolve (co-evolve) in ways which may not occur from domesticated species reared under artificial or controlled environmental conditions (Oldfield, 1989). This may be valuable in sustaining the productivity of the domesticated stock of the species. Some impacts of farming of a species on its conservation will be discussed in the next chapter.

5.4 Criteria for deciding on species to save from extinction

Economic development (economic growth) has led to the widespread disappearance of species and varieties of different species. The extent of biodiversity in the world is being reduced rapidly. This is a matter of considerable economic concern because for all practical purposes the disappearance of species is irreversible. While genetic engineering may allow limited reversibility, its scope is still very restricted. Furthermore the potential for genetic engineering is likely to be less the smaller is the stock of genetic material (the basic building blocks) available.

While the disappearance of species is a normal evolutionary phenomenon, the scale and rate of disappearance today is unprecedented and is largely due to human activity. Loss of species and their varieties is of economic concern because (1) some species and their varieties already have sufficient economic value to warrant their preservation and (2) many have *potential* economic value e.g. to maintain the economic productivity of domesticated species, to provide medicines, to satisfy changing curiosity-interests about nature, and their disappearance closes off options for the future possible use.

Given uncertainty and a changing world, the maintenance of flexibility and the retention of options can be (indeed, is likely to be) of economic value (Tisdell, 1968, 1970; Pearce, Markandya and Barbier, 1989). It is worth making some economic sacrifice (but not an unlimited sacrifice) to keep options open. But due to market failures, amongst other causes including institutional failures, species may not be preserved even when their currently known economic value is positive, let alone their potential value. Thus some positive action may be needed by the community, or its leaders, to conserve genetic diversity (McNeely et al., 1990).

While reducing the rate of economic growth and of the growth rate of human populations and modifying the path of economic development can assist with the general conservation of nature, there is unlikely to be sufficient progress in this regard to eliminate man-induced extinctions in the near future (See Chapter 12). Possible choices about whether or not to save a particular species or which species to save will need to be considered. A number of approaches to such decision-making have been proposed in the literature. These include approaches suggested by ecologists, for example in the World Conservation Strategy document (IUCN, 1980), the approach taken in cost-benefit analysis (CBA), the safe minimum standard (SMS) view, the suggestion of Randall (1986) and other approaches. Apart from the following discussion of these approaches, there is additional discussion of the issues involved in Tisdell (1990b, Ch.6).

In the *World Conservation Strategy* (IUCN, 1980) *priorities* for saving species are based upon the imminence of loss of the species (the degree of its rarity) and the (biological) size of loss is indicated by whether the loss of the species would involve the loss of a family, genus or just the species itself with other species of the genus surviving. It is suggested that top priority should be given to conserving species which are vulnerable or endangered and the sole representatives of their family whereas lowest priority should be afforded to conserving those species which are rare or vulnerable but which belong to a genus which consists of several species. Thus the priority for conserving a species is determined by its degree of uniqueness in relation to the biological system of classification and the imminence of its loss.

However, this ignores the size of the possible economic value of a species. A species which is the sole representative of its family may have little economic value whereas a species which is one of many in a genus may have a high economic value and its loss would result in a very high economic loss. Furthermore, it may not always be rational, all other things being equal, to concentrate on trying to save species the loss of which is most imminent. To do so may be very costly and indeed intervention could be too late in any case to save the species. It may sometimes be more sensible to concentrate on conserving species for which the loss is less imminent but which in the absence of positive conservation action will become endangered.

Cost benefit analysis (CBA) is favoured in mainstream economics for social decision-making about resource utilisation and conservation (Smith and Krutilla, 1979). The aim of this approach is to express the cost and benefits of conserving a species or one of its varieties in terms of monetary units alone. In that sense, it takes a unidimensional rather than a multidimensional approach to valuation. The usefulness of CBA depends upon the extent to which the benefits and costs of conserving a species can be accurately expressed in monetary terms.

When the availability of a species supplies material goods such as meat e.g. fish, this part of its value can be assessed relatively easily in economic terms but the economic value of non-marketed or imperfectly marketed attributes of species, such as existence value, are less easy to assess in monetary terms. Nevertheless, a number of methods of assessment have been suggested. Most of these depend upon the stated or inferred willingness of individuals to pay for the availability of the desired characteristics (See Chapters 3 and 7). However, willingness to pay can only be directly assessed in terms of the current preferences of the present human population. Preferences of future populations can at best be imperfectly known and the tastes of existing populations may be subject to unpredictable change.

A common practice in CBA has been to attempt to treat uncertainty as if it is risk, that is by assigning probabilities to future possible events. But there is considerable debate about whether uncertainty can reasonably be treated as risk and in particular whether in such cases expected gain or expected utility should be maximised. Proponents of the safe minimum standard (SMS) approach reject the expected gain or expected utility approach under such conditions (Ciriacy-Wantrup, 1968; Bishop, 1978). This alternative approach will be discussed shortly.

Benefits and costs associated with conservation generally occur over a long period of time. Usually, in economic terms, benefits obtained in the future are considered to be worth less than the same amount of benefits received now because the latter could be invested to earn interest and return the capital *plus* interest at the later date. To take account of this in economic decision-making, future benefits and costs are usually discounted in CBA using the rate of interest. However, there is considerable debate about the appropriate level of interest to use. Some economists argue that from a social point of view a zero rate of interest should be used. This implies no discounting of the future (Brown and Jackson, 1986; see also Chapter 3).

CBA recommends that taking into account both tangible and intangible benefits those species be saved from extinction for which the discounted present benefits from saving them exceeds the discounted present costs of doing so, that is those for which the net present value of saving them is positive. If insufficient resources are available to save all species which satisfy this rule, then preference is given to saving those species the continued existence of which yields the highest (discounted) benefit to cost ratio.

As for uncertainty about benefits and costs, this may be taken account of in a variety of ways, none of which may be entirely satisfactory especially in a social setting. For example, probabilities may be assigned to the possible events and one may proceed to maximise expected net benefits or in certain cases expected utility. Or certainty equivalents may be used and one may proceed to maximise discounted net benefits based on the certainty equivalents. The certainty equivalent corresponding to an uncertain economic gain is the certain sum of money which

TABLE 5.2
Ciriacy-Wantrup/Bishop type of matrix for determining the desirability of saving a species from extinction

	S_1	S_2	Maximum loss
E	0	$-Y$	$-Y$
SMS	$-C$	$Y-C$	$-C$

is received by an individual and is considered by the individual to be equivalent to the 'gamble' (Tisdell, 1968).

The criterion of maximising expected net gains does not take account of an individual's attitudes to bearing risk or uncertainty - it is risk neutral. However, if expected utility rather than expected gain is to be maximised, account is taken of the individual's attitude to risk-bearing. The certainty-equivalent approach does take account of an individual's attitude to the bearing of risk and uncertainty but in a social context we encounter the problem that different individuals often have different attitudes to the bearing of risk and uncertainty, different perceptions about what is possible and the 'degree' to which it is possible. In the case of decisions about the conservation of a species all members of society may collectively bear the consequences of any decision made. In these circumstances, should one apply the Kaldor-Hicks criterion to social choice and blindly respect individual preferences when collective public (environmental) goods are involved?

Given that individuals are to be subjected to collective risks or uncertainties, should all be treated equally in deciding what should be done (Cf. Tisdell, 1983)? Should, for example, the wishes and views about what should be done of the 'ill-informed' count just as much in social choice as those of the 'better-informed'?

Considerable social and natural uncertainties exist as a rule about the likely future benefits from saving species. Those advocating the safe minimum standard (SMS) approach to the preservation of species believe that these uncertainties are so great that CBA is inadequate as a technique for determining the conservation of species. The SMS approach furthermore implies a conservative approach to risk-bearing. In effect is adopts a *minimax* strategy – a strategy of minimising the maximum possible loss given the presence of uncertainty. The use of this criterion tends to favour the conservation of species in comparison to CBA. In a collective risk situation, SMS subjects the risk-averse to less risk.

Ciriacy-Wantrup (1968) and Bishop (1978) suggest that as a rule the *possible* benefits from saving a species from extinction far exceed the costs of doing so and the cost of saving many species is actually very low. Therefore on the whole conservation is to be favoured given the SMS approach. The decision structure of the problem can be appreciated from the Bishop-type matrix shown as Table 5.2. The choice problem illustrated by Table 5.2 is extremely simplified.

Two available alternative strategies and two possible states of nature are indicated. The two available alternative strategies are (1) E, to do nothing and allow the species to become extinct and (2) SMS, to preserve the population of the species at a safe minimum level. The two possible states of nature are s_1, the species proves to be of no (economic) value and s_2, the species proves to be of very great economic value. Let C represent the cost of ensuring the continued existence of the species and let Y represent the value of the species if it turns out to have economic value in the future. The entries in the body of Table 5.2 represent the possible payoffs to mankind given the alternative strategies and possible states of nature. If for example, s_2 prevails and strategy E is adopted Y is forgone so that in effect there is a loss of Y.

Ciriacy-Wantrup and Bishop argue that normally Y > C. Therefore, the maximum possible loss is minimised when the SMS strategy is adopted. By comparison, it can be seen that CBA based upon expected gain is less supportive of conservation than SMS. For example, suppose that Y = 4C where C > 0. Then if the probability of s_2 is less than 0.2, e.g. 0.1, CBA will favour non-preservation of the species whereas SMS will still favour its preservation.

Randall (1986) has suggested that decisions about saving species from extinction might be made using a combination of CBA and SMS. For those cases in which knowledge is sufficient, he recommends that CBA be applied to make the decision and that SMS be applied to the remainder of the cases .

But it is not only CBA which raises difficulties. In the case of SMS, the necessary level of population or standard of environmental provision to ensure survival of a species can be uncertain. Different population levels or habitat standards may make a species' survival 'more or less probable' but none may guarantee its continued existence. Furthermore if only a *fixed* amount of resources is available for species' preservation and these criteria are applied subject to this constraint, we need to consider the different array of species which they select for preservation (Tisdell, 1990b, Ch.6). *In those circumstances*, one would want to debate further which criterion is appropriate or whether a different criterion should be used. Note that in this case the overall amount of resources for conservation is not variable and SMS cannot therefore be used as a lever to increase the amount of resources devoted to conservation. Its application in this case is purely to divide up a given pie for conservation purposes – it has no influence on the size of the pie (Tisdell, 1990b).

However, decisions about preservation of species are much more complicated than is apparent from the above. For example, decisions to save a species cannot always be taken in isolation from the conservation of other species because populations of species are often interdependent. Randall (1986) observes that some conservationists argue that species are so interdependent that the removal of any one may ultimately lead to the extinction of all. However, there appears to be little evidence to support this point of view even though the removal of one species may set in motion a chain reaction resulting in the demise of other species.

If the extreme instrumentalist position were to hold, we would already be on the road to the extinction of all species and our only choice now would be how to delay or modify the chain of extinctions on the way to ultimate extinction of all living things.

5.5 Concluding comments

The economic value of wildlife and of biodiversity has not been fully appreciated in the past. It is only now that the many economic values of wildlife and the economic significance of biodiversity are being more fully appreciated. Biodiversity is important to sustain production based on living resources and to keep options open for new economic developments which may make use of living resources.

In the very long-term, the main burden of maintaining economic production and standards of living is likely to fall on biological resources. These resources are renewable and can sustain production unlike irreplaceable resources such as coal, oil and many minerals, the stock of which is inevitably reduced as they are used in production. As non-renewable resources are depleted, mankind will be increasingly forced to rely on living resources for survival. This provides biological resources with special significance for the economic future of mankind. Georgescu-Roegen (1976) has suggested that if a sustainable economic society is to be achieved, the level of economic production must be adjusted so that it can be sustained by the use of biological resources alone. Long-term economic sustainability may require not zero-human population growth but an actual reduction in levels of human population. This issue will be taken up in Chapter 11 and discussed further in Chapter 12.

References

Bishop, R.C., 1978. Endangered species and uncertainty. The economics of a safe minimum standard. American Journal of Agricultural Economics, 60:10–18.

Brown, C.V. and Jackson, P.M., 1986. Public Sector Economics, Third Edition. Basil Blackwell, Oxford.

Christiansen, F.B. and Fenchel, T.M., 1977. Theories of Populations in Biological Communities. Springer-Verlag, Berlin.

Ciriacy-Wantrup, S.V., 1968. Resource Conservation: Economics and Policies (Third Edition). Division of Agricultural Science, University of California, CA.

Clark, C.W., 1976. Mathematical Bioeconomics: The Optimal Management of Renewable Resources. John Wiley, New York.Georgescu-Roegen, N., 1976. Energy and Economic Myths: Institutional and Analytical Economic Essays. Pergamon Press, New York.

McNeely, J.A., 1988. Economics and Biological Diversity: Developing and Using Economic Incentives to Conserve Biological Resources. IUCN, Gland, Switzerland.

McNeely, J.A., Miller, K.R., Reid, W.V., Mittermeier, R.A. and Werner, T.B., 1990. Conserving the World's Biological Diversity. IUCN, Gland, Switzerland.

Oldfield, M.L., 1989. The Value of Conserving Genetic Resources. Sinauer Associates, Sunderland, Mass.

Pearce, D., Markandya, A. and Barbier, E.B., 1989. Blueprint for a Green Economy. Earthscan Publications, London.

Plucknett, D.L., Smith, N.J., Williams, J.T. and Anishetty, N.M., 1986. Gene Banks and the World's Food. Princeton University Press, Princeton, N.J.

Randall, A., 1986. Human preferences, economics and the preservation of species. In: B.G. Gordon (Editor), The Preservation of Species: The Value of Biological Diversity, pp. 79-109. Princeton University Press, Princeton, N.J.

Smith V.K. and Krutilla, J.V., 1979. Endangered species, irreversibilities and uncertainty: a comment. American Journal of Agricultural Economics, 61:371–375.

Tisdell, C.A., 1968. The Theory of Price Uncertainty, Production and Profit. Princeton University Press, Princeton, N.J.

Tisdell, C.A., 1970. Implications of learning for economic planning. Economics of Planning, 10:172–192.

Tisdell, C.A., 1973. Kangaroos: the economic management of a common-property resource involving interdependence of production. Economic Analysis and Policy, 4(2):59–75.

Tisdell, C.A., 1979. Wildlife: A national asset or a pest to be managed? In: Department of Science and the Environment, Environmental Economics, pp. 79–87. Australian Government Publishing Service, Canberra.

Tisdell, C.A., 1983. The law, economics and risk taking. Kyklos, 36:3–20.

Tisdell, C.A., 1990a. Ecological economics and the environmental future. Paper presented at the Fourth International Congress on Environmental Future: Surviving with the Biosphere, Budapest, April, 1990. To be in J. Burnett and N. Polunin (Editors), Surviving with the Biosphere. Edinburgh University Press, Edinburgh.

Tisdell, C.A., 1990b. Natural Resources, Growth, and Development: Economics, Ecology, and Resource-Scarcity. Praeger, New York.

Chapter 6

Common property and natural resource management

6.1 Types of property and general consequences

The nature of ownership of resources, that is the nature of ownership of property, can have important consequences for the conservation of resources and the economic efficiency with which resources are used, protected and developed. If wildlife is a common-property resource, a resource to which all have free access and if it is valuable for direct use, its existence can be threatened and paradoxically the more valuable it becomes the more likely is it to be brought to the brink of extinction by overharvesting. The property of all is frequently the concern of none and usually such property is not adequately protected and husbanded.

The nature of ownership of resources may take many forms. At one extreme, ownership may involve a single owner with the exclusive right to enjoy (or to exchange) any product flowing from that resource, to use up the stock of that resource and to assign the resource together with improvements (and the rights attaching to it) to others. This is an extreme case of private property. More complicated cases arise when a resource is jointly owned by a number of persons as in a partnership, co-operative or company and when the group has the same rights as mentioned above for a single owner. These cases are complicated because we cannot assume that a group will act in the same way as an individual. The way in which a group can be expected to behave will depend on the size of the group, its articles of association and the nature of the organisation for conducting its business. Private rights, however, to use a resource may be restricted or use may not be entirely exclusive. The use of a property may be subject to conditions or covenants imposed by the State or by vendors or those assigning property in some cases.

At the other extreme to pure private property is common property to which all have common access. In the common-access case, everyone is free to use the resource. Individuals or groups of individuals gain no property rights from conserving the resource or undertaking investment to increases its economic value or its productivity. Such property is sometimes described as *res nullium* - a thing belonging to no one.

This contrasts with *res communis* – a thing belonging to a community. In this case, access and use of the resource is regulated by the community. In our society, public parks might be considered to be *res communis* because the purposes for which they can be used are regulated. In some traditional societies, community-use of natural resources was regulated by conventions and by rules imposed by village councils. On the other hand not all state property is *res communis* because members of the community or the public do not have access to it e.g. in the case of state-owned power stations.

The nature of property rights can be extremely varied and this together with the great diversity of possible institutional arrangements for use of property results in a wide range of cases each with differing consequences for the conservation and utilization of resources. All cases cannot be covered here. Attention will be focused on the common-property case involving common-access because this provides a contrast to the pure private-property case involving a single owner.

Institutional arrangements for the ownership and management of property, especially natural resources have altered with the passage of time. To some extent, economic factors determine the nature of such historical changes. For example, private property is more likely the greater are the economic gains of individuals from its creation and use. Private property is more likely to arise the lower become the costs of exclusion of non-owners of the resource and the larger the profit or gain to be made from the exclusive use of the resource. For example, technological change may (1) reduce the costs of exclusion (consider, for instance, the advent of steel wire and steel post fencing) or (2) raise the profitability of exclusive-use of resource, for instance consider methods which increase productivity of a species under conditions of domestication or cultivation. In Australia and USA for instance the development of steel wire fencing led to enclosures of many grazing properties that were previously unfenced. In Australia, the knowledge that superphosphate fertiliser could be used to increase the productivity of agricultural land resulted in an extension of privately owned properties for farming purposes.

Other influences increasing the profitability of possessing *private* property, apart from the impact mentioned above of technological change on land or resource enclosure, can include an increase in the demand for produce from the resources involved, reductions in the cost of production using the resources involved and improvements in the legal system which make it less costly to enforce property rights. Also in a society having moral respect for private property, transgression of property rights may be less common. Less frequent violation of property rights, will increase the owners gain from possessing private property and provide an encouragement to its creation.

In some cases, the value of property rights, such as national exclusive economic zones in which a nation has exclusive fishing rights will depend on its ability to detect violation of property rights and enforce appropriate penalties or violations. For example, small island nations although the frequently have very large exclusive fishing zones often find it difficult because of lack of aircraft etc. to keep their zones under surveillance. Furthermore, they are often in a weak position to extract penalties from violators e.g. to confiscate fishing vessels of foreign nations fishing illegally (Sutinen and Anderson, 1985: McKee and Tisdell, 1990, Ch. 11).

Note that private property is not always an ideal economic form of ownership of a resource. The cost of maintaining private property can be so high that such property is uneconomic. The cost of excluding straying livestock in earlier times may have been so high in some areas as to make it uneconomic and thus communal grazing of land was the rule. Taking into account the costs involved in enforcing property rights some economists argue that socially appropriate forms of property rights and ownership of resources evolve over time, and that property rights and institutional arrangements which exist at any point of time tend to be the most efficient available from an economic viewpoint. Thus common property involving common access while not leading to absolute economic efficiency may at a point in time be the most efficient form of property ownership available but at a later time may be replaced by private property as the economic viability of this increases due to technological change, changes in demand or other relevant factors affecting profitability.

Some writers argue that appropriate institutional arrangements from an economic point of view evolve naturally and that state interference to create property rights is usually unwarranted, even in the case of resources involving common access. 'Forced' attempts by the state to change institutional and property arrangements may involve considerable transaction costs and when these are taken into account no net economic gain may arise from the changed institutional arrangements (Furubotn and Pejovich, 1972). This view supports a laissez-faire position because existing institutional arrangements are believed on the whole to be the best available in the circumstances. This is not to say that their appropriateness may not change but the role of the state in relation to any change is seen as being minimal.

To some extent this point of view differs from that which recommends that governments take an active leading role in the creation of private property rights and competition in order to solve economic and environmental problems (Cf. Coase, 1960). At the same time, many of these private-property activists believe that with economic development the natural evolution of property rights is increasingly towards private property rights. They wish to see this process speeded up. But they give less attention to the costs of state intervention than do those who favour a more evolutionary approach to property rights (Furubotn and Pejovich, 1972).

6.2 Common access: economic failures and their consequences

Assume for simplicity that the value of a natural resource depends only on the market value of the produce which it supplies, that is on the private goods supplied by it. For example, it is possible that the value of some fish depends only on their meat. Thus they have no intangible benefits such as existence value. In such a case, common access to the natural resource results in market failure. It leads to a social economic loss for two main reasons: (1) An excessive quantity of resources are allocated to its harvesting or utilisation, and (2) there is failure to adopt appropriate measures to conserve the resource and sustain it and to undertake investment to improve its economic productivity (Tisdell, 1972, 1982, Ch. 15; Tietenberg, 1988, Ch. 12). When common-access occurs, resources are not allocated in a Paretian optimal manner within the economy – in *principle* a Paretian improvement in welfare would be possible by allocating fewer resources to the exploitation of a common-access natural resource and by adopting more appropriate investment and conservation policies.

Thus the main economic argument against common access to resources is that it fails to maximise the economic value of resource-use. From an ecological point of view, common- or open-access to a resource results in harvesting levels and practices which may seriously reduce the stock of the natural resource. Thus the population of a harvested species may be reduced to such a low level as to threaten the species' continued existence. Furthermore, economic changes such as rising demand for the produce from the common-access resource or falling costs of harvesting may lead to a *perverse* long-term supply response. The changes just mentioned result in greater harvesting pressures on the resource, a falling population or stock of the harvested species and eventually lower levels of supply from it. The above propositions can be illustrated by simple analysis.

First take the proposition that an excessive amount of resources (from a Kaldor-Hicks standpoint) is likely to be used to harvest or exploit a common-access resource. Suppose that the price of the product (obtained from a common-access resource) is independent of the quantity of its supply and let x represent the quantity of a resource (labour, capital, bundles of capital/labour in fixed combination, sometimes described as 'units of effort') allocated to the harvesting of the resource. Furthermore in Figure 6.1 let the line identified by VMP represent the value of the marginal product of the resource when it is used in harvesting an open-access resource and let the line identified by VAP indicate the value of its average product. Let the horizontal line FG represent the per unit cost of purchasing the resource used in harvesting the natural resource e.g. species. It is the marginal cost of using each unit of the resource used in harvesting. Assuming a perfectly competitive economy, it is also the value of marginal production forgone elsewhere by allocating an additional unit of the harvesting resource to exploitation of the common-access resource.

In order to obtain a Paretian optimal allocation of resources, a resource used in exploiting a common-access resource should be employed up to the point where the value of its marginal product equals its price per unit. Thus in the case shown in Figure 6.1 the quantity x_1 of the harvesting resource should be employed. But because of common-access, the amount of the exploiting resources employed in the common-access industry will be such that the value of its average product is equal to its price. In Figure 6.1, this occurs when the quantity x_2 of the harvesting resource is used in the common-access industry. When less than x_2 of the harvesting resource is employed in the industry, revenue will exceed cost and resource-users will find it profitable to transfer additional resources to harvesting the common-access resource. This results in a Kaldor-Hicks social deadweight loss equivalent to the area of the hatched triangle shown in Figure 6.1. If, on the other hand, the common-access resource happened to be privately owned and owners could without cost enforce their property-rights, a rent would emerge for the exploited resource or price for entry of the exploiting resource would occur of FH per unit. Thus resource-owners would earn a rental income equivalent to the dotted rectangle shown in Figure 6.1.

Resources used in exploiting a common-property resource are likely to be misallocated as between areas or regions. This is because they are allocated to each region or area so as to equalise the marginal cost of exploiting the open-access resource with the value of their average product in each area. Consequently too many resources are allocated to areas with the highest average productivity, such as 'good' fishing grounds, in comparison to those areas with lower productivity.

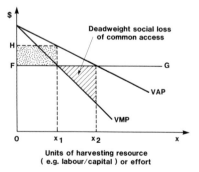

Figure 6.1. Common- or open-access results in resources being allocated in accordance with the value of their average product rather than the value of their marginal product and this leads to a deadweight social-loss indicated here by the hatched triangle.

Thus, because marginal costs are not equated to the value of *marginal* product in each area the total production (or value of the catch in the case of fisheries) is not maximised relative to the total amount of the exploiting resources employed (Gordon, 1954).

Secondly, a common-access resource is unlikely to be conserved and sustained and invested in in a way which maximises the value of production. Since all can share equally in any future increase in value or productivity of a common-access resource, no individual has an incentive as a rule to adopt actions now which will increase or sustain its value or productivity. Any individual who takes beneficial action to conserve an open-access resource can, at most, appropriate a very small fraction of the benefits from this action. Thus the immature and most productive members of the population of a species may be harvested even when their harvest is not in the collective interest. User costs are not taken into account, that is, the value of resource benefits forgone in the future because of current resource-use or practices are ignored.

Furthermore, environmental improvements which may increase the returns from the common-access resource may be neglected. For example, in some cases the provision of permanent water supplies, e.g. by building small dams, may beneficially increase the supply of cropped wildlife in some areas. Indeed, individuals may adopt actions which lead to destruction of environments complementary to the productivity of a common-access resource. They may do this because (1) they can earn profit from appropriating the complementary environmental goods or (2) because the use of environmentally damaging techniques reduces the private costs of harvesting or utilizing the common-access resource, e.g. driftnet fishing or fishing techniques that damage the sea floor.

The economic response to market signals in the common-access case is often a perverse one (Turvey, 1964; Copes, 1970; Clarke, 1973; Anderson, 1977; Wilen, 1985). Instead of market signals leading to greater conservation of a resource for which demand is increasing as is likely to occur in the case of a pure private commodity, in the case of a common-access resource less conservation occurs. Those exploiting a common-access resource are as a rule motivated only by their immediate individual gain.

Apart from the economic problem of an excessive amount of resources being devoted to harvesting a common-access resource, population levels of a harvested species, such as fish, may be reduced to levels which do not minimise the cost of the actual harvest achieved. This can be illustrated by Figure 6.2.

Assume that the sustainable harvest, X, of the species is a function of the level of population, N, of the species, that is $X=f(N)$. Suppose that this function has a single maximum (is unimodal). Then the sustainable supply of the harvest under conditions of common-access might be as indicated by the backward-bending curve SS in Figure 6.2. When the demand curve is D_1D_1, market equilibrium exists at E_1. The corresponding equilibrium level of the harvest is X_1 units per

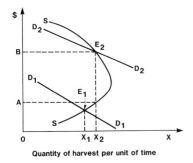

Quantity of harvest per unit of time

Figure 6.2. Backward-bending supply curve for the harvest of species to which there is common-access. This can result in perverse conservation decisions and a smaller population of the species than is desirable for minimising the cost of the actual harvest.

period of time. If, however, the demand curve for the common-access commodity should shift up to D_2D_2, a new market equilibrium is established at E_2. This equilibrium involves a harvest per unit of time of X_2 at a cost per unit of supply of OB. It also results in a reduction of the population level of the species to such an extent that the cost of the actual harvest is not minimised. With a larger population of the species, a harvest of X_2 per unit of time can be sustained with less cost per unit of the harvest, namely at a cost of OA per unit. From Figure 6.3 it can be seen that a harvest of X_2 can be sustained either with a population level for the species of N_1 or a population level of N_2 given the nature of the net population growth function $f(N)$.

Note that both equilibria in figure 6.2 are stable given Marshallian reaction functions. But if the demand curve should cut the downward sloping portion of

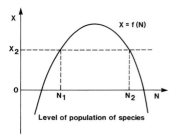

Level of population of species

Figure 6.3. Sustainable harvesting levels as a function of the level of population of a species.

the supply curve from above, the top equilibrium is unstable to its left side and an appropriate disturbance can be expected to result in increased harvesting pressure which eventually drives the species to extinction. The reaction is economically perverse assuming that demand for the species is expected to be maintained in the future.

Technological progress in a common-access industry which reduces the per unit costs of harvesting the common-access resource does not necessarily increase economic welfare (see, for example, Lindner, 1989). Indeed in some circumstances, it reduces economic welfare. This can be illustrated by Figure 6.4.

In figure 6.4, curve S_1S_1 represents the common-access supply curve in the absence of technological progress whereas the curve marked S_2S_2 represents this supply curve after technological progress. If the demand curve for the common-access commodity is D_1D_1, technological progress results in the market equilibrium shifting from E_1 to E_2. As a result, consumers' surplus increases but producers' surplus remains unaltered because it is zero under common-access. In this case, economic welfare increases if the decrease in the stock or population of the common-access resource is itself without any social welfare consequence.

However, in the case of a *heavily* exploited common-access resource, welfare can be expected to decline as a result of cost-reducing technological progress. For example, if the demand curve in Figure 6.4 is D_2D_2, technological progress which shifts the supply curve from S_1S_1 to S_2S_2, alters equilibrium from E_3 to E_4. Consequently, the price of the common-access commodity rises, its sustainable supply falls and consumers' surplus is reduced with producers' surplus remaining at zero. The stock or population of the species being harvested is reduced.

Note that improved technology may cause a shift in the market equilibrium from the lower branch of a supply curve to an its upper branch. In some cases the after-innovation supply curve may cut the demand curve from below or the

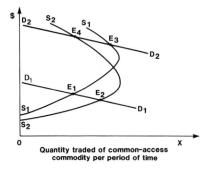

Figure 6.4. In an open-access industry, technological progress which reduces per unit harvesting costs *might* reduce economic welfare and threaten the existence of a species.

new supply curve actually be below the demand curve. In the former case, the instability of the market equilibrium makes it likely that a common-access population will be driven to extinction. In the latter case the harvested species is certain to be driven to extinction.

6.3 Policies for managing common-access resources

A number of policy measures or economic instruments have been suggested in the economic literature for correcting the economic problems associated with common-access resources (Turvey, 1964; Tisdell, 1972, 1973, 1974; Anderson, 1977). While the use of economic instruments may be intended to increase the economic efficiency of resource-use, they may also be used purely for conservation reasons. In the latter case the measures may be designed to limit or to stop economic trade in the open-access resource in order to conserve it, for instance, at not less than a safe minimum level (Bishop, 1978).

One way to control the harvest or utilisation of a common-access resource is to impose a tax on its use. If in Figure 6.5 curve S_aS_a represents the supply curve of the 'harvest' under common-access and S_cS_c represents the supply curve assuming an efficient allocation of resources, economic efficiency can be theoretically achieved by imposing a tax of BF on each unit of the harvest, assuming no differences in productivity and costs by area of origin of the harvest. This would result in market equilibrium altering from E_1 to E_2 and the level of the harvest per period falling from X_3 to X_2. Theoretically this result could also be achieved by having a quota on the maximum per period harvest equal to X_2 and the government making this quantity available by bidding or tendering. This method in-

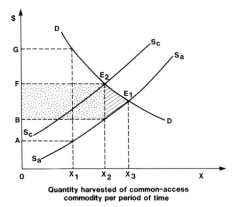

Figure 6.5. Taxes on the catch or tradeable permits may be used to improve allocative efficiency in the case of an open-access resource. But if economic gains are to be made the cost of administering such schemes must not exceed the benefits otherwise obtained.

volves the creation of a market in harvesting rights or permits. Under competitive conditions, the right to harvest one unit of the resource would sell for an amount BF and lead to the same result as with a per unit tax of that amount. In either case the government would obtain revenue equal to $BF.X_2$.

But if this government revenue is absorbed by the government in higher administration costs, the costs of promoting greater allocative efficiency may be a reduction in the level of economic production and a reduction in economic welfare. For example, the net economic benefit of costless optimal regulation of the harvest is as indicated by the hatched area in Figure 6.5. But if all the government revenues obtained (as indicated by the dotted rectangle) are used up in administering the regulatory system, e.g. monitoring, enforcing and improving the regulations, undertaking research on the regulations and so on, the value of production forgone elsewhere as a result of resources drawn into these activities *may* be equal to this dotted rectangle. In the case shown, the 'allocative' benefit of the regulation (the hatched area) is less than the dotted area. Thus the value of production forgone as a result of administration costs for the scheme could exceed its allocative benefits. In some cases the costs of monitoring and enforcing the above solutions may be so high as to make these measures uneconomic (Tisdell, 1983, 1990, Ch. 9).

Note that the above regulations (taxes and marketable or tradeable permits) do not ensure efficiency in *investment* or in husbanding a common-access resource for the future. They do not ensure that full account is taken of user costs. If a large number of economic agents can share in the future harvest of the industry, no individual has an incentive to increase that harvest by forgoing current profitable action. For this reason the above measures are often supplemented by additional measures, e.g. regulations on the minimum size of fish to be taken.

The harvesting of a species may be limited not primarily to attain economic efficiency but to ensure that the population of the species survives or survives at a minimum degree of abundance. In the case illustrated by Figure 6.5, the last mentioned conservation goal might be achieved if the level of harvesting per period is not allowed to exceed X_1. Theoretically, this aim could be met by imposing a tax of AG on each unit of the harvest or by introducing an aggregate quota of X_1 on the annual harvest which could be auctioned to achieve efficiency. However, as mentioned before, such measures can be costly or difficult to enforce especially in developing countries.

There is a further problem: The knowledge of the government about market supply and demand conditions and of relationships between the level of catch and the degree of abundance of the species may be imperfect. This will be especially so when these relationships fluctuate over time. Hence, harvesting policies have to be devised as a rule under conditions of uncertainty. Consequently attitudes to the bearing of risk or uncertainty need to be taken into account. For example, the greater the risk-aversion of policy-makers in relation to maintaining the existence of the species or its degree of abundance, the lower is likely to be the harvesting rate permitted for it.

Sometimes it is not practical to regulate the quantity of the harvest of an open-access resource directly. Restrictions may then be placed on the amount of effort by regulating the harvesting gear used or the number of entrants. Generally, this results in some economic inefficiency, that is in higher cost of attaining the actual harvest than is necessary. However, taking account of monitoring costs and enforcement costs involved using alternative regulations, such regulations can sometimes be defended from an economic viewpoint.

The creation of property rights can, as mentioned earlier, often assist in the appropriate economic management of common-property resources. The extension for example of the exclusive fishing zone to the 200 nautical mile limit around sovereign states has made it possible for national governments to regulate fishing catches to a greater extent than in the past. However, the mere declaration of an exclusive zone is not enough to ensure optimal management. Access by nationals to the exclusive economic zone may need to be regulated by the government and it must consider the extent to which it is economic for it to detect and exclude foreign poachers (Sutinen and Anderson, 1985). In the case of transboundary or transfrontier species (e.g. of highly migratory fish) that is, species which move across national boundaries or frontiers, different nations need as a rule to co-operate to ensure optimal harvesting and conservation of the species.

When the main goal of economic regulation is to protect a species from extinction or maintain its abundance on conservation-grounds, its harvesting may be totally banned, or the use of specified techniques for its harvest may be disallowed or the markets for its harvest may be restricted. For example, the Convention on International Trade in Endangered Species (CITES) basically bans trade in endangered species and their products between the signatories (Lyster, 1985). This reduces the legal market for the harvest of endangered species and in normal circumstances can be expected to result in reduced harvesting pressures. But in itself it is not *the* solution to saving all endangered species. This is because most are threatened by habitat destruction as a result of economic change and development. CITES *may* make it more difficult for ranching or farming of wild species to develop. Farming *may* provide a means to help conserve some wild species.

6.4 Ranching and farming as means to overcome common-access problems and conserve species

Ranching is the practice of capturing the young of a species and rearing them in captivity. Techniques may be used in rearing the captured young which ensure a greater survival rate, faster growth rate and higher biomass for the species involved than that normally attained under natural conditions. For example, in some countries, such as Ecuador, shrimps (prawns) are maricultured under these conditions. The young are captured in the wild and raised in privately controlled artificial ponds. Common access continues for capture of the young.

While this practice *could* in special cases raise supplies available from the natural population of a species, it appears usually to result in a reduction in the level of population of the ranched species in the wild. This is because the profitability of raising captured wild stock may increase the demand for capturing natural stock for this purpose. In addition, sites selected for raising captured stock may be those most sought after under natural conditions by natural stock. These are sometimes the natural breeding and hatchery grounds of wild stock. This is so in the case of shrimp farming in Ecuador.

In Ecuador the construction of new ponds for shrimp not only leads to demands for more postlarvae shrimp from the wild but reduces their availability from the wild because it destroys the breeding ground of the shrimp. Consequently, in Ecuador despite an approximate doubling of effort to catch postlarvae of shrimp in the wild to satisfy the area of cultivation of shrimps, the number of semilla (postlarvae) caught has barely risen (Meltzoff and LiPuma, 1986). Thus, this form of ranching/mariculture appears to have led to a reduction in the population of shrimps in the wild.

Farming of a species is sometimes seen as a means for preventing extinction of a species and of increasing supplies of products obtained from it. Farming normally involves a closed breeding cycle unlike ranching and usually requires farmers to have private property rights if it is to be an economic success. By contrast ranching does not involve a closed breeding cycle and the rancher only has property-rights over a limited part of the life cycle of the species and then only for captives.

Scientists are investigating possible systems for farming many wild species. Both

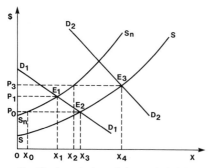

Quantity of species harvested per period of time

Figure 6.6. While farming may favour the conservation of wild stock of a species, it is not bound to do so. This is because it can increase demand for the use of the species and it may cause the supply schedule of supplies from the wild of the harvested species to move upward and to the left. (Note that this shift in the supply schedule is not illustrated.)

terrestrial and aquatic species are targets for possible farming. Various types of deer are for example now farmed. A number of species are also bred on farms for amateur hunting purposes. In marine areas, the farming of seaweed has developed considerably in many countries. The possibility of farming giant clams and turtles has also been established in recent years (Copland and Lucas, 1988; Tisdell, 1986). However, controversy exists about the effectiveness of farming as a means of saving species from extinction and relieving pressure on natural stocks. Proponents of farming argue (1) that farming is likely to relieve harvesting pressure on wild stocks and (2) that in certain cases some species are bound to disappear in the wild and that farming may be the only viable way of conserving them.

The issues involved are complex but Figure 6.6 is useful for analyzing them. Suppose that curve marked S_nS_n represents the supply curve for the harvest of a species from the wild and let D_1D_1 represent the demand curve for that harvest. Market equilibrium is established at E_1 with the quantity X_1 being traded at a price P_1 per unit. Suppose now that farming of the species becomes possible and adds to total supplies so that the new supply curve becomes SS. The difference between curve SS and S_nS_n represents the supply from farmed sources. Market equilibrium now shifts to E_2 and equilibrium price falls to Po. The total supply of X_3 consists of X_o captured in the wild plus $X_3 - X_o$ available from farming. In this case, farming does relieve pressure on wild stocks and their population increases. But this may give too favourable a view.

Opponents of farming and trade in the products of farmed species which are endangered in the wild have argued that farming, by leading to a larger and more regular supply of the farmed products, results in demand for the products being stimulated. It results in the demand curve being shifted upwards. It may, in relation to Figure 6.6, for example, result in the demand curve shifting up from D_1D_1 to D_2D_2 and the new market equilibrium being established at E_3 rather than at E_2. In that case, harvesting pressure on wild stock increases. The harvest of wild stock rises from X_1 to X_3 per period, and the level of the wild population is reduced. Indeed the wild stock could become seriously endangered by the harvest from the wild may be forced on to the backward-bending section (not shown) of a natural harvest supply curve.

Wild stocks may in addition be adversely affected in other ways (Tisdell, 1991, forthcoming). Farmers, for example, may appropriate sites which are favoured by wild stocks and exclude wild stocks from these. Consequently, the wild population may decline as it is denied resources appropriated for the farming of cultivated stock. This for example has occurred in the case of shrimp culture and appears to be a common occurrence. In effect, this pushes the curve S_nS_n upward and to the left.

While it is true that farming may help to save a species which would otherwise become extinct, it need not be favourable to the conservation of wild stocks of the species. In the long term, however, the continuing economic success of farming may depend upon genetic diversity being maintained in the wild (See Chapter 5). In this respect, both use and conservation need to be reconciled from the point of view of economic benefits from farming.

Commercial farming of species should be distinguished from programs designed to breed species in captivity to supplement wild stock. Programs, for example, to rear giant clams in captivity to restock reefs depleted of natural stock, or programs designed to give turtles a 'head start' by protecting the young for a time before allowing them to enter the sea are designed to add directly to natural stocks of the species involved. They are a supplement to natural forces.

6.5 Concluding comment

While common-access to resources can create problems for the efficient economic utilisation and conservation of resources and for their preservation generally, the creation of private property is not always economical and in some cases is itself inimical to conservation. Unfortunately, there is no single universally optimal institutional arrangement for the ownership and management of property whether this is judged purely on the basis of narrow economic goals or on the basis of narrow conservation goals. This, however, is not to say that institutional arrangements are immaterial nor that we cannot judge in particular instances. Indeed, we can judge and we can usually at least reject some institutional arrangements as inferior either from an economic or a conservation viewpoint. We should proceed in an open-minded manner, weigh up the evidence in each case and take account of the type of analysis and the issues discussed above. This also applies to choice of economic instruments for improving the management of natural resources, including open-access resources.

References

Anderson, L.G., 1977. The Economics of Fisheries Management. Johns Hopkins Press, Baltimore.

Bishop, R.C., 1978. Endangered species and uncertainty. The economics of a safe minimum standard. American Journal of Agricultural Economics, 60:10–18.

Clark, C.W., 1973. The economics of overexploitation. Science, 181:630–634.

Coase, R., 1960. The problem of social cost. The Journal of Law and Economics, 3:1–44.

Copes, P., 1970. The backward-bending supply curve of the fishing industry. Scottish Journal of Political Economy, 17:69–77.

Copland, J.W. and Lucas, J.S. (Editors), 1988. Giant Clams in Asia and the Pacific. Australian Centre for International Agricultural Research, Canberra.

Furubotn, E.G. and Pejovich, S., 1972. Property rights and economic theory: a survey of the recent literature. Journal of Economic Literature, 10:1137–1162.

Gordon, H.S., 1954. The economic theory of common property resource: the fishery. Journal of Political Economy, 62:124–142.

Lindner, R.K., 1989. A framework for priority-setting for fisheries research. In: H. Campbell, K. Menz and C. Waugh (Editors), Economics of Fishery Management in the Pacific Islands Region, pp. 150–158. Australian Centre for Agricultural Research, Canberra.

Lyster, S., 1985. International Wildlife Law. Grotius, Cambridge.

McKee, D. and Tisdell, C.A., 1990. Developmental Issues in Small Island Economies. Praeger, New York.

Meltzoff, S.K. and LiPuma, E., 1986. The social and political economy of coastal zone management: shrimp mariculture in Ecuador. Coastal Zone Management Journal, 14(4):349–380.

Sutinen, J.G. and Anderson, P., 1985. The economics of fisheries law enforcement. Land Economics, 61(4):387-397.

Tietenberg, T., 1988. Environmental and Natural Resource Economics, 2nd Edition. Scott, Foresman and Company, Glenview, Illinois.

Tisdell, C.A., 1972. The economic conservation and utilisation of wildlife species. The South African Journal of Economics, 40(3):235–248.

Tisdell, C.A., 1973. Kangaroos: the economic management of a common-property resource involving interdependence of production. Economic Analysis and Policy, 4(2):59–75.

Tisdell, C.A., 1974. On population effects, wildlife and management of kangaroos. Economic Analysis and Policy, 5(2):8–11.

Tisdell, C.A., 1982. Microeconomics of Markets, Wiley, Brisbane.

Tisdell, C.A., 1983. Conserving living resources in Third World countries: economic and social issues. The International Journal of Environmental Studies, 22:11-24.

Tisdell, C.A., 1986. Conflicts about living marine-resources in Southeast Asian and Australian waters: Turtles and dugongs as cases. Marine Resource Economics, 3(1):89–109.

Tisdell, C.A., 1990. Natural Resources, Growth and Development: Economics, Ecology and Resource-Scarcity. Praeger, New York.

Tisdell, C.A., 1991. Development of aquaculture and the environment: coastal conflicts, and giant clam farming as a case. The International Journal of Environmental Studies (forthcoming).

Turvey, R., 1964. Optimisation and suboptimisation in fishery regulation. American Economic Review, 54:64–77.

Wilen, J.E., 1985. Bioeconomics of renewable resource use. In: A.V. Kneese and J.L. Sweeney (Editors), Handbook of Natural Resource Economics, 1:60–124. Elsevier Science Publishers, Amsterdam.

Chapter 7

Economics of conserving natural areas: national parks and protected areas

7.1 Introduction: nature and availability of natural areas

With economic growth, development and change, Man has modified or radically altered most natural terrestrial areas on the Globe and many marine areas as well, particularly those in the coastal zone. The extent of this modification reflects Man's increased ability through use of new technology, his effort and investment to transform and utilise nature, as well as the substantial worldwide effects of increased and increasing human population, economic production and consumption. The area of the Earth not modified by the activities of man is now extremely small and continues to shrink so that the reduced availability of natural areas is now a global concern.

There is no single adequate indicator of the extent of loss of natural areas because both qualitative and quantitative dimensions are involved. For example, compared to pre-agriculture times, approximately 13 per cent of natural terrestrial areas have been lost to cultivation. While forest cover accounts for just under 32 per cent of existing land use, this cover has been much reduced, especially in temperate zones, and the type of forest cover has been altered, e.g. by the expansion of monocultural forest plantations. (Based on statistics given in World Resources Institute and IIED, 1986, pp. 92, 93.) Together with woodland and shrubland, forest cover accounts for just under 50 per cent of land cover. But even woodlands and shrublands have been greatly changed in nature by increased intensity of grazing by livestock and reduced density of cover, e.g. as a result of use of shrubs for firewood in developing countries (Timberlake, 1985). Deterioration in the natural qualities of such areas is much greater than is evident from global land-use statistics.

A substantial increase in the number and the total size of protected areas has occurred globally in the last 100 years or so since the founding of the first national park, Yellowstone National Park in the United States. Nevertheless, a global net loss of natural areas, especially in many less developed countries, has occurred. In 1985, 3.2 per cent of the Earth's terrestrial area was allocated to major protected areas according to IUCN estimates quoted in *World Resources 1986* (World Resources Institute and IIED, 1986, p. 282). But this percentage varied widely between countries, continents and regions. On average the percentage is highest in the countries with higher per capita incomes and in temperate areas. This may be a reflection of both demand and supply factors. Citizens in more developed and high-income countries may have a greater demand for the use and preservation of natural areas. Furthermore, natural sites in such countries may be at considerable risk in the absence of being given a formally protected status. In less developed countries many areas remain in a relatively natural state, despite the absence of formal protective status, because available technology, capital and access to markets has been insufficient to make it economic to transform them. But this is changing. The original natural protection of relative isolation of such areas from the global economy is disappearing and posing increasing threats to their retention (Tisdell, 1989, 1990, Ch. 4).

Note that available statistics on the size of protected areas conceal another problem. Countries vary in their ability to protect those areas legally declared to be protected. Thailand, for example, has 'protected' a high percentage of its land area but in many cases settlers have settled (squatted) in 'national parks' and have seriously modified these.

Furthermore, the status and nature of protected areas varies. IUCN recognises ten categories of protected areas and the statistics above refer to areas listed in categories I-V only. These are: I. Scientific reserves and strict nature reserves. These are generally closed to public access. II. National parks and provincial parks. These are relatively large areas that are not materially altered by humans. Although visitors are encouraged to use these areas for recreation and study, access is controlled. III. Natural monuments and natural landmarks. These areas may contain special animals or plants or unique geological formations, and public access is usually restricted. IV. Managed natural reserves and wildlife sanctuaries. They are managed for wildlife conservation purposes. V. Protected landscapes and seascapes.

Other categories include Multiple Use Management Areas (Category VIII). In these large areas, renewable resources such as timber and game are used and recreation potential is managed to ensure sustainability of resources. Other categories of protected areas include Biosphere Reserves (Category IX) and natural World Heritage Sites (Category X).

Biosphere Reserves are approved by the International Coordinating Committee of UNESCO's Man and the Biosphere (MAB) Program. Biosphere Reserves include a strictly protected core area, surrounded by buffer zones of less strictly protected areas, followed by even less protected areas such as multiple-use management areas which may include cultivation. Such a system of reserves recognises that interconnectedness of land use can be important for the survival of many species. Island-like national parks and highly protected areas are often too small to provide adequate protection to some species targeted for protection and these species need to spill out on to nearby areas. Where this is not possible, protected areas may need to be increased in size to achieve the target and this could result in greater cost and economic hardship to local communities.

A recent IUCN publication (McNeely, et al., 1990, p. 61) points out that 'strictly protected categories [of land use areas](categories I, II, III) will not be able to conserve all - or even most – species, genetic resources, and ecological processes. Far greater expanses are required for conservation than modern societies are willing to remove from direct protection'. In these circumstances, integrated land-use along the lines suggested for Biosphere Reserves may constitute the best hope for conservation of nature.

Note that land-use patterns such as those indicated by Biosphere Reserves require land-use planning and control. This suggests that land use cannot be left entirely to free market forces. Consequently it raises the question of the efficiency and desirability of alternative social mechanisms for regulating land-use.

In Australia, the Great Barrier Reef Marine Park is similar to a Biosphere Reserve because it includes strictly protected areas, for example, for scientific use; protected recreational areas in which natural resource harvesting is not permitted; and other areas in which natural resource harvesting e.g. of fish, is allowed subject to conditions which, in a large measure, are intended to ensure the sustained harvesting of the resource (Tisdell and Broadus, 1989).

7.2 Benefits and uses of natural protected areas

As pointed out by McNeely (1988, Ch.2), natural protected areas can have a wide range of economic benefits and uses. They may provide products for direct consumption, e.g. fish and game, as well as raw materials for production, such as timber and fish. But here we are concerned mostly with the non-exploitative benefits and uses of protected areas.

Benefits received from a natural area may be classified into two sets: Those that can only be achieved by visiting the site and those which are obtained off-site. Outdoor recreational benefits from a natural area can only be had for example by actually visiting the site. On the other hand, hydrological advantages from a natural site such as more regular flows of streams used for water supply are external to the site as such. Existence, option and bequest values can also be obtained independently of visits to a natural area.

But the benefits from conserving natural areas do not always neatly fall into two sets – on-site and off-site. Even in the case of outdoor recreation, the existence of the natural area may result in more fish, game or wildlife for recreational activity outside the protected area. Thus there would be a favourable externality generated for outdoor recreation.

Furthermore the potential benefits from protecting a natural area for genetic diversity may largely be obtained off-site when the gene bank of species or varieties preserved on the site are used for commercial application, e.g. on farms. A small amount of living material may be removed from the protected site for propagation or multiplication off-site. While many examples are available of the ways in which protected areas have yielded economic benefits via their preservation of species or varieties which became of commercial value for food, medicine, fibre, timber and so on, (Oldfield, 1989) it is very difficult to predict the exact value of a site for this purpose in advance. Nevertheless, this type of productive option value can be substantial.

In developed countries, protected natural areas appear to be used principally for outdoor recreation and non-consumptive purposes. While these areas are sometimes used for similar purposes in less developed countries, in less developed countries local inhabitants appear to make greater use of natural areas for consumptive purposes e.g, as a source of food, of fuel for domestic purposes and of building materials.

Methods of estimating the value of natural areas (which have been mainly developed in Western countries) tend to concentrate on non-consumptive values. Economic evaluation of such areas in developed countries tends to concentrate on their value for recreation but also increasingly their existence, option and bequest values. For the purpose of economic evaluation various methods have been developed. These include the travel-cost method, contingent valuation methods and hedonic price methods. Let us discuss each of these in turn.

7.3 Travel cost method of estimating the value of a natural area

This method was initially suggested by H. Hotelling in the 1930s as a potential means of valuing national parks. However, it was not until the 1950s onward that it was developed operationally, largely as a result of the research of Marion Clawson (1959) and Jack Knetsch (1963, 1964) in the USA (Clawson and Knetsch, 1966). The travel cost method is now applied relatively widely in assessing projects which involve an outdoor recreational element. For example, apart from its application to national parks, forested areas and similar areas used for recreation, it is frequently used to assess the value of dams or reservoirs which may cater for outdoor recreation such as fishing, boating or picnicking as a part of their benefits.

Basically, the travel cost method uses the costs which individuals incur in travelling to an outdoor area as surrogates for prices of their visits. If visitors are drawn from a large catchment area, the cost per visit of those coming from further afield can be expected to be higher than those located closer to the natural area. This cross-sectional data together with relative frequency of visits can be used to estimate a demand curve for visits to the natural area (McConnell, 1985, pp. 683–701; Hufschmidt et al., 1983, pp. 216–232; Tisdell, 1977).

More specifically, the catchment area for visitors to an outdoor attraction is divided into zones, transition from one zone to another being dependent on the travelling distance to the outdoor attraction. At the entrance to the natural attraction, individuals may be interviewed to determine the origin of their journey so that they can be allocated to a catchment zone. For example, in the simple case shown in Figure 7.1 where point A represents the attraction and the space represents travelling distance, the space has been divided into three zones by concentric circles and it is assumed that no visitors come from outside zone 3. Supposing that entry to the outdoor site is free, the average cost of travelling from each zone may be used as an indicator of the effective 'price' to be paid by a visitor for visiting the recreational site.

The frequency of visitors from each zone is recorded. The relative frequency of visits from each zone can be determined by dividing the number (frequency) of visits from each zone by the population of each zone. The relative frequency of visits from each zone can then be plotted against the average cost of travel from each zone and the line or curve of 'best' fit can be obtained. This is an estimate of the demand curve for relative frequency of visits. We would expect it to have the normal properties of demand curves e.g. we would expect the relative frequency of visits to be greater the lower is the cost of each visit.

From the demand curve for relative frequency of visits, the demand curve for

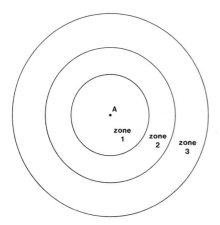

Figure 7.1. Zoning of areas depending upon travel distance to an outdoor attraction A.

the absolute number of visits to the outdoor area as a function of the possible price of entry to the outdoor area can be computed. As the price of entry is varied the relative frequency of visits from the various zones will alter – the relative frequency of visits from more distant zones will tend to decline. The aggregate number of visits to an outdoor attraction corresponding to any price for entry to the attraction can be found by multiplying the relative frequency of visits from each zone (as found from the demand curve for relative frequency of visits) by the total population in the zone, and summing these amounts for all the zones. Hence, by allowing the price of entry to vary, an aggregate demand curve for visits to the outdoor recreation area can be constructed.

The basic procedure can be clarified by a simple example. Suppose that the travel costs per visit from zones 1, 2 and 3 are respectively $2, $3 and $4 and that the respective relative frequency of visits during a period of time from these zones are 0.3, 0.2 and 0.1. These points are identified in Figure 7.2 by (1), (2) and (3). They fall on the line

$$c = 5 - 10r$$
$$\text{or } r = 0.5 - 0.1c$$

where c is the average cost of travel from a zone and r is the relative frequency of visits from a zone. They give rise to the demand curve for relative frequency of visits identified by line AF in Figure 7.2

Suppose that 100,000 people live in each zone. Where there is no entry fee to the natural area, the number of visits from each of the zones during the selected period of time is found by multiplying this figure by the relative frequency of vi-

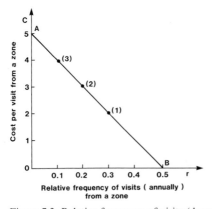

Figure 7.2. Relative frequency of visits (demand for visits per capita) as a function of the (travel) cost per visit.

sits from each zone. This gives 30,000, 20,000 and 10,000 visits from zones 1 – 3 respectively and a total number of visits of 60,000.

If an entry fee to the natural area of $1 per visit is introduced this will add $1 to the cost of visits from each of the zones. Now it will cost $5 to visit from Zone 3 and no visits will be made from this zone. The relative frequency of visits from zones 2 and 1 will be 0.1 and 0.2 respectively. So at this price of entry 30,000 visits should take place per unit of time. At a fee of $2 per visit to the natural area, the only visitors will be from zone 1 and 10,000 visits per period of time will occur. At a fee of $3 per visit to the outdoor area no visits will occur. Thus four points on the demand curve for visits to the outdoor area as a function of the entry fee are identified. These are shown respectively as points A, B, C and D in Figure 7.3 and are consistent with the demand curve shown.

Given that the curve ABCD in Figure 7.3 represents demand for visits annually, the annual economic value obtained from this natural area for visits is usually measured by the area under the demand curve if there is no entry fee to natural area. It is the amount of consumers' surplus obtained by visitors and is represented by the hatched area in Figure 7.3. If no other benefits are obtained from the natural area and if no costs are involved in maintaining it, this surplus will provide a measure of the (on site) net recreational value of the area if the site is preserved in its natural state assuming that it is already in a natural state. This can be compared with the net value of the area for alternative possible uses of the area to decide which form of use provides the greatest economic net value (Tisdell, 1972). Thus it can form the basis for a comparative cost-benefit analysis of land use.

In this respect, however, note that the world is not static (stationary) but in a constant state of change. Population levels in catchment zones a natural area may alter, the relative frequency or per capita demands to visit such an area may change and alternative uses of the land and returns from these may alter. Land-use planning would require estimates or predictions to be made about such vari-

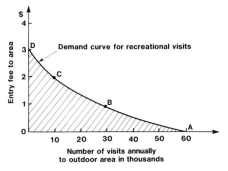

Figure 7.3. Demand curve for visits to an outdoor area. Consumers' surplus in the absence of an entry fee is shown by the hatched area.

ables. Furthermore it is the stream of future benefits from alternative uses that needs to be assessed. This may call for discounting of future benefits (e.g. use of net present values) in the decision-making about land use. But in that respect account needs to be taken of possible irreversibilities in land use, e.g. the difficulty or impossibility of restoring a natural site once it has been transformed for agriculture or similar uses, as well as controversies about appropriate discount rates.

Apart from the problems already mentioned above (such as the failure of the method to measure values obtained off-site for a natural area), a number of other problems can also be encountered in using the travel cost method as a means to value the benefits of an outdoor area such as a national park or similar area. These include:

(1) Non-homogeneity of relevant attributes of population in different zones. The travel-cost method assumes that individuals on average in the different zones exhibit the same demand patterns for visits to the outdoor attraction. This may not be so, for example, because of differences in income or educational levels between zones.

(2) Journeys to the outdoor area are assumed to be for the sole purpose of visiting it, that is a single purpose. But often journeys are for multiple purposes. They may be a part of a journey which involves visits to several areas so that in effect a joint product is consumed. For example, many travellers from zone 3 may visit sites in zone 1 or 2 in their journey to the outdoor attraction under consideration.

(3) No utility or disutility from the process of travelling is supposed. The full costs of the travel are assumed to be reflected in actual transport costs.

(4) Usually because of the costs of collecting data, information or visitors to an outdoor area (e.g. collected by interviews at an entry point) will be limited to a sample. The survey may involve data collection over a limited period of time, e.g. a month, or on some randomised basis. The question then is how representative is the sample? If the frequency of visits is seasonal and data is collected in the on-season and projected for the whole-year demand, demand will tend to be overestimated and vice-versa if data is collected only in the off-season or a slack season. Also visits to a site may follow a cyclical pattern of change over several years, and results will be influenced by the part of the cycle in which data is collected.

(5) In the cases where curves have to be fitted to the data, there is the usual problem of deciding on the appropriate form of the function to fit and determining the 'goodness' of its fit to the data.

(6) The economic value of a park or natural site very often does not depend solely upon visits to it. A number of off-site benefits are possible. On the one hand these include benefits like existence, option and bequest value and more material benefits such as hydrological benefits outside the area, and in some cases waste absorption e.g. CO_2 absorption. Contingency valuation methods go some way to taking account of such additional values.

7.4 Contingency valuation of natural areas

Contingency valuation methods are widely and increasingly used to value environmental goods including natural areas such as national parks (Wilks, 1990; Loomis and Walsh, 1986; McConnell, 1985, pp. 701–706; Hufschmidt et al., 1983, pp. 232–254). Usually their purpose is to determine the *willingness* of individuals *to pay* to avoid a particular environmental change, to retain an environmental asset, or to bring about a particular environmental change. The payment is contingent upon some desired environmental state occurring. An alternative approach is to ask individuals what payment they would require (*willingness to accept payment* or monetary compensation) to allow a particular environmental variation to occur. The latter approach appears to be less commonly adopted.

The simplest methods of contingency valuation are so called *single-bid games* and *multiple-bid games*. [For more information about alternative methods and for additional references see Wilks, 1990 and McConnell, 1985, pp. 701–706]. In the former case individuals are asked how much they are willing to pay (the maximum) to ensure that a particular environmental good is provided e.g. a natural area protected as a national park, or alternatively they are asked how much they would have to be paid as a minimum to forgo such a possibility. The amounts provide two different measures of consumer surplus.

In the case of multiple-bid games, the interviewer uses trial-and-error to determine the maximum amount which a respondent is willing to pay for an environmental good, such as a national park, or the minimum amount which must be paid to the respondent to forgo such an environmental good. Other methods of contingency valuation have also been developed (Hufschmidt et al., 1983; Sinden and Worrell, 1979) but these simple methods highlight the nature of this approach, and its limitations. Note that in all cases that contingency valuation relies on the valuations of the individuals interviewed so, in that respect, it is a 'democratic' method in which all individuals have a chance to count.

A number of standard limitations of this approach have been mentioned in the literature. Hufschmidt, et al. (1983, p. 153) classify these as (i) strategic bias, (ii) information bias, (iii) instrument bias and (iv) hypothetical bias.

Strategic bias refers to the possibility that respondents will vary their answer in an attempt to influence the occurrence of their desired outcome. For example, if a respondent strongly desires the establishment of a national park in an area he/she may exaggerate the sum which he or she would be prepared to pay for its establishment.

Information bias can arise from the way in which the alternatives are presented to respondents. Especially if individuals have not visited or seen a natural area which is being considered for protection, they may be largely dependent on the interviewer's description of the area for their knowledge. If this is not accurate, bias may occur.

Instrument bias refers to bias which may occur in relation to the method (instrument) used to finance provision of the public good. This may take several forms: There may be failure to appreciate the fact that provision of the environmental good may call for extra taxation for its supply. Again, the method of collection of funds to finance provision of the environmental good (purchase of land for protection, for example) may influence responses. If financing is from *general* public revenues, it will not be closely related to the willingness of individuals to pay for provision of the environmental good. In effect, those most willing to pay will obtain a subsidy, and this may give them an incentive to exaggerate their willingness to pay in order to influence the resulting policy (that is, increased strategic bias occurs). Even if a special tax is introduced to finance the environmental good, payment of the tax by individuals is unlikely to be exactly related to their willingness to pay.

Hypothetical bias can arise because although respondents have been provided with unbiased information, their past experience is limited in such a way that they cannot fully appreciate the benefits to them of the environmental good that is being offered. For instance, a respondent may have no first-hand experience of a rainforest and his/her answer about willingness to pay for its preservation may be to some extent hypothetical.

Other biases may occur. It has been noted in the literature that multiple bidding games seem to be subject to *starting-point bias*. For example, if the interviewer asks respondents first whether they are prepared to pay a very high sum for the provision of an environmental good such as a national park, the eventual amount determined by trial-and-error questioning may be different to where the starting-point is a low price. Fatigue or costs to the respondent in time forgone in answering questions involving multiple interaction with the interviewer may lead to truncated responses by the respondent who can become impatient to end the interview, rather than provide truthful or accurate answers.

There are, however, some other serious problems that can arise in relying entirely on contingency valuation methods to make decisions about land use. The most serious of these is determining what the bidder or respondent *assumes about the provision of other environmental goods* (and other commodities) in making the bid. Does the respondent, for example, assume that everything else remains the same? Or is it assumed that all similar environmental goods disappear? Or is some intermediate situation assumed by the respondent such as continuance of historical trends in the disappearance of environmental goods. It is essential to know the basis upon which the response is made and it may be important to 'standardise' this basis in interviewing respondents.

Suppose that the responses are made on the ceteris paribus, other things unchanged, assumption. This can lead to a *dangerous bias* as far as conservation is concerned, especially if a number of natural areas are being assessed simultaneously, or almost so, for possible preservation. A simple example will serve to illustrate the problem.

Suppose that three natural areas A, B and C are being considered for protection. Each area can be developed for the production of non-environmental goods and it is estimated that each area would give a net benefit of 100 monetary units from this use. Individuals are also interviewed and asked how much they would be willing to pay for the protection of each natural area. Suppose that in aggregate this is found to be 80, 90 and 95 monetary units for areas A, B and C respectively. On this basis, the optimal land-use decision from an economic point of view might *seem* to be to develop all three areas, that is, *not* to protect them.

But this decision could be incorrect. Assume that all the areas under consideration are in a natural state at the time when the matter is being considered. Respondents may have 'bid' for the protection of each area on the basis that all other areas remain as they are, that is, in a natural state. But if any one of the areas should be altered from a natural state, bids to retain the other areas in a natural state could increase, assuming that the areas in the minds of respondents are to some extent substitutes. Suppose, for example, that area A is developed. Aggregate bids for protection of areas B and C may rise, say, to 105 and 115 monetary units. This would indicate that they should be protected on economic grounds.

The extent of complementarity and substitutability between environmental goods should be taken into account in bidding games or contingency valuation. In the land-use case all combinations of possibilities should be considered. In the above case, for example, we might consider willingness to pay for protection of the following combinations: (1) only A, B or C; (2) A and B, A and C, B and C; and (3) the complete set of A, B and C and compare this with the alternative benefits from development.

The second problem when we rely upon evaluation by individuals is the state of their knowledge and variations in it. The willingness of individuals to pay for the protection of an area is dependent upon their *perception* of the consequences and subsequent benefits from its protection or the loss which will occur if it is not protected. Opinions may differ about consequences. For example, opinions differ about the greenhouse effect, the extent to which it is present, how economic change will influence it and the exact consequences of local environmental changes to be expected from it. In some cases, individuals' assessments may be heavily influenced by media reports, sensational reporting and so on. Thus individual assessment may not be based on reliable information. Indeed, it may be impossible to obtain fully reliable information – it may be impossible to eliminate many uncertainties.

This inevitably raises the question of what weight should be placed for social decision-making on individual evaluations based on imperfect information, or reflecting different attitudes of individuals to the bearing of risk and uncertainty. If the decision were merely an individual decision as in the consumption of a private good, the problem would be of a smaller magnitude. But in this case a collective decision is being made on the basis of aggregate willingness to pay (or to accept compensation). The willingness of uninformed individuals counts just as much as the informed. Thus the informed could be subjected to the tyranny of the uninformed, even if we gloss over the difficulty of deciding who is informed or knowledgeable. The individualistic liberal approach, which seems to underlie contingency valuation methods, cannot be realised in applying this method because the provision of collective or public goods is involved.

A practical difficulty in applying contingency valuation methods is how to select the sample of individuals to be interviewed for determining valuation. From what population should they be drawn and how? To what extent should individuals throughout the world be given a chance to bid on the preservation of a natural site? Sometimes bidding is confined to a region or a nation. Is this on the basis that others have little or no interest in the area being considered for protection, or is it basically a political decision? In Australia for example, the Resources Assessment Commission has been asked to make its assessments on the basis of Australian interests.

Again, future generations are not available to participate in interviews, so their demands will have to be inferred. This will require prediction of future population levels and the tastes of future generations, variables which are likely to be uncertain up to a point. Furthermore, even the valuations of the living can alter with the passage of time and this also adds to uncertainty.

The above points indicate that we should be circumspect about making use of contingency valuations for land-use decisions. That is not to suggest that they are useless, but merely to point out that it would be unwise to place too much weight on a contingency valuation without carefully examining the underlying basis of its estimation.

7.5 Hedonic price valuation of natural areas

The hedonic price method of valuation mostly uses cross-sectional data to infer the prices which individuals are willing to pay for environmental goods, even though in some circumstances time-series data can also be used for this purpose (Streeting, 1990; Rosen, 1974; Hufschmidt, et al., 1983, pp. 196–216). It relies on the hypothesis that the prices which individuals pay for commodities reflect both the environmental and non-environmental characteristics provided by them. If these characteristics can be identified and measured objectively, then it may be possible from available statistical data to infer how the valuation of a commodity varies as the environmental characteristics made available by purchasing it vary. For example, the prices of houses or dwellings of the same size and quality may vary by neighbourhood with variations in air quality in the different neighbour-hoods. From this data it may be possible to infer the household demand for air quality.

This method has not been widely used for estimating the value of natural areas, primarily because it is likely to yield inferior results to other methods when ap-plied to this assessment. For instance, variations in property values in relation to their proximity to a natural area may not reflect or fully reflect the value of the natural area to the community. In fact, agricultural properties in the vicinity of a protected area, other things equal, may be somewhat lower in price if animal 'pests' use the protected area as a refuge and as a result of straying do agricultu-ral damage on nearby properties. While property values may, other things equal, be higher in relation to a natural scenic attraction, e.g. beach or coastal protected area, this extra valuation is unlikely to capture the full value of the natural asset to the community. For instance, it will not capture the value which day visitors place on these attractions and, of course, it will not capture off-site values, such as existence value.

It might be thought that the willingness of individuals to pay for different types of package tours could form a basis for hedonic-price analysis of the value of natural areas included in the package. But it is often very difficult to specify ob-jectively the bundle of characteristics provided by package tours. In any case, a natural area is likely to be visited by persons other than those on package tours. Furthermore, even if the only visitors are those on package tours, there is still the valuation of those not visiting the natural area to consider.

7.6 Back to some fundamentals of economic valuation

It needs to be emphasised that all the economic methods outlined above are man-centred or anthropocentric. They rely on the ability of individuals to express their values in money terms. But they do permit individuals to value the existence of other living things for other than materialistic reasons and to express this in terms of their willingness to pay or accept payment. The expression of the valuation is either through willingness to pay for a change or to accept compensation for an environmental change. In practice empirical evidence indicates significant dis-parities between measures of willingness to pay and willingness to accept compen-sation (Pearce and Markandya, 1989, p. 39; Gregory, 1986; Knetsch and Sinden,

1984) even though economic theory predicts little divergence (Willig, 1976). Valuations having been done, the most common economic approach to social choice is to apply the Kaldor-Hicks principle: if the gainers from the change can compensate the losers and still be better off than before the change, the environmental change is judged to be desirable. Otherwise it is judged to be socially undesirable.

It ought, in particular, to be noted that what is being considered is willingness to pay or to accept compensation relative to the existing distribution of income. The Kaldor-Hicks or potential Pareto improvement criterion is applied relative to this distribution. This is an extension of Pareto's (static) principle that economic efficiency in satisfying human wants or desires is not satisfied if, relative to any distribution of income, someone can be made better off without making another worse off. In practice, this tends to reinforce the status quo or the dominant position of those on higher incomes in determining resource use. Those on higher incomes are able to pay more to avoid a change which they dislike or to require a large compensation to permit such a change when their feelings are of equal intensity to those on lower incomes.

Applying a willingness to pay rather than a willingness to accept compensation approach can result in conflicting policy advice. Take the case illustrated in Figure 7.4. This supposes that there is an area of land which is currently in a natural state. The social decision which has to be made is to determine what proportion, if any, of this land should be allowed to be used for development e.g. agriculture or housing.

For simplicity suppose that interested groups can be divided into two sets: those favouring 'development' of the area and those opposing it and favouring its protection in a natural state. Suppose further that those in favour of development of the area are prepared to accept an amount in compensation for not developing a proportion of the area equal to the amount which they are willing to pay for

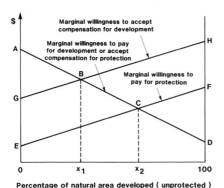

Figure 7.4. Marginal evaluation curves of conservationists and developers in relation to the percentage of natural area developed.

permission to develop it to this extent. Let line ABCD in Figure 7.4 represent the developers' marginal evaluation of development of the area.

In the case of conservationists, let us suppose that their willingness to accept compensation for development of the area differs from their willingness to pay for its protection. The marginal willingness of conservationists to pay for protection of the area might be as indicated by curve ECF and their marginal willingness to accept compensation for development might be as shown by curve GBH. This relationship could occur if those conservationists on lower incomes are more intensely in favour of conservation of the area than those on higher incomes. In this case, if it is agreed that conservationists should be compensated for development, the Kaldor-Hicks criterion will result in a greater degree of protection of the natural area than if conservationists are required in principle to pay developers to forgo development. In the former case, it is socially optimal to develop x_1 per cent of the area and in the latter case x_2 per cent. Of course, in some circumstances the curve GH could be above line AD in which case no development is optimal even though line EF intersects AD, and development is optimal given the willingness to pay approach.

This raises the question of who should compensate whom. If private property rights exist and are to be respected, the matter might be clear. However, in the case of environmental goods the property rights of the parties in these goods are often not well defined. Consequently basic ethical decisions need to be made about who, if any, should be entitled to compensation. These decisions are essentially non-economic ones (Mishan, 1981) but they have important implications for resource-use and the distribution of income or interpersonal welfare levels.

7.7 Concluding comments

If economic tests such as those discussed above indicate that the optimal policy is to develop a natural area,should we as individuals accept that this is necessarily so? It is merely the case from one point of view. 'The' economic solution may not be unique. Further, it may not be effective in conflict resolution, if the compensation of losers is purely hypothetical. So we also have to examine environmental choices in the context of effective resolution of social conflict. Also as mentioned earlier the valuations obtained for example by contingency valuation methods are subject to a number of serious limitations and this needs to be taken into account in coming to a land-use decision. Given such uncertainty there appears to be a strong case in environmental decision-making to err in favour of flexibility or decisions which keep options open. Because of irreversibilities, this is often achieved by erring in favour of conservation.

138

References

Clawson, M., 1959. Methods of measuring the demand for the value of outdoor recreation, Reprint 10. Resources for the Future, Washington.

Clawson, M. and Knetsch, J.L., 1966. Economics of Outdoor Recreation. Johns Hopkins University Press, Baltimore.

Gregory, R., 1986. Interpreting measures of economic loss: evidence from contingent valuation and experimental studies. Journal of Environmental Economics and Management, 13:325–337.

Hufschmidt, M.M., James, D.E., Meister, A.D., Bower, B.T. and Dixon, J.A., 1983. Environment, Natural Systems and Development: An Economic Valuation Guide. Johns Hopkins University Press, Baltimore.

Knetsch, J.L., 1963. Outdoor recreation demands and benefits. Land Economics, 39:387–396.

Knetsch, J.L., 1964. Economics of including recreation as a purpose of Eastern water projects. Journal of Farm Economics, 46:1148–1157.

Knetsch, J.L. and Sinden, J.A., 1984. Willingness to pay and compensation demanded: experimental evidence of an unexpected disparity in measures of value. Quarterly Journal of Economics, 99:507–521.

Loomis, J.B. and Walsh, R.G., 1986. Assessing wildlife and environmental values in cost-benefit analysis: state of the art. Journal of Environmental Management 22:125–131.

McConnell, K.E., 1985. The economics of outdoor recreation. In: A.H. Kneese and J.L. Sweeney (Editors), Handbook of Natural Resource and Energy Economics, Vol.II. Elsevier Science Publishers, Amsterdam.

McNeely, J.A., 1988. Economics and Biological Diversity: Developing and Using Economic Incentives to Conserve Biological Resources. IUCN, Gland, Switzerland.

McNeely, J.A., Miller, K.R., Reid, W.V., Mittermeier, R.A. and Werner, T.B., 1990. Conserving the World's Biological Diversity. IUCN Publications, Gland, Switzerland.

Mishan, E.J., 1981. Introduction to Normative Economics. Oxford University Press, New York.

Pearce, D.W. and Markandya, A., 1989. Environmental Policy Benefits: Monetary Valuation. Organisation for Economic Cooperation and Development, Paris.

Oldfield, M.L., 1989. The Value of Conserving Genetic Resources. Sinauer Associates, Sunderland, Mass.

Rosen, S., 1974. Hedonic prices and implicit markets: Product differentiation in perfect competition. Journal of Political Economy, 82:35–55.

Streeting, M.C., 1990. A Survey of the Hedonic Price Technique. Australian Resource Commission Research Paper No. 1. Australian Government Publishing Service, Canberra.

Sinden, J.A. and Worrell, A.C., 1979. Unpriced Values: Divisions Without Market Prices. Wiley, New York.

Timberlake, L., 1985. Africa in Crisis: The Causes, the Cures of Environmental Bankruptcy. International Institute for Environment and Development, London.

Tisdell, C.A., 1972. Provision of parks and preservation of nature - some economic factors. Australian Economic Papers, 11:154–162.

Tisdell, C.A., 1977. National Parks: economic issues. In: D. Mercer (Editor), Leisure and Recreation in Australia, pp. 111–119. Sorrett Publishing, Melbourne.

Tisdell, C.A., 1989. Environmental conservation: economics, ecology and ethics. Environmental Conservation, 16:107–112, 162.

Tisdell, C.A., 1990. Natural Resources, Growth, and Development: Economics, Ecology, and Resource-Scarcity. Praeger, New York.

Tisdell, C.A. and Broadus, J.M., 1989. Policy Issues Related to the Establishment and Management of Marine Reserves. Coastal Management, 17:37–53.

Wilks, L.C., 1990. A Survey of the Contingent Valuation Method. Australian Resource Assessment Commission Paper, No. 2. Australian Government Publishing Service, Canberra.

Willig, R.D., 1976. Consumer's surplus without apology. American Economic Review, 64:589–597.

World Resources Institute and the International Institute for Environment and Development, 1987. World Resources 1986. Basic Books, New York.

Chapter 8

Forestry, trees and conservation

8.1 Introduction: forest cover and uses

As mentioned in the previous chapter, forest and shrubland account for the largest percentage of 'land-use' of the terrestrial areas of the globe. Nevertheless, there is widespread concern amongst conservationists about forest and shrubland. The rapid disappearance of tropical and semi-tropical rainforests in Amazonia and elsewhere, the removal of shrubs and denudation of shrubland in Africa (the Sahel), the clearfelling of Australian native hardwood forests to supply chips (primarily to Japan) for the production of high quality paper (used largely for the production of quality photocopying paper and computing paper) and the replacement of native mixed forests by plantations of single species, often introduced from abroad, have all been areas of concern.

The basis of concern about the disappearance of forests and tree-cover are several. They include:

(1) The non-sustainable logging of forests or trees for commercial or subsistence needs, that is practices resulting in yields of timber or timber products being unmaintained.

(2) The direct destruction of species and of ecosystems as a result of forestry.

(3) The indirect destruction of species due to loss of forest or wooded habitat or in some cases food resources on which a particular species depends or a number of species depend. As a result, genetic diversity is likely to be reduced with consequences of the type discussed in a previous chapter.

(4) The loss of tree-cover can result in an increased rate of soil erosion with adverse environmental consequences both on-site and off-site.

(5) There may be a loss of opportunities for outdoor recreation and tourism dependent on the forested or wooded area.

(6) Adverse hydrologic effects usually occur as the result of loss of tree cover. These include changes in the levels of underground watertables, greater irregularity in the volume of surface water flows and reduced maintenance of flows over a period of time.

(7) Local climatic conditions may alter if the removal of tree cover is widespread. For example, rainfall may be reduced or become more irregular and local temperatures may alter.

(8) The availability of trees to act as sinks (stores) for carbon emissions is reduced and if the burning of the timber is involved this will add to carbon dioxide emissions. Thus tree destruction may add to the rise in global atmospheric carbon dioxide levels and accelerate the occurrence of the greenhouse effect.

(9) The loss of forests and tree-cover may reduce the incomes of rural families dependent on the collection of natural resources from such areas. Often the economic value of hunting and gathering in such areas is underestimated by urban dwellers and harvesting or destruction of the woodland area can lead to a net national loss (in economic terms) and a more inequitable distribution of income (Cf. Caldecott, 1988).

(10) Forests and wooded ares sometimes provide security reserves for rural communities. They provide reserves to draw upon in times of need e.g. if crops fail or yields from agricultural activity fall below normal levels (Chambers, 1987; Clarke, 1971).

(11) The presence of trees on farms sometimes increases productivity on the farm. For example, shelter belts may result in higher crop yields or higher weight gains or economic performance by domestic livestock (Tisdell, 1985).

Trees have a wide range of uses (Oldfield, 1989, Chs. 5–7). They are not only used for timber and for pulp for paper, but they can be sources of serums and drugs, and in many less developed countries are extensively used for firewood. Trees or shrubs are also grown or used for their fruit, honey, rubber, beverage production (e.g. cocoa and coffee), oil production and as forage for animals. In the tropics coconuts, for example, have multiple uses. Trees may also be planted to improve soil quality. Some species of trees and shrubs have the ability, in association with bacteria, to fix nitrogen into the soil. Trees and shrubs play an important role in some forms of sustainable organic agriculture (RamaKrishnan, 1987, 1988). They are utilised for instance in shifting agriculture in semi-arid Rajasthan, India, in tropical areas and in Papua New Guinea, hill tribes plant casuarina trees to improve the fertility of their home gardens (Clarke, 1971).

8.2 Commercial forestry for timber production

The objectives followed in forest management and the way in which forests are managed are likely to depend on the nature of the ownership of forests, that is, whether they are private property, state property, collective property or common property.

One would expect forests which are private property to be managed or exploited so as to yield maximum profit or net present value to their owners. This appears to be the major objective of private resource-owners in modern market economies and many texts on silviculture provide advice on this basis. In simple models, advice is given about the optimal length of replanting or regeneration cycles to maximise the net present value of operations from the forest owner's point of view (Cf. Hartwick and Olewiler, 1986, Ch. 11).

Silviculture or forestry operations can be quite complex. Logging may rely on forest plantations or natural stands of trees. In both cases, sustainable logging may be possible - the maintenance of plantations being dependent on replanting, and the maintenance of natural stands being dependent on natural regeneration of trees. In the simplest case, operations would consist of planting or regeneration of the forest followed by harvest of the complete stand after a number of years. In these circumstances the quantity of timber in the forest area, y, from the replanting or commencement of regeneration is likely to follow a logistic curve. Let

$$y = h(t)$$

represent the quantity of timber in a forested area as a function of time elapsed, t, from the date of planting or regeneration. The optimal period of time to hold a stand, or the optimal length of the replacement cycle is $y/t = h(t)/t$ *if* maximum yield of timber per unit of *time* from the available area is desired. This is true assuming that the *yield function does not alter* for future replanting or regeneration cycles.

However, the yield function could alter if, as a result of tree removal, the quality of the soil for tree growing deteriorated. Actual silviculture practices could make the current timber yield function $y = h(t)$ inapplicable to future cycles and this would need to be taken into account. Models which fail to take this into account would give a false impression of the degree of sustainability which exists in practice for forest operations. Unwittingly, therefore, shorter cycles than are optimal for sustaining yields or inappropriate silviculture practices may be recommended because of myopia about long-term effects.

Let the timber yield (production) function, h(t), for a forest stand be represented by curve OBCDF in Figure 8.1. The quantity of timber on the forested area reaches a maximum after t_2 years of growth and for simplicity is assumed to remain constant after that if not harvested. But if timber yield per unit of time, h(t)/t, is to be maximised (that is maximum sustainable yield is to be achieved), the optimal length of the cycle (period between planting or regeneration and harvesting) is t_1 years for the case illustrated in Figure 8.1. This is a shorter period than the period required to maximise the volume of timber on the land, that is t_1 t_2. Thus, under a policy of maximising sustainable yield of timber, the average standing stock of timber is likely to be reduced compared to that under natural conditions, assuming that natural climax for the forest occurs for t_2 or greater. Consequently the average age of trees in a commercially harvested forest can be expected to be less than under natural conditions.

However, as already noted, the production function for the forest may not remain stationary over time. For example, the production function for future cycles may depend upon the length of previous rotations or cycles. A shortening of the rotation period, or the period between commencement of a forest crop and its harvest, may lower future productivity of the area, e.g. through loss of soil nutrients, humus, and poorer soil structure. In the case of natural regeneration, the availability of an appropriate tree-seed bank in the soil, and the ability of the main species of trees being harvested for timber to compete in regeneration with other species, would also influence the future productivity of the forested area, thereby affecting the optimal length of harvest cycles, or leading to variations in their optimal length.

From an economic viewpoint, it is not so much maximum sustainable yield that is of interest but maximum sustainable economic yield (or, more generally, maximum economic yield). In the case where biological yields of timber are sustain-

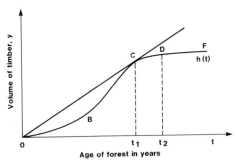

Figure 8.1. Quantity of timber production available from a forest as a function of its age.

able, economic considerations tend to reduce the optimal length of the harvest cycle or rotation period. Trees will tend to be harvested at an age younger than required to maximise commercial timber yield. This will be so if the price of timber does not vary significantly with the age of the wood (tree), if the rate of interest is positive and no substantial costs are involved in regenerating or re-planting the forest after harvest. Basically a positive rate of interest shortens the optimal harvesting cycle or rotation period (Cf. Hartwick and Olewiler, 1986, Ch. 11; Bowes and Krutilla, 1985). If the unit value of the timber tends to rise with the age of a tree, this will tend to lengthen the cycle. Also large re-establishment costs after the harvest of a forest will tend to lengthen the optimal growing period for the forest before harvest (Cf. Bowes and Krutilla, 1985; Tietenberg, 1981, Ch. 11).

Let $v = g(t)$ represent the net standing value of the forest to its owner after de-duction of any necessary cost involved in maintaining it and let k be the initial cost of establishing the forest stand. Then where r represents the rate of interest, the aim of the owner, assumed to be a profit-maximiser, is to establish a rotation or cycle which maximises the net present value of operation, that is ensures maxi-mum economic yield. The net present value of a forest stand of age t to the owner is

$$W = g(t)e^{-rt} - k$$

and the optimal length of the harvest cycle is that which maximises W/t, that is net present value *per unit of time*. [Note that the actual situation is more compli-cated because if the rate of interest is positive, future cycles will have a smaller

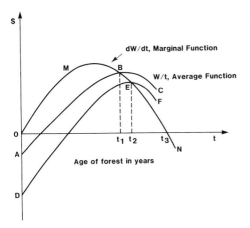

Figure 8.2. Determining the optimal growing period or harvest cycle for a forest in order to maximise economic sustainable yield.

net present value than the current one (Bowes and Krutilla, 1985). So the model here can be taken as heuristic or an approximation.] Assume that curve ABC in Figure 8.2 corresponds to W/t for a particular case and that curve OMBEN is the corresponding marginal curve, that is dW/dt. In this case, the optimal length of the harvesting cycle is t_1 years. Note that this is less than the age, t_3, or the growing period which would maximise the net present value of a single crop of trees not taking account of rotation. [The optimal aging of wine case which is commonly mentioned in the literature does not apply because it ignores the fact that available space is fixed in quantity (Cf. Henderson and Quandt, 1971, pp. 323–324).]

As mentioned previously, a rise in the rate of interest tends to shorten the optimal length of the growing period of a forest crop, the period of rotation. This is because it becomes profitable to convert the forest into cash at an earlier date to earn the higher rate of interest by investing the funds obtained.

An increase in the initial establishment cost of the forest also lengthens the optimal length of the growing period of the forest crop, the rotation period. This can be seen from Figure 8.2. Suppose that initial cost of establishing the forest rises from OA to OD, everything else unchanged. Because only initial or fixed costs alter, the marginal net present value curve OMBEN is unchanged and the maximum of the 'new' average curve, W/t, occurs to the right of point B. In the case shown, it occurs at point E and the optimal length of time to grow a tree crop before harvest increases from t_1 to t_2. Note that initial cost may occur not only in the case of replanting of plantation forests but in assisting the natural regeneration of forests, because selective removal of competitive trees and shrubs (pests or weeds) may be required.

Observe that while the optimal age for harvest in the infinite period rotation model is influenced by the level of costs of establishing or re-establishing a forest stand, in the single period model this is not so. This is because dW/dt does not vary with fixed costs or set-up costs.

Once again it should be noted that the function describing the net present value of a forest as a function of its age may not, in contrast to the assumption above, remain stationary. It may alter, for example, because productivity cannot be sustained for the reasons noted above. Also a change in economic conditions such as in the rate of interest or costs of silviculture may, for instance, alter the length of the optimal forest growing cycle.

The above model assumes that forests are treated in the same way as many farm crops. The crop is planted or regenerated at a particular time and clearfelled at harvest time.

The practice of clearfelling can have serious environmental consequences. It may be destructive of the habitat of wildlife and may make it difficult for a forest to regenerate naturally. It can expose the forest floor to serious erosion risks. To reduce this problem, corridors of the forest stand may be left unlogged, or the timing of clearfelling of a forest stand may be staggered.

In some natural forests, logging is a selective, almost continuous, process. Only trees of an appropriate age are logged from an area and forest trees of mixed ages occur in each area. Environmentally this may be superior to cropping and clear-felling, even though it might be less economic from the operator's point of view, assuming that selective logging involves extra costs in harvesting. In such forests, a more natural, even if somewhat disturbed vegetative cover, continues to be present. Yields for timber may not be as high as under conditions of intensive silvicul-ture, but yields may be sustained over a longer period and the forest may play a more positive role in meeting community environmental objectives.

Nevertheless, a forest managed for timber production is likely to have some ad-verse impact on natural flora and fauna. 'A managed forest is a less suitable habi-tat for much wildlife than the original vegetation. Old trees with numerous nest-ing hollows are removed and the stands of trees of different ages tend to become stands of uniform age of the one species. The ground cover is reduced or removed to reduce the danger of fire. All these practices reduce diversity and operate against wildlife populations' (Frith, 1973, p. 99). The introduction of exotic tree species for monoculture, such as *Pinus radiata* or *Pinus elliotti* in Australia, tends to be extremely unfavourable to natural wildlife (Frith, 1973; Bell, 1978, p. 100).

In managing the forest attention has to be given to such factors as fire control, access (e.g. roads and erosion), and control of pests such as weeds, insects or mammalian pests. One would expect a private owner to manage all of these as-pects with an eye to maximising the anticipated net present value of the forest en-terprise to him or her. In doing so he/she will not take account of externalities unless required to do so by law or unless fearful of social criticism.

While profit maximisation may provide an incentive for owners of private forests to manage them on a sustainable basis, this will not happen in all circum-stances. If, for example, the rate of increase in the value of a forest or the forested land is at a very slow rate in relation to the rate of interest, the most profitable strategy may be to harvest the existing tree crop and *not* replace it, or to replace it entirely by a different but faster growing species of tree. In the first case, the area may be left deforested and, for example, used for grazing which may prevent reafforestation of the land. In the second case, slow-growing species of trees may be brought to extinction and replaced by faster growing ones (Clark, 1973).

In the case of common-access or common-property forests the situation is worse. There is no incentive for individuals to harvest or manage common-access forests on a sustainable basis. As with other common-access resources, users take no account of the future, that is user costs. It can happen that when the economic value of greater conservation of these forest increases, less conservation occurs (Cf. Tisdell, 1972).

The way in which state-owned forests are managed is likely to depend upon the policies adopted by the government in relation to state forest authorities and any guidelines given to them. These can vary widely from country to country as can the extent of discretion left to state forest authorities in the management of forests.

Some state forest authorities may see it as their almost exclusive role to meet the timber needs of their clientele. Principally, their forests are managed for timber supplies. In *other* cases, forests may be managed for multiple community objectives e.g. timber production subject to provision of various recreational opportunities, or subject to retention of selected areas in relatively undisturbed state for conservation of wildlife or retention of particular types of trees on which some species of wildlife are dependent for their existence, (e.g. in Australia, koala bears are dependent on the leaves of particular gum trees for food, many Australian parrots require tree boles or hollows for nesting which usually occur only in older trees) or subject to account being taken of externalities such as those resulting from soil erosion which could occur if particular silviculture practices are adopted, or failure to control mammalian pests such as feral pigs which roam to surrounding farms and do agricultural damage.

Political factors are liable to influence the behaviour of state forest authorities. State forest authorities have been 'captured' in some cases, it has been said, by large sawmillers dependent on log supplies from state forests. As a result such sawmillers have, it is claimed, obtained preferential royalty rates and access to timber from state forest authorities. The interest of sawmillers and processors of forest products is not necessarily one of sustaining supplies in perpetuity.

8.3 Multiple purpose management of forests

The suggestion is often made that forests, especially state-owned forests, should be managed to satisfy multiple purposes or uses (Tietenberg, 1988; Bowes and Krutilla, 1985). It is true that forests and forested land can be used for multiple purposes, but whether that is an ideal policy would seem to depend upon the particular circumstances of the forest.

Privately-owned forests are only likely to be managed to satisfy multiple purposes if mixed use maximises the owner's profit from the forested area or its net present value. In some cases, for example, agroforestry may be pursued in the forested area. For instance, grazing of livestock in the forest may be a part of the owner's land-use pattern. The optimal pattern will depend on production possibilities, costs involved in managing the resources and the market values of the commodities produced (Filius, 1982; Tisdell, 1985).

Other things equal, the more competitive are the commodities which can be produced on the land, the less likely is it that mixed land-use will occur. For example, Figure 8.3 shows three alternative possible product transformation curves for a land area in terms, say, of sustainable production. If the trade-off between timber and meat production is as indicated by curve ABC (which is strictly convex) mixed land use is less likely than when the trade-off is linear (as is shown by curve DEF) and less likely than when the production possibility frontier is strictly concave (curve GHJ). However, mixed land use may be profitable in any of these cases depending on the nature (shape and curvature) of the relevant iso-profit curves. If for example the iso-profit curves are strictly convex it is possible for maximum profit to occur at a position such as B, although this would clearly be impossible if the iso-profit curves were linear or concave. Only in cases where strong complementarity in production between products is present can we say that mixed land-use is optimal on the basis of production conditions alone, and that is assuming that profit increases with the level of production. Thus, if the product function is like KLMN in Figure 8.3, efficient production must always occur along the segment LM. This implies mixed land-use.

The land-use or mixed land-use of a forested area under private control will not necessarily be socially optimal. Also it is unlikely to accord with that desired by groups of conservationists. This raises the question of whether forests should be managed to achieve multiple social objectives.

If that is so, then government restrictions on the use of privately owned forested land may be necessary. For example, the government may consider restrictions on the clearing of forests, taxes on the clearing of particular forested areas or subsidies for the retention of particular forested areas in view of the social benefits involved, e.g. favourable externalities obtained.

In the case of state-owned forests, forest managers may be directed to manage them on a multiple-use basis to serve social ends. In developed countries, state forests are being increasingly managed to take account of social objectives, such as outdoor recreation demands and demands for nature conservation. In some re-

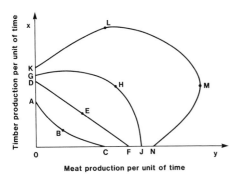

Figure 8.3. The economics of mixed land-use (multiple purpose use of forested land) depends only partially on biological production possibilities. But if the production transformation curve is of the form of KLMN economic efficiency requires mixed production and mixed land-use.

cent cases, conservationists have come into intense social conflict with loggers and those dependent on logging for their livelihood. In Australia, conservationists and loggers have clashed several times in Tasmania; they have done so in Southern New South Wales over the clearfelling of forests for chips for export for paper production; over the logging of rainforests in parts of Australia and, recently, in relation to logging on Fraser Island in Queensland.

Government may direct managers of state forests to manage them so as to achieve social objectives. But there is a problem. Social objectives are rarely clearly defined, and dominant objectives may change from time to time depending on the political situation. When there is conflict about social objectives, as is not uncommon, clear guidelines may be unavailable for resolving the conflict or allowing for it. Consequently, state forest managers may become uncertain and confused about the objectives which they are expected to pursue. A directive to take into account social objectives in managing forests is too vague a guideline for operational purposes.

8.4 Forests and trees in less developed countries

The state of forests and tree cover in less developed countries varies greatly. In some less developed countries, substantial stands of natural forest still remain. These stands include tropical rainforests in a number of tropical less developed countries such as in Brazil, several South East Asian countries, New Guinea and the Solomon Islands, as well as in several Central African countries. But these forests are being logged and reduced in size at a rapid rate. As a result, particularly in the case of rainforests, there is a considerable loss of biodiversity, soils are being exposed to greater erosion, local (sustainable) incomes may be reduced and there are fewer trees and plant matter available to act as a storehouse for carbon dioxide.

However, not all less developed countries, even those in tropical areas have rainforests or had these. In some cases their land area is arid or semi-arid. The natural vegetation of some areas is sparse and conditions are such as only to support scattered shrubs. In other cases, natural vegetation is of a savanna type because of the occurrence of monsoonally influenced wet and dry seasons each year. While in these cases stands of commercially loggable timber are not present, tree and shrub cover plays a valuable role in retarding soil erosion, providing habitat for wildlife, fuel for subsistence needs, fodder for grazing domestic animals such as goats, provides timber supplies for some household needs other than fuel and may provide some food supplements for humans, for example in the form of fruits, nuts or berries (Cf. Timberlake, 1985, Chs 5 and 6).

There are several reasons for the reduction in natural stands of forests and trees in developing countries. These include greater opportunities for profitably marketing timber internationally (the extension of the market with economic development) and the need for extension of agriculture so as to add to food supplies locally to meet increasing subsistence needs, expanding principally as a result of rising human populations in less developed countries. However, in addition to this there is pressure on subsistence communities to obtain cash through market exchange (Tisdell, 1983, 1986). There are three pressures at least in this respect: (1) The formation of central national governments in less developed countries has led to the imposition of taxes (payable in cash) on rural people who have had little or no previous involvement in the cash economy. Hence, this has forced many to commence or increase their production of saleable goods so as to obtain cash to pay taxes. (2) Central government (and improved communications) have imposed new obligations on rural communities such as payment for basic eduction of their children and this is usually required in cash rather than kind. (3) Income aspirations have risen and opportunities to consume a wider range of commodities have been expanded as a result of improved communications. Many of the additional commodities now available and wanted in developing countries are produced commercially and can only be obtained in exchange for cash. These factors, together with expansion of the markets, the introduction of new technology and population growth have all conspired to place growing economic and environmental pressures on natural resources, including forest and tree resources in developing countries.

Loss of forested and wooded areas in less developed countries results from the following activities:

(1) *Commercial forestry*. While this may involve selective logging without any alternative land-use for the area in mind, such logging is often a prelude to use of the area for agriculture. Much of the timber harvested is exported to developed countries (See for example, McKee and Tisdell, 1990, Ch. 11). But the greater part of wooded areas lost in less developed countries is being lost to agriculture and associated activities.

(2) *Extension of agriculture* is still occurring in many less developed countries. Forested areas continue to be cleared for the extension of agriculture. This is true in Brazil, for example, in the Amazon. Indonesia also has a scheme for transmigration – the movement of its population from the more densely settled islands to islands more sparsely settled and, in many cases, naturally vegetated. Forests in such areas are being cleared to make way for agricultural activities by migrants. In arid and semi-arid areas, the margin of agriculture has extended and soils have been exposed to wind erosion.

(3) *Intensification of agriculture* in less developed countries is also leading to loss of tree and shrub cover. Trees and shrubs can compete with annual crops for nutrients, water and sunlight, and sometimes grass cover. Available pasture, for example, for grazing cattle can often be increased by reducing tree or shrub cover. In those cases where modern Green Revolution technologies are being applied, intensification of agriculture results in substantial tree and shrub loss because there are strong economic incentives to remove trees and shrubs in order to increase returns. In these communities which rely on shifting agriculture, increasing population pressure is leading to reduction in the length of time between cultivation of the same area. This reduces the overall stock of tree and shrub vegetative matter in such areas and can be expected to result in the longer term in falling agricultural yields. Increases in domestic livestock numbers and grazing are increasingly preventing regeneration of natural forests and woodland. Overstocking and overgrazing by livestock is a serious problem, for example, in parts of Africa (Timberlake, 1985).

(4) *More intensive use of trees and shrubs for firewood and subsistence needs.* With an increase in population in rural areas of many less developed countries, and loss of trees and shrubs for reasons such as those mentioned above, remaining stands are being more intensively utilised for firewood and subsistence needs and this is further accelerating loss of tree and shrub cover. In some instances, this means greater use of animal dung for fuel which, of course, has an unfavourable impact on soil fertility. Women in Africa find increasingly that they must travel or walk longer and longer distances to collect firewood to meet basic fuel needs. This means that they have reduced time for attending to other economic needs. Strategies to deal with these problems include the development of improved fuel combustion systems and the planting of woodlots (Timberlake, 1985, Ch. 6).

(5) *Loss of forested and wooded land for or as a result of economic developments other than those mentioned above.* Developments such as increased urbanisation, provision of dams for irrigation and drinking water, and salinity problems caused as a result of irrigation or tree clearing, roads, engineering and other man-made facilities have also been a source of loss of tree cover in less developed countries, as well as developed ones.

While it would be rash to claim that less developed countries should not harvest their forests to obtain income and foreign exchange for investment and economic development, they do not always do this to their own advantage. In utilising such forests they are drawing on their natural wealth. Unless the gains from this are invested in assets which can sustain or improve their incomes over a longer period, less developed countries are engaging in non-sustainable consumption.

In some cases, urban elites have arranged for the logging of forests in rural areas to obtain benefits for themselves. In some cases the net cost to the local rural community is greater than the benefits obtained by the urban elite. The urban elite may or may not be aware of such a situation. In the former case naked income redistribution is involved. In the latter case ignorance may be involved. For example, the full value of the forested area to local communities, for instance for subsistence needs, may not be fully realised by the urban elite. In India this has been one of the reasons for the growth of the Chipka movement, the movement for 'the hugging of trees' (Sinha, 1984). It is easy to underestimate the subsistence value of forests to rural people. Often they provide food and income security in times of need for rural people (Chambers, 1987). They are backstop resources to draw upon when agricultural yields are below normal levels (Clarke, 1971). If they disappear, they undermine the social security of rural people, especially the landless or near-landless.

It should however be observed that the growing of tree crops in developing countries is widespread. This includes the growing of coconuts, oil palm, rubber, coffee and cocoa. Such crops may be environmentally less damaging than the growing of annual crops in tropical areas and in some cases, such as with coconuts, mixed agricultural systems can be established which may be relatively sustainable, and intercropping and other cultivation practices can be adopted with beneficial environmental effects. However, the extension of tree crop cultivation is often at the expense of natural forests.

8.5 Economic policies, pollution, forests and trees

In the past economic policies have not always been favourable to the conservation of forests and trees. While this may be less so now than in the past, policies still exist which are unfavourable to retention of forests and tree cover. For example, the Common Agricultural Policy of the European Common Market artificially maintains the price of agricultural products. By doing so it encourages the use of rural land for agriculture. Consequently marginal areas are used for agriculture which could be more economically left as forest or shrubland. In Australia in the past subsidies and tax concessions were provided for land clearing for agriculture in some areas. In Indonesia subsidies are provided for transmigration of individuals and their establishment of agriculture in areas initially in a natural state. In the United States and other countries, subsidies for agriculture have had, and continue to have, an effect in extending the area of land allocated to agriculture, at the expense of forested and tree-covered land.

Acid rains have been a source of tree losses, particularly in developed countries such as Germany. These acid rains often occur as a result of international or transboundary air pollution. Burning of coal with a high sulphur content and combustion of fossil fuels can be the source of sulphur dioxide and other gases which are transported over long distances and result in acid rains. For example, combustion of fossil fuels in the United Kingdom can contribute to acid rains in Central and Northern Europe. Similarly, fossil fuel combustion in the United States can contribute to acid rains in Canada. Tree losses are only some of the possible environmental effects of acid rains. Other environmental impacts include soil and lake acidification. This case raises questions about the extent to which such international pollution should be controlled and about the appropriate economic methods or instruments for their control.

The matter is complicated when different nation states are involved, particularly because a number of alternative economic control methods or instruments are available. While different instruments can result in the same *efficient* international solution, they often have quite different income distributional consequences. This can be illustrated by Figure 8.4.

In Figure 8.4, curve ECF represents the economic benefits to country A of being able to emit air pollutants resulting in acid rain in country B. Curve OCD represents the marginal cost of damage caused to country B as a result of these emissions. Applying the Kaldor-Hicks criterion internationally, the optimal quantity of emissions of air pollutants in country A is x_1, assuming that the adverse environmental effect is one way – from A to B. In the absence of international agreement, country A will emit x_2 units of relevant air pollutants.

The Kaldor-Hicks solution can be achieved in two different ways. Country A can compensate country B for damages caused or alternatively country B can pay country A to reduce its emissions. The first solution requires A to make a minimum payment to B equivalent to the dotted area, whereas the second solution requires a payment from B to A corresponding to the hatched area in Figure 8.4.

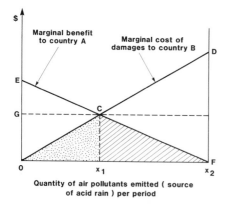

Figure 8.4. Solutions to transboundary or transfrontier pollution, such as air pollution causing acid rain, are difficult to achieve. The polluter may either pay to pollute or be paid not to pollute. The Kaldor-Hicks solution can be achieved by either policy but the income distributional consequences are different.

The first solution is more advantageous to B than A in income distributional terms whereas the reverse is so for the second solution.

Note that if a per unit tax of OG is placed on pollution emissions, the cost to polluters in country A will be higher than if polluters pay the minimum sum needed to bring about the Kaldor-Hicks result. Similarly, if a subsidy of OG per unit reduction is paid to polluters to reduce pollution, the payment to polluters in country A exceeds the bare minimum payment necessary to bring about the Kaldor-Hicks solution.

The possibility has been mooted of introducing an international carbon-use tax. The prime purpose of such a tax would be to reduce carbon dioxide and other gaseous emissions adding to the greenhouse effect. Note, however, that although such a tax might partially relieve acid rain occurrence, it would not be an efficient tax for that purpose. This is because the combustion of carbon fuels per se is not so much the source of these rains as the combustion of carbon fuels containing sulphur. Thus if the policy aim is solely to reduce the incidence of acid rain, one does not want to discriminate equally against all carbon-based fuels.

However, important policy issues are raised by the possibility of an international carbon tax. If we suppose that the only reason for imposition of such a tax is to reduce the rise in atmospheric carbon dioxide levels with a view to reducing the onset of the greenhouse effect, the impact is a global one involving the control of a pure public 'bad' (Lowe, 1989). This would suggest that a uniform carbon dioxide emission tax is desirable on economic efficiency grounds. But the *real* impact of this in income distribution terms is liable to be greater in less developed countries than developed ones. Less developed countries may therefore find such an approach unacceptable unless there is compensating income redistribution in their favour.

Another problem is that the impacts of the greenhouse effect, such as possible sea level rises and weather pattern changes, may not be strictly a pure public 'bad' (interpreted as the opposite of a pure public good). Some nations may gain, for example the United Kingdom, from such changes whereas others may be very adversely affected, e.g. China, Bangladesh and Egypt. Who should make economic sacrifices in these circumstances? To what extent should beneficiaries be required to pay?

A possible way of restraining rises in atmospheric carbon dioxide levels is to provide more environmental sinks for it. Trees can act as environmental sinks for carbon dioxide. By planting and conserving trees, one provides a sink for the storage of carbon dioxide (Lowe, 1989). Thus, on this basis a case can be made out for subsidising tree planting and restricting the destruction of trees and forests. That, however, is not to claim that such action would be sufficient in itself to absorb all carbon dioxide likely to be released from projected fossil fuel combustion in the foreseeable future.

It has been suggested that sustainable environmental development requires that portfolios of projects be such that their *overall* environmental impact is zero (Pearce, Markandya and Barbier, 1989, pp. 127–129). Thus, a company engaging in a set of environmentally destructive projects may be allowed to do this provided this group is counterbalanced by a set of projects which enhance the quality of the environment. I do not wish to debate the merits or limitations of this criteria here (it will be discussed in Chapter 11) but it is pertinent to note some policy applications. For example, electricity authorities in the Netherlands burning coal are engaging in 'compensating' tree planting in the Netherlands and in South America, presumably to limit global carbon dioxide increases (Byron and Davies, 1990, p. 7). Whether the compensation is sufficient is another matter. But the planting of trees or the setting aside of areas for natural tree regeneration can at least provide a partial environmental offset for some types of development projects.

8.6 Concluding remarks

In the past, national income accounting has failed to take adequate account of depletion of natural resources, including reductions in natural (capital) stocks of timber. Indeed, in the early stages of economic growth the unsustainable exploitation of stocks of natural resources may show up as an increase in GDP and therefore apparent welfare on the part of those who tend to judge welfare by GDP or GDP per capita. This is now being rectified by the increasing use of natural resource accounting to at least supplement traditional national accounts (See, for example, Pearce, Markandya and Barbier, 1989). This is a desirable practice which may result in a less exploitative attitude towards natural forests. In order to assess accurately the wealth and well-being of a nation, account must be taken not only of its man-made wealth and income flows from this but also account must be taken of the state of the nation's natural resource stocks, of its environment and of the benefits provided by these.

In conclusion it might be observed that it is risky to disturb forest environments severely. In many cases, the long-term consequences are unknown. Empirical evidence about the impact of such disturbance is often lacking because forestry experiments typically have to be carried out over several decades at least, given the longevity of trees and the period required for disturbed forest ecosystems to stabilise. It seems that in the tropics, rainforests are being replaced by agricultural systems without substantial knowledge of the long-term economic and environmental impacts of such decisions. This at least suggests that caution is required.

The role and environmental benefits of trees on farms has not been discussed in detail above. This topic will form part of the discussion in the next chapter of agriculture and the environment, and more information on that subject can be found, for example, in Tisdell (1985).

References

Bell, F.C., 1978. Forest Systems: Their Future in N.S.W. Total Environment Centre Publications, Sydney.

Bowes, M.D. and Krutilla, J.V., 1985. Multiple use management of public forestlands. In: A.V. Kneese and J.L. Sweeney (Editors), Handbook of Natural Resource and Energy Economics, II:531–543. Elsevier Science Publishers, Amsterdam.

Byron, N and Davies, R., 1990. Sustainable Forestry: Past trends and future directions. Centre for Forestry and Research Development, Australian National University, Canberra (Mimeo). Paper presented at a National Workshop on 'Moving Toward Global Sustainability: Policies and Implications for Australia'. University House, Canberra.

Caldecott, J., 1988. Hunting and Wildlife Management in Sarawak. IUCN, Gland, Switzerland.

Chambers, R.J., 1987. Trees as savings and security for the poor. IIED Gatekeeper Series, SA3:1–10.

Clark, C.W., 1973. Profit maximisation and extinction of animal species. Journal of Political Economics, 81:950–961.

Clarke, W.C., 1971. Place and People: An Ecology of a New Guinean Community. Australian National University Press, Canberra.

Filius, A.M., 1982. Economic aspects of agroforestry. Agroforestry Systems, 1:29–39

Frith, H.J., 1973. Wildlife Conservation. Angus and Robertson, Sydney.

Hartwick, J.M. and Olewiler, N.D., 1986. The Economics of Natural Resource Use. Harper and Rowe, New York.

Henderson, J.M. and Quandt, R.E., 1971. Microeconomic Theory: A Mathematical Approach, 2nd Edition. McGraw-Hill, New York.

Lowe, I., 1989. Living in the Greenhouse. Scribe Publications, Newham, Victoria.

McKee, D.L. and Tisdell, C.A., 1990. Developmental Issues in Small Island Economies. Praeger, New York.

Oldfield, M.L., 1989. The Value of Conserving Genetic Resources. Sinauer Associates, Sunderland, Mass.

Pearce, D., Markandya, A. and Barbier, E.B., 1989. Blueprint for a Green Economy. Earthscan Publications, London.

RamaKrishnan, P.S., 1987. Shifting agriculture and rainforest ecosystem management. Biology International, (15):17.

RamaKrishnan, P.S., 1988. Successional theory: implications for weed management in shifting agriculture, mixed cropping, and agroforestry systems. In: M. Altieri and M. Liebman (Editors), Weed Management in Agroecosystems: Ecological Approaches. CRC Press, Boca Raton, Florida.

Tietenberg, T., 1988. Environmental and Natural Resource Economics. Scott, Foresman and Company, Glenview, Illinois.

Timberlake, L., 1985. Africa in Crisis: The Causes, the Cures of Environmental Bankruptcy. International Institute for Environment and Development, London.

Tisdell, C.A., 1972. The economic conservation and utilisation of wildlife species. The South African Journal of Economics, 40(3):235–248.

Tisdell, C.A., 1983. Conserving living resources in Third World countries: economic and social issues. The International Journal of Environmental Studies, 22:11–24.

Tisdell, C.A., 1985. Conserving and planting trees on farms: lessons from Australian cases. Review of Marketing and Agricultural Economics, 53(3):185–194.

Tisdell, C.A., 1986. Conflicts about living marine-resources in Southeast Asia and Australian waters: turtles and dugong as cases. Marine Resource Economics, 3(1):89–109.

Chapter 9

Agriculture and the environment

9.1 Introduction

Most of the world's food today is obtained from agriculture, that is from culti-vated and grazing land. Cereals supply the major portion of this (Harlan, 1976). While modern agriculture has enabled large increases in food supply to be achieved with greater certainty and with enhanced stability of supplies, it does seriously disturb natural ecological systems and create artificial environments (Cf. Oldfield, 1989). Of all human activities, agricultural activity has probably been re-sponsible for the greatest loss of genetic diversity, mainly through habitat destruc-tion but also in other ways discussed below. The question is being increasingly raised of whether modern agricultural systems are sustainable (Conway, 1985, 1989).

Modern agricultural systems are typically high energy-using, high chemical-using, require intensive management, place a high premium on uniformity rather than diversity of both products and environments, and appear to be dependent on the results of continuing research for the maintenance of their productivity. Both energy and chemical inputs in agriculture are mainly obtained from non-renew-able resources such as oil and natural gas, which are exhaustible. In the long-term, modern agricultural systems would appear to be unsustainable in their pres-ent form (Cf. Oldfield, 1989).

The topics to be considered in this chapter in relation to agriculture and the en-vironment are: externalities, sustainability, biodiversity, the 'Green Revolution', pest control, organic agriculture and permaculture, trees on farms and the conser-vation of wildlife on farms.

9.2 Externalities and agriculture

Traditionally economists have analysed environmental impacts of agricultural activity in terms of the theory of externalities or environmental spillovers. Indeed, much of the early theoretical literature on externalities draws on agricultural examples (Coase, 1960; Meade, 1952) for illustrative purposes. While environmental economics today consists of much more than the application of the economic theory of externalities, it is still an important consideration in environmental management and policy-making. Therefore let us consider externalities specifically in relation to agriculture, concentrating on unfavourable production externalities which are assumed to be one way (not reciprocal).

Divide the universe into commodities supplied by the agricultural sector, A, and into commodities supplied by non-agriculture, B, which can include those supplied by non-agricultural industries as well as the supply of environmental services. In these circumstances at least six possibilities for unfavourable externalities exist:

(1) Some part of agriculture may have an unfavourable externality on another portion.

(2) Some part of agriculture may have an unfavourable externality not only on another portion of agriculture but elsewhere.

(3) Activity in the agricultural sector may have an unfavourable externality on non-agriculture.

(4) Activity in one portion of the non-agricultural universe may have an adverse externality on the supply of commodities elsewhere in the non-agricultural universe.

(5) The situation in (4) may hold but in addition there may be an unfavourable external effect on agricultural production.

(6) Activity in the non-agricultural universe may have an unfavourable externality on agricultural production.

Examples of each of these six types of externalities are easy to find. Let us consider cases (1), (3) and (6) in some detail.

9.2.1 Agricultural externalities on agriculture

A variety of productive activities in one part of agriculture can have negative externalities on other parts. Such activities include chemical pesticide-use by some farmers (for instance when chemicals are sprayed, chemical drift may damage the crops of neighbouring farmers), nitrogenous fertiliser use (for example where this results in contamination of ground water shared with other farms), or tree-clearing by some farmers which results, for example, in rising water-tables and the salting of the soil on nearby properties. As a result of such salting only very salt-tolerant crops or grasses may grow. In extreme cases, the soil may become virtually barren. The removal of trees in some areas can lead to increased salinity of streams to such an extent that they can no longer be used for irrigation or the watering of livestock. Salinity externalities of this type have for example arisen in Western Australia and Victoria but also occur elsewhere (Tisdell, 1985a; Mulcahy, 1983).

In areas with sufficient rainfall, removal of natural vegetation as a result of agricultural activity usually results in more variable water run-off. Vegetation may be removed by overstocking, by land-clearing and cultivation. Where these practices occur in the catchment areas of rivers and streams, more frequent flooding (including flash flooding) tends to occur not only because the volume of water to be carried by streams after rain is higher, but they often become sedimented due to erosion, which means that they break their banks more easily. Increased flooding has an adverse impact on farmers downstream, who may find also that relatively infertile soil or sand is deposited on their properties because of increased soil erosion. In more arid regions, removal of natural vegetation exposes soils to wind erosion. Soils which are fallowed for cereal crops are often at considerable risk. However, overgrazing can also provide scope for wind erosion in such areas. As a result farmers in regions away from the wind-erosion site may be damaged. For example, unwanted soil and sand may be blown on to their properties, or the growth of crops may be reduced by the presence of air-borne dust. Other examples, such as those involving agricultural pests and diseases, could be given (See for example, Auld, Menz and Tisdell, 1987, Ch. 8).

At a more general level, if the activities of agriculturalists in an area result in loss of genetic diversity, this may have an adverse impact on farmers in other localities, if they rely on some of the species for their livelihood and wild relatives or cultivars are lost. For example, the intensification or extension of agriculture in the Middle East could lead to the loss of wild varieties and relatives of wheat (Baker, 1978). This could eventually have an adverse impact on wheat production in developed countries. The wild relatives or varieties of wheat lost could have proved to be valuable in increasing or sustaining wheat production in developed countries through genetic manipulation (Oldfield, 1989).

The impact of an externality from one part of agriculture on another part can be modelled in a simple case in the way indicated in Figure 9.1. The curve ABC represents the value of the marginal product obtained by a group of agriculturalists, say Group I, from engaging in an activity say, land-clearing. But this has an adverse effect on the agricultural production of a group of agriculturalists,

162

Group II. The marginal loss in the value of their production as a result of the environmentally damaging activity by Group I is shown by the difference between curve ABC and ADE. Hence, although curve ABC represents the value of the marginal product of the activity to Group I, after allowing for unfavourable spillovers on Group II the value of the social marginal product is as indicated by curve ADE.

If line FC represents the marginal cost to Group I agriculturalists of engaging in the environmentally damaging activity, they will, in the absence of regulation, engage in the activity up to the point where this marginal cost equals the value of their marginal product. In the case shown this will be done to extent x_2 and, consequently, a deadweight economic loss indicated by the hatched area occurs. The socially optimal level of the activity from a Kaldor-Hicks point of view is x_1 because, at this level, the marginal cost of the activity equals its marginal social value.

Theoretically, the 'ideal' solution could be achieved by a number of alternative policies. A tax of GF might, for example, be levied on Group I agriculturalists for each unit of their environmentally damaging activity, or rights to engage in total in x_1 of this activity might be auctioned, thereby creating an artificial market in rights to engage in the environmentally damaging activity. However, this is only an optimal approach if the spillover depends *solely* on the aggregate quantity of the activity. If the extent of the spillover is affected by the *location* of its occurrence, a uniform price for engaging in the environmentally damaging activity will not be optimal from a Kaldor-Hicks point of view (Cf. Tisdell, 1983).

In some cases there are quite direct natural resource spillovers within agriculture, as in the case of shared water resources. Suppose, for example, that the agriculturalists along a river are sharing its water for irrigation purposes. If the demand to use the water exceeds the available supply, an allocation problem exists.

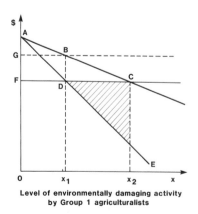

Level of environmentally damaging activity
by Group 1 agriculturalists

Figure 9.1. A case in which activities by one group of agriculturalists has negative spillovers on another group of agriculturalists.

In the absence of control, agriculturalists on the lower reaches of the river are likely to be left with a smaller supply of water than is optimal from a Kaldor-Hicks point of view. This can be illustrated by means of Figure 9.2 in which, for simplicity, the agriculturalists along a river or stream are divided into two groups, Group I (upstream agriculturalists) and Group II (downstream agriculturalists).

Curve ABCD represents the value of the marginal product of irrigation water to upstream agriculturalists and curve EFGHJ that for downstream agriculturalists. Suppose that x_1^3 is the total supply of water available for irrigation along the stream and assume that the cost of pumping water from the stream and distributing it is OL per unit of water. In that case upstream farmers will use x_1^2 of the water per period if access is free. Although downstream farmers would use x_2^3 units of water if it were available, only x_2^1 units will be available to them (x_2^1 = $x_1^3 - x_1^2$).

Consequently, the value of the marginal product for water use by downstream farmers will exceed that for upstream farmers. Hence, the available quantity of water is not allocated so as to maximise the value of its contribution to production. For this to occur, the supply of water must be allocated so as to equate the value of the marginal product obtained by all users of the water, given the limited supply of water that occurs when x_1^1 of water is allocated to upstream farmers and x_2^2 is allocated to downstream farmers. This leads to an increase in the value of production of an amount equivalent to the hatched area, less the dotted area, in Figure 9.2.

Note that if the total available quantity of water is $x_1 > x_1^2 + x_2^3$, water is not in scarce supply for irrigation and it will be optimally used if farmers are free to access it as they wish. In practice of course, the matter is likely to be more complicated than this because both the quantity and the quality of the water downstream may be affected by the amount of water used upstream. If, for example,

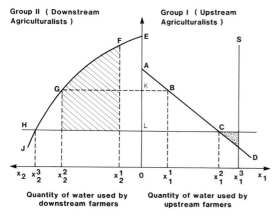

Figure 9.2. Economic loss resulting from negative spillover on downstream agriculturalists of water use by upstream agriculturalists.

the flow of water downstream is reduced, the salinity of downstream water may increase.

Policies which may be used to rectify the situation include: (1) The imposition of a user charge on water of KL per unit, (2) The auctioning of the rights to the use of the total quantity of available water x_1^3, and (3) the introduction of transferable (marketable) quotas for the use of water, the aggregate quantity of water allocated by the quotas being x_1^3. In practice, non-transferable quotas are often used by government water authorities to allocate rights to use water. Such a practice is not always most efficient from an economic point of view because the quotas are rarely allocated so as to equate the value of marginal product obtained by all waterusers.

On the other hand, taxes and the creation of water markets do not necessarily result in optimality either. The tax must be adjusted if the demand to use water or the available supply alters and this requires flexibility in the tax and may call for forecasting. Forecasters are not infallible. Even water-markets may not always operate efficiently, for example, due to errors of judgment by market participants or in some cases the small number of participants. Nevertheless, public action leading to an improvement in resource-use or conservation can be justified even if the results are not perfect. It is irrational to avoid social action on the basis that it will not yield perfect results.

Because water is a natural resource which is being placed under greatly increased pressure as a result of globally increasing population and economic growth, it is worthwhile considering another agricultural case involving water-use. Consider underground aquifers or water supplies. These are important sources of water supply for agriculture as well as for other uses. The nature of such aquifers varies considerably and the examples considered here are particular cases. Where there is free access to drawing on such underground sources of water supply, the water resource is unlikely to be used efficiently from an economic viewpoint.

Suppose that the underground source of supply is not an underground stream (in this case the previous example can be adapted) but an underground basin of water which, for simplicity, is assumed to be a uniform depth below the ground level and of uniform difficulty to access. In practice, the last two conditions are rarely met. If they are not met, conditions for optimal water-use are more complex. Also assume that underground water stocks are supplemented at a constant rate by natural seepage of rainwater, seawater, etc. The spillover problem to be expected given free access to this resource can be illustrated by Figure 9.3. (Note that the example can also be applied to shared aboveground lake-water.)

In Figure 9.3 curve ABCD represents the demand of water-users for the underground supply of water which is assumed to be supplemented from natural sources at a rate of x_1 per period. Assuming that only agriculturalists are involved in the use of the water, curve ABCD might be the aggregate of the value of their marginal product from using the water. OF represents the per unit cost of obtaining the water (e.g. by tube-wells and pumping) initially. In these circumstances, in the absence of control, initially x_2 units of water per period will be pumped. But this is not sustainable because the rate of off-take from the basin exceeds rate of inflow. Water levels in the basin will drop, tube-wells will need to be extended in depth and the cost of pumping each unit of water will rise. Eventually, in this case, a new equilibrium will be reached where the cost per unit of water drawn equals OK. This situation is not economically efficient. While an initial extra benefit equal to the dotted area in Figure 9.3 is obtained by an off-take of water, x_2, which cannot be sustained, eventually this results in extra costs indicated by the hatched area. The discounted extra benefit obtained early is likely to be less than the discounted cost subsequently imposed by this free access policy.

The sustainable least cost solution could be achieved by initially imposing a fee of FK on each unit of water drawn from the underground source or by creating a market for the rights to draw water from the underground source. The rights, or certificates for rights, should be such as to auction or market the sustainable supply x_1 per period. In many places in the world, however, especially in less de- veloped countries, free access to underground water resources is resulting in eco- nomically inappropriate use of the resource.

The above example is a particular one. The cost of pumping or access to the underground water basin may not be uniform for all agriculturalists. As uncon- trolled pumping proceeds, the level of the underground water supply may drop and water may no longer be available to individuals in areas where the under- ground basin is not so deep. In some cases these may be the areas which can use the water most productively, or have lower costs in bringing it to the surface if it is available. Not only may the cost per unit of the pumping of the water rise but the average value of production obtained from use of the water may decline as a result of a policy of free access to the underground supply. Furthermore, when

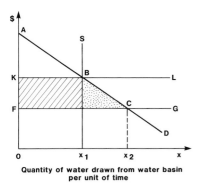

Figure 9.3. Free access to water from an (underground) water basin can result in inefficient reduction in the availability of the resource.

free access is the case, no allowance is made by individual users for the future value of conserved supplies, that is user costs. While it may be optimal to reduce the resource or stock of water in an underground supply or in a common pool, this will not occur at an optimal rate if free access is the case. Both in developed and less developed countries policy-makers have all too frequently ignored such issues with unfortunate natural resource and agricultural consequences.

9.2.2 Agricultural spillovers on non-agricultural sectors and interests

Just as agriculture can give rise to spillovers within agriculture, it may also have spillovers on other sectors and social interests. For example, leaching of nitrates from artificial fertiliser used in agriculture or from animal dung in cases of intensive livestock husbandry, can contaminate surface or underground water used for human consumption, affect the quality of water for industrial use, result in excessive weed growth in streams and waterways (thereby 'choking' them and increasing rates of water loss) and, in some cases, affecting navigation and accelerating eutrophication of ponds and lakes.

In some instances 'foul' smells from intensive animal husbandry can be offensive to nearby householders.

Removal of natural vegetation cover by agriculturalists may make a landscape less appealing to travellers and tourists, but this is not always so. Greater variability in stream or water flows as a result of vegetation removal can have adverse effects on the availability of potable water for urban areas, add to seasonal urban water shortages, and increase the frequency of urban flooding. The greater turbidity of the water may reduce fish numbers, detract from tourism and in areas where corals grow near river outlets, may lead to their destruction over an area because dirty fresh water during flood periods spreads over a wider sea area. Silting of harbours and of waterways may increase and add to the costs of navigation. Increased flash-flooding may cut roads with greater frequency and greater damage to roads may occur. One could add to this list. Loss of wildlife via habitat destruction is, for instance, a major loss given that many individuals value the existence of wildlife. In the past the use of some pesticides in agriculture such as DDT have been notorious in causing adverse spillovers via wildlife destruction.

9.2.3 Spillovers from other sectors on agriculture

Jut as agricultural activity can have an adverse effect on other sectors, spillovers from other sectors can have adverse spillovers on agriculture. Several examples can be given.

Water pollution from manufacturing industry, mining operations and from urban areas can impose major spillover costs on agriculture. Crops irrigated with 'polluted' water may die, or not grow so well and in certain cases livestock can be poisoned by drinking polluted water from such sources. Cases of this nature as a result of chemical wastes released from factories have, for example, been reported from China.

Urban water-users may fail to take full account of the costs imposed on agriculture by reducing water supplies for the agricultural sector. Just as upstream agriculturalists may use an excessive amount of water from an economic efficiency point of view, so can urban communities.

In some instances, removal of forests by the forest sector may result in negative spillovers on agriculture of a hydrological nature, e.g. more frequent flooding of agricultural land. Urban expansion can create a similar problem.

Air and related pollution is another possible cause of negative environmental spillovers on agriculture. Lead and heavy metal emissions from factories, dust from open-cut mines, fluoride emissions from aluminium plants, acid rains, and radiation fallout are all capable of having adverse impacts on the value of agricultural production.

Economic policy-means for dealing with externalities are similar no matter what is their source. The costs, however, of implementing different policies (the agency costs involved) may differ according to the source or nature of the externalities. For example, it may be difficult to place a tax on nitrate emissions from farms because they are not single point emissions and are difficult to measure.

9.3 Sustainability of agricultural systems

Already cases have been indicated in which agricultural systems may not be sustainable due to environmental spillovers or to related externalities e.g. due to removal of natural vegetation or depletion of underground water supplies. While sustainability of agricultural systems is not necessarily an absolute virtue, there is widespread agreement about the undesirability of some unsustainable agricultural systems.

Lack of economic sustainability is often associated with negative externalities. *Unwanted* lack of sustainability is likely to occur when negative spillovers exist because individual economic decision-makers do fully control their own economic future. For instance, the removal of natural vegetation in an arid or semi-arid zone as a result of individual landholders following their selfish interest may lead to desertification and climate change in a whole region. Even if one landholder in the area were to engage in practices designed to maintain natural vegetation on his or her property, he or she may be 'swamped' in the end by the negative environmental practices of other landholders in the area. Possibly the intensification of agriculture in areas bordering the southern Mediterranean was responsible for desertification and climate change in the area which was agriculturally very productive during the Roman era.

Lack of sustainability associated with negative production externalities or spill-overs is usually undesirable from an economic point of view. Such lack of sustain-ability may arise from factors such as loss of genetic reserves essential to main-taining agricultural productivity, hydrological impacts such as those mentioned above, the effects of acid rains in acidifying soils, externalities from chemical use in agriculture, such as the impact of pesticide-use in creating chemically resistant-pests and destroying natural predators of such pests, all of which may not only affect the users of the chemicals but also farmers not using them. While non-sus-tainability of economic activities is not invariably connected with *negative* envi-ronmental spillovers or externalities, in practice they frequently go hand in hand.

Because Chapter 11 deals with concepts of sustainability and their implications for economic policy in detail, only those aspects which are particularly relevant to agricultural systems are discussed here.

Conway (1985, 1987) in particular has argued that sustainability of yields or re-turns is a desirable property of agricultural systems (Cf. Tisdell, 1985b). He sug-gests that it is desirable to take into account four properties in assessing the desir-ability of alternative agricultural systems - (1) the level of yields or returns from alternative systems, (2) the degree of variability of these, (3) the sustainability of yields or returns for the alternative systems and (4) their impact on the distribu-tion of income. He claims that while modern agricultural systems usually give higher returns or yields than traditional systems, they are normally less sustain-able. He believes that modern agricultural systems are often less desirable than traditional ones when judged by taking account of the above-mentioned factors. (For a somewhat different viewpoint see Ruttan, 1988.)

For Conway, the sustainability of an agricultural system is judged on the basis of its ability to recover from environmental stress, that is, by its resilience. This can be illustrated by Figure 9.4. The yields or returns over time from two agricul-tural systems are shown – (1) a high yielding system (initially) or a modern system and (2) a lower yielding system. Between period t_1 and t_2 the systems are sub-jected to the same environmental stress which is then removed. Yields from sys-tem 1 follow path GHJKL whereas those from system 2 follow path ABCDF. Yields using system 2 recover from the environmental stress but when system 1 is used they recover only partially. Thus system 2 is more sustainable than system 1 in Conway's terminology.

Modern agricultural systems in order to achieve high yields rely on artificial en-vironmental conditions being created and maintained (Oldfield, 1989). When these conditions cannot be maintained yields plummet severely as a rule. High yielding varieties of crops, for example, when subjected to environmental stress during their growing period may become severely stunted, sensitive to pests and diseases and high plant losses may be experienced. If the stress which occurs before the crop matures should disappear before maturity, there may be very little recovery in expected crop yields. If, on the other hand, traditional varieties are subjected to the same stress, very little loss in yield may occur.

However, it should be observed that the dynamic properties of systems are complex and it may be desirable to take into account several characteristics of their response to 'disequilibrating' forces. These include (1) the size and nature of the shock needed to put the system into disequilibrium, (2) the extent of the response of the system to it and (3) the extent and speed of recovery from the shock. Different degrees of sustainability could be said to exist depending on these characteristics. Note that this concept appears to have much in common with the concept of stability of equilibria (Tisdell, 1988).

However, yields or returns from some agricultural systems may not be sustainable even in the absence of environmental shocks or disturbances. This may be because they are dependent on non-renewable resources, e.g. oil, or because they bring about unfavourable changes in life support systems, e.g. reduce soil nutrients, destroy other desirable properties of soil or its structure over time. This type of non-sustainability may arise solely from the effects of the agricultural system in its location (from endogenous factors) or largely from exogenous causes, e.g. a resource essential for an agricultural system may be depleted independently (or almost so) of its agricultural use. For instance, oil supplies are likely to be depleted even if oil is not used in agriculture.

Figure 9.5 illustrates the difference in sustainability of systems from this point of view. In the case illustrated, the returns from system 1 (traditional system?) are stationary but those from system 2 (the modern system?) decline over time. These flows of returns are respectively indicated by curves ABC and DBE. If a high premium is placed on sustainability, then agricultural system 1 will be preferred to agricultural system 2. However, if the discounted present value criteria is used, system 1 may be preferable to 2 if the flow represents net value. The higher the

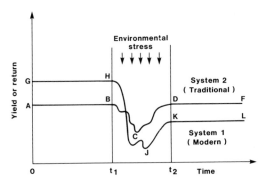

Figure 9.4. Two agricultural systems with different degrees of sustainability.

170

rate of discount, the more likely is technique 1 to be chosen by the net present value criteria.

The type of unsustainable situation depicted in Figure 9.5 by curve DBE could come about, for example, if there is a continual deterioration in soil quality with use of the system, or increase in pest populations due to growing resistance of the plant to pest controls, destruction of natural predators of pests, or the presence of more suitable (cultivated) hosts for pests, or continual deterioration in natural resistance of cultivated crops or husbanded agricultural organisms to natural environmental conditions (Cf. DeBach, 1974; Tisdell, 1990). For instance, the fact that modern agriculture occurs mainly under artificial environmental conditions could mean that naturally pest-resistant sectors of a cultivated population tend to be eliminated and that co-evolution fails to take place because husbanded agricultural organisms are shielded from evolutionary changes in their natural predators. Many examples exist both at the farm-level up to the global level. At the global level, for example, loss of natural biodiversity could make it difficult to sustain agricultural production in the long term because of a significant reduction in the gene pool. This gene pool may be essential for the maintenance of modern agricultural systems, e.g. maintaining relatives of cultivated varieties in the wild which retain resistance to disease and to pests absent from cultivated varieties.

Whether or not modern agricultural systems are less sustainable than traditional ones has been keenly debated. It is likely that some modern types of high chemical, high-energy using agricultural systems concentrating on monoculture are unsustainable in their present form. This lack of sustainability may become apparent in (1) declining yields with time, unless ever increasing amounts of energy and chemicals such as artificial fertilisers are applied, or (2) by the inability of their yields to recover satisfactorily from environmental stress. While one cannot generalise about all modern and traditional agricultural systems, the possible

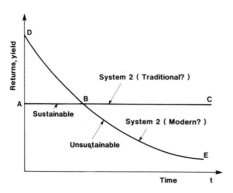

Figure 9.5. Sustainability or otherwise of agricultural systems from a different point of view to that considered in Figure 9.4.

limitations of present modern agricultural systems need to be recognised. In this context, it is worthwhile considering the 'Green Revolution', organic agriculture and permaculture.

9.4 The Green Revolution, organic agriculture, permaculture

The 'Green Revolution' involves bio-chemical packages and, as a rule, more controlled environments in agriculture through the use of chemicals, irrigation water and agricultural farm equipment powered directly or indirectly by carbon fuels. This Revolution has resulted in rising yields from agricultural land in developing countries and has provided some countries with a springboard for economic development. Much of this higher yield has arisen from an increased incidence of multiple-cropping as well as the enhanced responsiveness of high yielding varieties to artificial fertilisers, managed water availability, and control of competitors such as weeds and insects by pesticides (Alauddin and Tisdell, 1991). However, this raises the question of whether this form of agriculture (which is also the dominant form in the developed world) is sustainable.

There are reasons to doubt its long-term sustainability as far as yields are concerned. For example, increased multiple cropping tends to cause soil deterioration. It can do this because (1) more frequent cultivation of land leads to a breakdown in the tilth of the soil or desirable soil structure; (2) reduced organic or humus content in the soil because little organic matter may be left on the fields and there may be little or no scope for 'weeds', 'grass' and other organic matter to grow between periods of cultivation (such material can provide some natural 'green manure'); (3) soil erosion may increase as a result of more frequent cultivation and this may reduce the depth of fertile soil; (4) the growing of 'green manure' crops, at least in the early stages of the 'Green Revolution', may become economically less attractive; (5) mixed and rotational farming may become relatively less profitable and (6) livestock which provide a source of natural manure are more likely to be removed from the vicinity of intensively cultivated cropland. Chemical fertilisers may also cause long-term changes in the soil of an unfavourable nature, e.g. increase its acid content and/or kill valuable soil flora and fauna.

The use of artificial pesticides has also increased with the Green Revolution. Apart from spillover effects on wildlife, etc., their use can also have unsustainable consequences for yields, e.g. due to growing resistance of pests to the pesticides used (DeBach, 1974).

In some cases greater use of water, e.g. through irrigation, causes the leaching of nutrients from soils and results in yields not being sustainable. In addition, spillovers or externalities from irrigation are not uncommon, e.g. salting or flooding may occur on some properties because watertables are raised as a result of irrigation.

Another serious consequence of the 'Green Revolution' and modern agriculture has been the loss of genetic diversity. As the 'Green Revolution' has proceeded traditional varieties of many crops have disappeared, as farmers have 'swapped' to a smaller band of improved varieties. This means a loss in genetic diversity and may adversely affect the long-term viability of the crops in question. The impact of agriculture on biodiversity will be given further consideration in a later section.

Organic agriculture (and to some extent traditional agricultural systems) have been promoted by some social groups as an alternative to modern biochemical agricultural systems. The main reasons for promotion of organic agriculture appear to be its (claimed) superior consequences for health and its superior environmental consequences compared to chemical agriculture. In addition, organic agricultural systems appear to display greater sustainability than chemical agricultural systems, even though they may give lower yields in the short run. There is some evidence that organic agriculture can give higher returns than chemical agriculture for *some* types of agriculture (Wynen, 1989).

Possibly organic agriculture should be more common than presently is the case. Economic and development processes may have favoured chemical agriculture excessively. Some reasons for bias against organic agriculture include:

(1)   At least in the past, subsidies for the use of agricultural chemicals including fertilisers.

(2)   Because companies find it easier to patent inventions or advances in knowledge associated with chemical agriculture or protect such knowledge compared to organic agriculture, private research appears to have been distorted. There is often a follow-on effect as far as publicly funded or conducted agricultural research is concerned (Menz, Auld and Tisdell, 1984).

(3)   For similar reasons, promotion and advertising of non-organic agricultural methods has been most widespread (Tisdell, Auld and Menz, 1984)

(4)   Farmers (and often manufacturers of agricultural chemicals) have not been required to pay or to pay for the full amount of the environmental costs associated with the use of such chemicals.

Development has encouraged the growth of chemical agriculture because the value of uniformity of products and reliability of their supply rises with 'economic development'. When agriculture is conducted in artificial environments, greater uniformity in product and greater reliability of supply (in the short run) are likely. Possibly the growth of markets, specialisation in production and the transaction costs involved in doing business over long distances place a premium on uniformity of agricultural products. A buyer in a distant city ordering an agricultural product (sight unseen) would no doubt like it to be supplied uniformly in accordance with a particular standard. Today, supermarket retailing puts an even higher premium on uniformity of products.

A further reason for the decline in the incidence of organic agriculture in some countries is increasing urbanisation. Organic material sent from rural areas to urban areas is rarely returned for use in agriculture. In countries such as China, where nightsoil has been traditionally used as fertiliser, urban sewage is being less frequently used for this purpose. This is so for at least two reasons: (1) The cost involved in collecting and transporting organic wastes to the countryside is high. (2) Urban organic wastes are often contaminated with substances harmful to agriculture. Thus, as a result of urbanisation organic material is lost to agriculture and in urban areas is often disposed of at considerable cost by means that frequently pollute waterways. Furthermore, individuals in urban communities mostly do not bear the full cost of urban waste disposal and this is once again a distorting factor. It does not encourage productive use of 'waste' organic matter.

In the countryside itself, organic material is being more intensively utilised. For instance, on the Indian subcontinent cattle dung is being increasingly used for fuel as firewood becomes scarce. Therefore, dung is less frequently available as fertiliser.

Again, economic factors may discourage the use of organic agricultural methods as economic growth occurs. Organic agricultural methods appear to be more labour-intensive than chemically based ones. As wage rates rise relative to the price of other factors of production, this will discourage the use of organic methods.

Note that modern chemical agricultural methods can lead to irreversibilities of agricultural yields or reversibility only with difficulty. This can be illustrated by Figure 9.6. A chemically-based agricultural system may result in a flow of yields over time indicated by curve ABCDE whereas an organic system may give yields

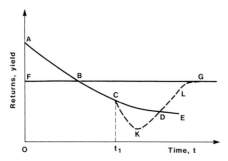

Figure 9.6. When chemical agricultural systems are adopted agricultural yields or returns become very dependent on them. Withdrawal of chemicals results initially in marked depression of these yields or returns. So agriculture tends to become locked into such systems once they are adopted.

indicated by curve FBG. However, perfect reversibility may not be possible between systems. For example, suppose that chemically-based agriculture has been adopted on a farm and it is decided at time t_1 to revert to an organic system. Yields may follow a path like CKDLG. At first, as the switch occurs, returns are depressed before recovering. This means that once chemical agricultural systems have been used, *an economic barrier is created to switching* to organic systems. On the other hand, if only organic systems have been used, an immediate high but not sustainable return is obtained by switching to an appropriate chemical system.

Observe that farmers acting in their own individual interest may adopt chemical-type agricultural systems in preference to organic systems when the private return from the former is only slightly higher than the latter. But once the chemical system is adopted, farmers tend to become locked into it. Even though the social return from an organic system may exceed that from a chemical one, it may prove to be very difficult to get farmers to switch to an organic one once a chemical one is adopted because there are extra costs involved in switching. Even the community may find it uneconomic to switch once a chemical agricultural system has been adopted, although the superior social choice initially would have been not to adopt the chemical agricultural system.

Organic and non-chemically based agricultural systems do of course vary widely in their returns. Both from the points of view of avoiding unfavourable externalities and from that of sustaining yields, organic systems are worthy of greater consideration than in the past. Even if complete organic systems are not adopted, the use of systems which involve fewer chemicals and more organic and natural methods may be environmentally advantageous.

Not all systems of organic or 'naturally' based agriculture can be discussed here, but mention might be made of permaculture (Mollison and Holmgren, 1978; Mollison, 1979). This is a form of mixed permanent agriculture heavily reliant on mixed perennials, such as fruiting trees and shrubs, but also including some annual and biennial plants, agricultural animals for recycling nutrients, pest control and so on. Its aim appears to be to create a living community of animals and plants valuable to man for consumption purposes which is close to a climax community. It involves, in its ideal form, mixed agriculture, an integrated system or ecological community that is stable, diverse and self-equilibrating and to a large extent self-contained, that is, requiring few external inputs.

Permaculture is claimed to have yield-sustainability and environmental advantages compared to most modern agricultural systems. These properties and its economic and ecological properties are certainly worth further study. However, permaculture is likely to be best suited to small communities and to economic situations not requiring the marketing of specialised products in large quantities over great distances. Because of the nature of permaculture, only small quantities of different agricultural products are liable to be ready for harvest on a property at any time. Economies of scale in marketing a standardised product are likely to be lost when permaculture is practised.

Many of the products most suited to permaculture, such as fruits, do not transport and store well. Cereals (the backbone of modern economies as far as food is concerned) are as a rule unsuited to permaculture, except that small amounts of cereal crops, such as maize, may be interspersed with other plants in permaculture systems. It seems likely that permaculture would be most suited to small subsistence communities such as those espoused by some alternative life-style groups in the West. It may also make a positive contribution to semi-subsistence communities which still exist in developing countries.

9.5 Pest and disease control in agriculture

Pest and disease control is an important part of protecting agricultural yields in modern agriculture. As mentioned earlier, several characteristics of modern agriculture make this form of agriculture susceptible to pests and diseases (Oldfield, 1989). Chemicals are widely used for the purpose of pest and disease controls and wherever possible domestic plants and animals are shielded from pests and diseases. Apart from the fact that in the long-term this could prevent the co-evolution of protected animals and crops, adverse environmental spillovers and human health impacts may be experienced.

The adverse environmental impact, for example, of the use of DDT and related substances are well documented. But they continue to be used in some less developed countries. Populations of birds and fish, for instance, are susceptible to such chemicals. Furthermore, their effectiveness as pest control measures are not always maintained. This is because in some cases the targeted pests become increasingly resistant to the pesticide and/or the pesticide destroys enemies or predators of the targeted pest. In addition other beneficial living things, such as beneficial insects, e.g. bees, may be killed. For these reasons agricultural yields may fail to be sustained when pesticides are used and many of the ecological changes which are brought about by their use may be irreversible (Cf. Tisdell, 1990, 1982).

The effects of the use of a pesticide may be slow or rapid in changing the ecological balance permanently. The mechanisms involved can be varied. The long-term consequence, however, is frequently a less economic situation than prior to the application of the pesticide. The pest-control system often becomes dependent on the development of new generations of pesticides in order to remain economic.

In some cases alternatives to using pesticides are available. For example, weeds may be destroyed by cultivation or mechanical means rather than herbicides. Even this can have some unfavourable effects e.g. by exposing the soil to erosion. Other approaches to control include biological control, the use of genetically pest-resistant species and integrated pest management. There may be less reliance on these methods in modern agriculture than is desirable. Partly this is because little or none of the benefits from marketing or promoting such methods can be appropriated by firms or companies that might market or promote them (Tisdell, 1990a; Tisdell, Auld and Menz, 1984).

In the case, for example, of classical biological control, the natural predator of a pest spreads once it is introduced to an area of its own accord and an externality is generated, the benefits from which cannot be appropriated by the person or company responsible for the original introduction of the predator. However, in the case of *inundative* biological control (which involves substantial introduction of the predator, or disease, of a pest to a limited area) there is scope for commercialisation and this is increasingly occurring. The benefits of classical biological control are largely of the nature of a collective good and therefore require, as a rule, government responsibility for it.

The protection or development of genetically pest-resistant plants may be encouraged commercially if they can be effectively protected for the developer or promoter in the market through plant variety rights. But often this is not possible because once the plant is available others may reproduce it secretly without paying royalties. Even when the rights are known to be flouted, it may be uneconomic for the holder of the rights to take legal action against all transgressors. Enforcing legal rights can be costly. Thus, unless there is co-ordinated international government action, many commercially valuable species and varieties which are genetically pest-resistant are likely to disappear.

In a commercial society, integrated pest management (IPM) may also not be promoted to the extent socially most economical. This is because such methods may result in few sales of commercial products. Furthermore, knowledge of the method may not be saleable or only be partially so, because once the method is known it may be communicated independently of the originator of it. Market failure is present.

Integrated pest management may, for example, involve changes in farm cultivation practices and the preservation of species which deter pests. This might be done, for instance, by retaining or creating suitable habitat for survival of these natural beneficial species throughout their life-cycle. This *can* require the preservation of some natural vegetation on a farm.

9.6 Agriculture, biodiversity, trees and wildlife conservation

While agriculture has preserved some species which would otherwise have been driven to extinction by hunting, gathering or human encroachment, agriculture has been responsible for a considerable loss of biodiversity, mostly through habitat destruction, but not entirely. This loss of species has occurred both with the extension and intensification of agriculture. Agriculture is sometimes a forerunner to built-environments, such as urban areas, which tend to be even less compatible with the preservation of biodiversity.

Modern agriculture systems reduce biodiversity because these systems usually create controlled micro-environments. Relatively uniform agricultural micro-environments emerge. In such environments, just one or a few varieties of a cultivated species are likely to give maximum yields and economic returns. Therefore, with advances in modern agriculture, including the 'Green Revolution', the number of different varieties of each crop and livestock species farmed has declined greatly (IUCN, 1980). This has reduced the gene pool available to agriculture.

Private economic efficiency in modern farming operations usually calls for specialisation and the removal of natural impediments to mechanical farming. Thus trees and shrubs are often removed to make operations with tractors and machinery easier, and in Europe many hedges have been removed to create large fields which can be more economically cultivated using larger tractors and machinery. In some areas, ponds and waterholes have been filled or swamps or wetlands drained to enable mechanical cultivation to take place. Such practices can have a deleterious impact on wildlife populations. The loss of ponds and wetlands can, for instance, adversely affect migratory birds and wetland birds. In the case of estuarine swampland, draining may lead to adverse external impact on fisheries since such areas may provide hatcheries or detritus for fisheries production.

Because of such impacts, environmental controls are being increasingly imposed on agricultural activity and 'developments'. In some countries and states, farmers are being restricted in their scope to affect habitat changes on their properties. Clearing, for example, of particular areas may be forbidden or only be permitted, if at all, after consideration by an environmental court which must weigh up the case for and against the proposed environmental change. Such measures recognise the external environmental impacts of agricultural activity.

The clearing of trees may be regulated because they are important for the survival of particular species of wildlife, or because various adverse environmental spillovers are expected from their removal. The removal of the trees may lead to greater erosion, faster run-off of rainwater with flooding and other hydrological effects downstream, and in some areas salting on nearby properties. Such clearing can, in principle, be controlled by a number of alternative policy instruments. These include taxes on tree clearing, auctioning tree removal rights, or subsidies on tree retention (Hodge, 1981; Tisdell, 1985a). But these measures may not show sensitivity between sites where the clearing occurs and to different species of trees having different spillovers or environmental benefits. The charges involved tend to be uniform for ease of administration. This is only optimal if the externality is not dependent on location of or species of tree. Where there is such a dependence, it may be necessary in practice to supplement such economic measures with administrative ones.

The question needs also to be raised of whether agricultural land should be more frequently used for multiple purposes including some social environmental purposes. Possibly a social case exists for placing covenants on parts of particular agricultural properties to protect wildlife, e.g. valuable wildlife breeding sites. For example, the yellow-eyed penguin is now a relatively rare or endangered species in New Zealand. One of the main reasons for its decline has been the loss in coastal habitat within less than a few hundred metres from the coastline, mainly due to clearing of coastal forest for farming and grazing which has reduced taller vegetative cover. This loss has severely affected the breeding of this species. By preserving a relatively small area, with little loss in the value of agricultural production, the preservation of this species might be secured (Tisdell, 1990b, Ch. 7). A case would seem to exist for covenants in such areas restricting land-use. They might come into force when a property changes ownership or owners may be compensated if immediate restrictions are imposed. Another interesting case is the management of kangaroo populations on agricultural properties, but there are many others (Tisdell, 1973).

There is also the related question of whether public access to agricultural land or to portions of it should be permitted for recreational purposes. In Britain, there are often public walkways through agricultural land and they appear to provide valuable possibilities for outdoor recreation. Also, in many places farm holidays, which essentially involve outdoor recreation, have become popular and may help to encourage nature conservation.

9.7 Concluding observations

Agriculture is both a cause of major environmental and ecological loss as well as a major potential beneficiary from the conservation of living things and their life-support systems. Thus it is a central concern in the economics of environmental conservation.

Sustainable economic development and the maintenance of biodiversity are central to present environmental concerns. An evaluation of agricultural systems in relation to their consequences for sustainable agricultural yields and their impact on biodiversity, provides valuable insights into the concept of sustainability and into the difficulties of even maintaining biodiversity to the extent that it is economically valuable to agriculture. Tourism, which is discussed in the next chapter, provides additional insights into the concept of sustainability.

References

Alauddin, M. and Tisdell, C.A., 1991. The Green Revolution and Economic Development: The Process and its Impact in Bangladesh. Macmillan, London.

Auld, B.A., Menz, K.M. and Tisdell, C.A., 1987. Weed Control Economics. Academic Press, London and Orlando, Florida.

Baker, H.G., 1978. Plants and Civilization, Third Edition, Wardsworth, Belmont, Cal.

Coase, R., 1960. The problem of social cost. Journal of Law and Economics, 3(Oct):1–44.

Conway, G.R., 1985. Agroecosystems analysis. Agricultural Administration, 20:31–35.

Conway, G., 1987. The properties of agroecosystems. Agricultural Systems, 24:95–117.

DeBach, P., 1974. Biological Control by Natural Enemies. Cambridge University Press, London.

Harlan, J.R., 1976. The plants and animals that nourish man. Scientific American, 253(3):88–97.

Hodge, I., 1982. Rights to cleared land and the control of dryland-seepage salinity. The Australian Journal of Agricultural Economics, 26:185–201.

IUCN, 1980. World Conservation Strategy: Living Resource Conservation for Sustainable Development. IUCN, Gland, Switzerland.

Meade, J.E., 1952. External economies and diseconomies in a competitive situation. Economic Journal, 62:54–67.

Menz, K.M., Auld, B.A. and Tisdell, C.A., 1984. The role for biological weed control in Australia. Search, 15:208–210.

Mollison, B., 1979. Permaculture Two: Practical Design for Town and Country in Permanent Agriculture. Tagari Books, Stanley, Tasmania.

Mollison, B. and Holmgren, D., 1978. Permaculture One: A Perennial Agricultural System for Human Settlements. Corgi Books, Ealing, UK.

Mulcahy, M.J., 1983. Learning to live with salinity. The Journal of the Australian Institute of Agricultural Science, 49(1):11–16.

Oldfield, M.L., 1989. The Value of Conserving Genetic Resources. Sinauer Associates, Sunderland, Mass., USA.

Ruttan, V.W, 1988. Sustainability is not enough. American Journal of Alternative Agriculture, 3(2+3):128–130.

Tisdell, C.A., 1973. Kangaroos: the economic management of a common property resource involving interdependence of production. Economic Analysis and Policy, 4(2):59–75.

Tisdell, C.A., 1982. Exploitation of techniques that decline in effectiveness with use. Public Finance, 37(3):428–437.

Tisdell, C.A., 1983. Pollution control: policies proposed by economists. Journal of Environmental Systems, 12(4):363–380.

Tisdell, C.A., 1985a. Conserving and planting trees on farms: lessons from Australian cases. Review of Marketing and Agricultural Economics, 53(3):185–194.

Tisdell, C.A., 1985b. Economics, ecology, sustainable agricultural systems and development. Development Southern Africa, 2(4):512–521.

Tisdell, C.A., 1988. Sustainable development: differing perspectives of ecologists and economists, and relevance to LDCs. World Development, 16:373–384.

Tisdell, C.A., 1990a. Economic impact of biological control of weeds and insects. In: M. Mackauer, J. Ehler and J. Roland (Editors), Critical Issues in Biological Control, pp. 301–316. Intercept Ltd., Andover, Hants., UK.

Tisdell, C.A., 1990b. Natural Resources, Growth, and Development: Economics, Ecology and Resource-Scarcity. Praeger, New York.

Tisdell, C.A., Auld, B. and Menz, K., 1984. On assessing the value of the biological control of weeds. Protection Ecology, 6:165–175.

Wynen, E., 1989. Sustainable and Conventional Agriculture: An Economic Analysis of Australian Cereal-Livestock Farming. Unpublished Ph.D thesis, School of Agriculture, La Trobe University, Melbourne.

Chapter 10

Tourism, outdoor recreation and the natural environment

10.1 Introductory issues, dependence of tourism on the natural environment

There are important links between tourism and the environment and vice versa. While all tourism does not depend on the natural environment, much of it does. A good deal of tourism relies upon resources or assets that cannot be reproduced or cannot be easily reproduced (Tisdell, 1984). This is true of much tourism dependent on the natural environment as well as tourism dependent on historical-cultural objects. On the other hand, some tourist attractions have been made by man recently and can be reproduced without undue difficulty.

Tourist attractions might be divided into two sets: Hecksher-Ohlin attractions and Ricardian-type attractions using the classification of Hufbauer and Chilas (1974) of traded goods. Essentially *Hecksher-Ohlin tourist attractions* are man-made attractions relying principally on labour and capital for their provision. They include, for example, shopping facilities, entertainment centres, restaurants, nightclubs and casino complexes which could be reproduced in almost 'any' part of the globe. The attractions of Singapore may largely be of this nature (Khan, 1986). *Ricardian-type tourist attractions* are unique or relatively unique and cannot be reproduced. Their supply and original properties are essentially fixed. In Ricardo's sense, they are gifts of nature. Apart from natural features, which are often Ricardian-type tourist attractions such as the Grand Canyon in the USA or the Great Barrier Reef in Australia, unique and irreplaceable man-made cultural objects from the past fall into this category. These include artefacts and works from ancient civilisations, such as the Egyptian and the Greek, as well as more recent irreplaceable works including buildings, e.g. the Forbidden City in China, St

Peter's in Rome. Possibly some living minority cultures could also be classified as Ricardian-type tourist attractions. Because of their uniqueness and the inelasticity of their supply, Ricardian-type tourist attractions are potential earners of rent or surpluses from tourists.

In practice not all tourist attractions can be divided neatly into one or the other of the above categories. Furthermore, the degree of attractiveness of an area to tourists may depend upon the available combination of Hecksher-Ohlin (man-made) facilities and Ricardian-type (natural or non-reproducible) attractions available. When visiting an area, region or country for a holiday, tourists are often seeking a suitable combination of both man-made and natural or similar attractions.

In many circumstances, the appeal of natural attractions to tourists depends on human modifications to the environment. In the case of natural outdoor areas, this may involve the construction of access roads, walking trails and limited shopping and accommodation facilities in the natural area or nearby. This should, of course, be done if possible without detracting from the essential natural features which draw tourists to the area.

In principle, it should be possible to determine the optimal combination of man-made and natural features to attract tourists to an area. However, the sole consideration in the use, conservation and development of an area is usually not tourism. Competing demands on the resources involved also have to be considered.

Tourism based on natural resources including living resources can be a powerful force favouring conservation. For example, the *World Conservation Strategy* document (IUCN, 1980) states that developing countries can earn income and foreign exchange by conserving their unique living and natural resources and by developing international tourism based on these, and this is an incentive for their conservation. Economic gains from tourism based on natural resources can provide a powerful incentive for conservation but unless there is co-ordinated planning by governments towards this end, conservation may not be translated into practice. Furthermore, in some cases, inadequately controlled tourism can destroy natural assets on which tourism relies and crowding from tourism may reduce the total benefits from it.

Let us consider this issue, the possibility that tourism development can lead to inadequate variety in tourism environments, the existence of tourism-area cycles in tourism development, conflicts about use of land for tourism, and pollution and tourism.

10.2 Tourism destroys tourism and tourist assets

The proposition is often heard that tourism can destroy tourism. Tourism can have an adverse effect on tourism in two ways: (1) crowding from a large number of tourists may reduce the total benefits received from tourism and deter some tourists from visiting an area; (2) tourist visits and facilities to cater for tourists may destroy or partially destroy the assets which attract tourists and reduce the number of tourist visits in the longer term. Consider the crowding case first.

10.2.1 Congestion or crowding and tourism

In the aversion to crowding case, the number of tourist-visitors to an area depends not only on the cost of visiting it but also on the number of other visitors, as well as on the attractions of the area which are taken as a given for this problem. This reflects the possibility that an individual's demand to visit the tourist area is not just a function of the price or cost of a visit but also depends on the number of other visitors likely to be present (Fisher and Krutilla, 1972; McConnell, 1985; McConnell and Sutinen, 1984). If individuals are averse to crowding then, other things equal, their willingness to pay for visits will fall as the number of other visitors increases. The situation is like that for snob goods (Leibenstein, 1950) and can be illustrated by Figure 10.1.

In Figure 10.1, curve ABC is the demand curve of tourists for visiting an area after account is taken of tourist reactions to increased crowding which may come about as the cost of visiting the area is lowered. The demand curve *relative* to any given number of tourist visits can be expected to differ from curve ABC. For example, the demand curve for visits assuming X_B visits per period might be as indicated by the curve marked $d_B d_B$. Assuming X_C visits per period, the demand curve may be as indicated by that marked $d_C d_C$ in Figure 10.1.

In the case shown, total consumers' surplus from visiting the area (indicated by the hatched areas) is smaller when the price per visit is OH than when it is OJ,

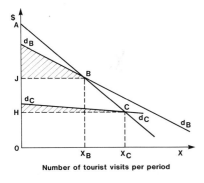

Figure 10.1. A case in which the number of tourist visits to an area is influenced by aversion to crowding.

184

that is when the price of (or cost of) a tourist visit is lowered in this example. While consumers' surplus would increase as the cost of a tourist visit is reduced if the total number of tourist visits did not alter, the number of tourist visits per period do increase. The increased crowding more than negates increased tourist benefits from the lowered cost of visiting in this case.

While for normal economic goods (those not subject to social effects) consumers' surplus rises as the price of the commodity is reduced, this does not necessarily occur in cases where demand is influenced by social effects like the snob effect or aversion to crowding effect in this case. In the aversion to crowding case, tourist or consumers surplus as a function of the price or cost of visit to an area may behave as indicated in Figure 10.2.

In the absence of restrictions on suppliers of facilities to cater for tourists (for example, the supply of accommodation), competition may result in the cost of a tourist visit being P_1 in the case illustrated in Figure 10.2. However, this will not maximise the surplus of tourists nor the surpluses of the tourist industry in the area. A price per visit of P_0 is required to maximise the surplus of tourists and this may also enable the tourist industry in the area to earn a rent or surplus.

The number of visitors to the area can be restricted in a number of different ways, depending on circumstances. For example, if accommodation is essential for tourism in the area, available accommodation can be limited e.g. by imposing a tax on tourist accommodation, restricting the number of construction permits for tourist accommodation, etc. In some cases, fees can be imposed or increased for entry to natural attractions which are the main drawcards for tourists, and thereby directly reduce overcrowding. In some areas, feeder transport to an area can be taxed to limit the number of visitors if this transport is mostly used by tourists and tourists have little alternative.

Note, however, that tourists are not always averse to other tourists. Indeed, in many cases *up to a point* tourists may derive greater satisfaction as a result of the

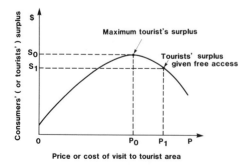

Figure 10.2. As the cost of visiting a tourist area declines, consumers' (tourists') surplus may not increase but decrease. This can occur if there is aversion to crowding because lower costs of a visit will usually bring more visitors.

presence of a greater number of other tourists. This case would be akin to Leibenstein's bandwagon effect (Leibenstein, 1950). Up to a point, tourists react positively to the presence of other tourists and there can be economies of scale in the supply of man-made complementary tourist facilities, all of which will tend to be favourable to greater tourism.

10.2.2 Destruction of tourism resources by visitors

Apart from tourism's adverse impact on tourism through crowding, it can destroy or damage assets which attract tourists (OECD, 1981; Tisdell, 1988). This destruction or deterioration may come about because of the physical impact of tourists on tourist attractions, e.g. wear and tear due to trampling or touching or 'souveniring'. For instance, corals can be damaged by trampling and by the taking of pieces for tourist souvenirs (Viryasiri and Tisdell, 1988). The hand of Michelangelo's statue of St Peter in the Vatican was being worn down, prior to its protection, by constant kissing of it by the faithful and the statue had to be protected by a glass screen to prevent this. Some animals refuse to breed if they are subjected to constant human intrusion. Wildflowers can be trampled under foot, sand and other formations can be denuded due to human trampling and can become subject to erosion. If tourists are involved in the taking of game or fish then, as the number of tourists increase, populations of the species used for recreational hunting, e.g. black marlin for game-fishing, may become endangered or seriously depleted. And we could add to the list of examples.

In addition, man-made *facilities* designed to cater for tourists can destroy tourist environments. These can include airports, roads, hotels and urbanisation resulting from the growth of tourist-based towns or the expansion of existing towns to cater for rising tourist demands. Provision of tourist facilities and the expansion of urban areas to cater for tourists is often at the expense of natural tourist assets. Yet it sometimes is worthwhile sacrificing some natural assets to provide space for other man-made assets which also have a role in attracting tourists. Nevertheless, the trade-off needs to be carefully considered. One should aim for an optimal mixture of assets and not leave the outcome to chance or naked individual self-interest Uncontrolled self-interest is likely to lead to excessive 'development'.

The relationship between the development of tourism, the destruction of tourist assets and the maintenance of tourism can involve many and varied complexities. Not all of these can be modelled here but we can consider a simple model (Cf. Tisdell, 1988a). Assume that the number of tourist visits to an area depends on the price or cost of visiting the area plus the quality of its natural tourist assets. For simplicity imagine that the demand curve for visits to the area is a function *only* of the cost of a visit and is of normal slope. However, suppose that the demand for visits to an area is a function of the quality of its tourist asset and declines as this quality declines. Furthermore, suppose that the quality of the tourist asset is determined by the largest number of visits of any previous period and that any deterioration in the tourist asset is irreversible (hysteresis is present). In addition, assume that complementary man-made facilities must be supplied for tourist visits to the area and that these facilities result in the supply prices (marginal cost of supply) indicated by curve SS in Figure 10.3. This is the marginal cost of supplying 'places' for visitors. Curve ABCD represents aggregate demand for visits to the area *taking account* of deterioration in the tourist asset. The extent of this deterioration depends on maximum number of visits which occur in any period.

Suppose that initially the area is a 'virgin' area for tourism. Initially it is of its highest quality for tourism. Relative to this quality, the demand curve for tourist visits is AFG. Planners may, therefore, believe that it would be socially optimal to build facilities to cater for x_2 tourist visits per period so as to achieve equilibrium at point F. But such planning does not allow for the adverse impact of tourism on the tourist asset. If planners proceed in this way, the quality of the asset will deteriorate. The demand curve will therefore shift downward. The new demand curve corresponding to the new quality of the asset will be HCK.

An avoidable deadweight economic loss indicated by the dotted area occurs if tourist facilities to cater for x_2 tourist visits are provided. Once the quality of the tourist asset is irreversibly reduced and demand curve HCK 'applies', it is socially optimal to reduce tourist facilities to the level which caters for x_0 tourist visits per period of time. Actually, after the deterioration, the new demand curve becomes in effect the kinked demand curve HCD rather than HCK.

Naturally, it would have been better not to have allowed the overexpansion of tourism in the first place. By appropriate planning in the beginning, the tourist area would have been able to sustain x_1 tourists per period and the tourist industry could have attained and sustained the equilibrium at point B. This would have given a socially preferable result, and could have been achieved by not allowing the number of tourist visits (and corresponding facilities to cater for them) to rise

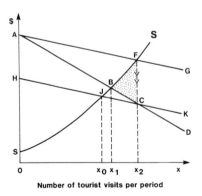

Figure 10.3. Consequences for tourism demand of deterioration of a tourist asset due to tourist visits.

above x_1 in the beginning. In this case, conservation, the community and the tourist industry all suffer if poor planning (or lack of planning) results in initial over-utilisation (non-sustainable use) of tourist assets.

Note that in this case, as in the crowding case (see Figure 10.2 and surrounding discussion), consumers' (tourists') surplus may decline after a point with increased visits, that is with movement along demand curve ABCD. In the above discussion, it is assumed that declining consumers' surplus does not occur for fewer than x_2 visits per period. If declining consumers' surplus occurs after a point with increased visits, this complicates the social optimality decision about tourist loads because it can be socially optimal to limit visits to fewer than those indicated by the intersection of curves SS and ABCD.

The above example is indicative of a wider range of problems. For instance, in some cases, deterioration of tourist assets may be a result of cumulative visits rather than the flow of visits, or may depend on a combination of both.

Interdependence between tourism and the environment may result in an initial large growth in tourism to a new tourist area followed by a slump in tourist visits as the tourist attractions of the area decline in quality due to the deterioration caused by the growth of tourism itself. The basis of this is apparent from the above model. Indeed, a typical cycle of tourism development of this type is claimed to exist (Butler, 1980). Let us consider this type of tourism cycle.

10.3 Tourism-area cycle and more on the dynamics of tourism

Butler (1980) considers that mainly because of the environmental impact of tourist loads, tourist areas in their evolution and development pass through a cycle in terms of the number of visitors to them. He suggests that a typical pattern for the number of tourists visiting an area which to begin with is 'newly discovered' for tourism is like that shown by curve ABC in Figure 10.4. In his model, the turning

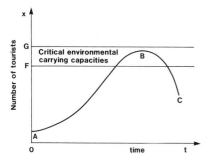

Figure 10.4. Typical tourism-area cycle according to Butler (1980).

point in the number of tourists to a tourist area comes about because the number of tourists to the area exceeds the initial carrying environmental capacities of the area and causes its environmental attractions to deteriorate. In the case shown in Figure 10.4, when the number of tourists visiting an area exceed OF one or more of the initial environmental carrying capacities for the area are assumed to be exceeded. All these carrying capacities are exceeded if the number of visits exceeds OG.

Butler believes that uncontrolled tourist development is usually unsustainable. He suggests that the typical pattern of tourist development is as follows: A new tourist area is discovered by the adventurous, it then becomes a mass tourist destination and subsequently, because the tourist *environment* deteriorates, tourist visits eventually decline. Only by redevelopment can this decline be staved off or avoided by preventing tourism reaching levels within the critical carrying capacity 'zone'.

Butler associates with this cycle a local community-cycle involving the cohesion of the local community and its control over its own affairs and involvement in tourism development. In the early phase of tourism development of an area, the local community is unaffected by tourism, then there is some local community investment and involvement in tourism, until this is displaced by outsider control over tourism development of the area. Only in the stagnation and decline phase of tourism to the area does local community control begin to be reasserted again. Thus, apart from environmental sustainability, community sustainability (see also Chapter 11) is affected by the tourism area cycle.

Butler (1980) draws the following conclusion from his analysis:

'These observations also suggest that a change of attitude is required on the part of those responsible for planning, developing and managing tourist areas. Tourist attractions are not infinite and timeless but should be viewed and treated as finite and possibly non renewable resources. They could then be more carefully protected and preserved. The development of the tourist area could be kept within predetermined capacity limits and its potential competitiveness maintained over a longer period. While the maximum number of people visiting an area at any one time under such arrangements may be less than most present policies of maximum short-term development, more visitors could be catered for in the long-term. In a few localities already, limits to the growth of tourism have been adopted' (Butler, 1980, pp. 11–12).

While some tourist areas may exhibit Butler's cycle, not all exhibit this cycle or some may exhibit a similar cycle for reasons other than those suggested by Butler. While the turning point in his model comes about because tourist numbers exceed certain environmental carrying capacities for the area, considerable difficulty may be encountered in defining carrying capacities in advance and even in principle, as pointed out by Tisdell (1988a).

Furthermore, a tourist area may exhibit a cyclical pattern of tourist visits for reasons other than environmental ones. This pattern may, for example, be related to the product cycle. If a tourist attraction or attractions in an area are *newly* discovered (or developed), a product cycle may occur for normal reasons (Cf. Reekie, 1975, Ch. 4). Once this type of tourist attraction is found to be successful, other areas may be able to open up similar attractions. This gives rise to a product cycle of the type indicated in Figure 10.5. Or the main attraction(s) of the area may be such that most tourists are satisfied by a single visit, e.g. viewing of unusual land formations, unique animals and so on.

In such cases, there may in the beginning be a large/latent number of individuals wishing to visit the area, but once this group has visited, future demand may depend on such factors as population growth and repeat visits which may be few. Existing latent demand may give rise to an initial boom in visits but eventually the number of visits stabilizes in the way indicated in Figure 10.5 by curve ABCD. Note that in both the product-cycle and the single-visit case a cycle has occurred but not because initial environmental carrying capacities have been exceeded. Apart from some natural attractions, new museums and similar man-made attractions often have visitor patterns of the nature shown in Figure 10.5 and repeat visits are heavily dependent on changes in exhibits in such cases.

10.4 Impact of pollution and environmental damage on tourism and benefits from pollution control

Pollution from sources external to the tourism industry, such as other industries, can adversely affect the tourist industry. Both tourists and tourism companies can be damaged. This needs to be taken into account. The extent of the damage to the tourist industry as a whole might be measured by the reduction in producers' surplus plus the reduction in consumer' surplus (Grigalanus et al., 1968; Tisdell,

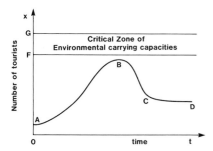

Figure 10.5. Tourism-area cycle not caused by environmental damage due to tourist loads.

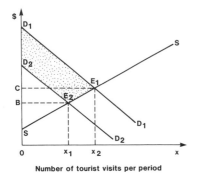

Figure 10.6. Illustrations of loss caused to the tourist industry and to tourists by pollution.

1988b). This can be illustrated by Figure 10.6.

In Figure 10.6, the demand curve for visits to a tourist area in the absence of pollution from sources external to the tourist industry is assumed to be D_1D_1 and the supply curve dictated by facilities assumed necessary for visits is SS. In these circumstances the industry would be in equilibrium at E_1. But suppose that pollution from an external source e.g. water or air pollution, occurs which adversely affects tourism. The demand of tourists to visit the area then declines from the level indicated by curve D_1D_1 to that indicated by curve D_2D_2, and the industry equilibrium shifts from E_1 to E_2. Hence, as a result of pollution, the surplus obtained by tourists and that obtained by suppliers of tourist services (assumed to be necessary for tourist visits) falls in total by an amount equal to the dotted area. The surplus obtained by suppliers of tourist services (necessary for tourist visits) falls by the equivalent of the area of quadrilateral BCE_1E_2.

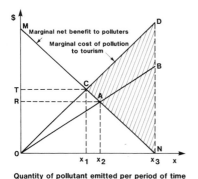

Figure 10.7. A case in which pollution from sources outside the tourism industry imposes external economic costs on tourism in terms of losses in producers' and consumers' surpluses.

If the tourist industry is adversely affected by pollution from other industries this may require their control of the pollution from an economic viewpoint. But it does not necessarily call for the elimination of such pollution. This can be seen from Figure 10.7, assuming that the only external damage caused by polluters is to tourism (Cf. Burrows, Rowley and Owen, 1974).

In Figure 10.7, curve MCN represents the marginal benefits to polluters, e.g. of polluting industries, of their being able to use the environment to dispose of their wastes. Curve OAB represents the marginal loss of profits (surplus) by supplies of tourist services as a result of this pollution. Curve OCD indicates the marginal gains to suppliers just mentioned plus the marginal loss in surpluses by tourists.

In the absence of restrictions on pollution emissions, x_3 units of pollutant will be emitted per period of time and will result in a social loss equivalent to the hatched area. However, applying the Kaldor-Hicks criterion, the socially optimal amount of pollution per period is x_1. This situation could be achieved, for example, by imposing a tax on each unit of pollutant emitted of OT or auctioning pollution rights equal to x_1 units in total. Of course this assumes that tourists and the suppliers of tourist services should count equally (in terms of their financial benefits) in the social decision about pollution control.

If the tourists are foreign tourists and only national gains are to count, it is possible that a social decision will only take account of gains in surplus of suppliers of tourist services. In this case x_2 units of pollution would be optimal. Thus a slightly higher level of pollution would be tolerated, when the interests of tourists per se are ignored.

In some cases, the tourist industry may find it worthwhile overall to undertake expenditure to protect the environment, or this may be worthwhile generally because of gains in the tourism sector. Consider the following case: The crown-of-thorns starfish destroys coral reefs which are important tourist attractions in some

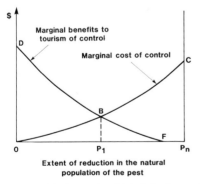

Figure 10.8. A case in which defensive environmental expenditures (on pest control) are economic because of their impact in increasing tourism.

parts of the world, and in some areas their populations appear to have increased. The crown-of-thorns starfish is a pest to the tourist industry. This is considered to be the case on the Great Barrier Reef.

Suppose that the population of this species of pest can be controlled at a cost by human intervention. Let curve OBC in Figure 10.8 represent the marginal cost of reducing the population of the pest to levels below that which it would prevail in the absence of intervention. Let curve DBF represent the marginal economic benefits to tourism of this intervention to control the pest population. The socially optimal level of reduction in the pest population is then P_1. Empirical economic analysis of the control of the crown-of-thorns starfish on the Great Barrier Reef has in fact been undertaken by Hundloe, Vanclay, Carter (1987) and Hundloe and Parslow (1988). Other defensive types of environmental expenditures which benefit tourism can be evaluated in a similar way.

10.5 Conflicts between tourists, variety in tourist areas, public finance issues and national gains

Tourism and recreational activities associated with it are extremely diverse. Different types of tourism and recreational activities can easily result in conflict between individuals or groups undertaking them or planning to do so in the same area. For example, off-road vehicle use may be largely incompatible with the use of a natural area for bushwalking, enjoyment and conservation of visual amenities, etc. Use of an area for boating may be incompatible with its safe use for swimming and so on. Thus mechanisms need to be found to determine the socially optimal pattern of land-use for recreation and tourism. In many cases, zoning has been used as a means to separate relatively incompatible outdoor recreational activities, at least at a localised level, and is a matter worthy of further study (Tisdell and Broadus, 1989).

Another matter worthy of study is the maintenance of adequate or optimal variety of tourist areas. Each tourist area is characterised by a bundle of environmental goods - some natural and some man-made. There seems to be a tendency for areas to become more uniform mainly because of the man-made element (Tisdell, 1987). Whether this is so and optimal needs consideration. Because of neighbourhood effects the pattern of tourism development which occurs naturally or globally may not be optimal (Cf. Mishan, 1967). It may lead to a product (including a built environment) which is excessively standardised from a social point of view.

Because tourism relies on many goods which are of a public or quasi-public nature (as opposed to pure private goods), it is sometimes difficult for governments to appropriate revenue from it. Because of this it is possible for foreign tourists to be left with a considerable surplus. Domestic suppliers of private tourist services may only be able to appropriate a small fraction of the benefits received by foreign visitors from their visit to a country. The government of a country may therefore find it desirable to consider the scope for taxes on foreign tourists (e.g. entry or exit taxes) to help recoup its outlay for tourist infrastructure and/or to increase national economic gains. Complicated public finance issues can be involved (Tisdell, 1984).

10.6 Concluding observations

Tourism can be either the friend or foe of nature conservation. Its role depends on the type of tourism which is being catered for and the nature of the tourism development. Furthermore, as indicated by Butler (1980), local communities which see tourism as a means of economic development, may find that the socio-political dynamics of tourism development results in the local community largely losing control over its own affairs and its cohesion as a social group. In this sense, it may result in unsustainability of the local community. In addition, tourist development may prove to be unsustainable because it results in environmental degradation of assets which attract tourists. Tourism development can be a motive for nature conservation, but sometimes it conflicts with nature conservation. Even when conservation intentions are good, this motivation may not be translated into practice because *supporting* public or social decisions and actions are not or cannot be implemented.

References

Burrows, P., Rowley, C. and Owen, D., 1974. Torrey Canyon: a case study in accidental pollution. Scottish Journal of Political Economy, 21(3):237–258.

Butler, R.W., 1980. The concept of a tourist area cycle of evolution: implications for management of reserves. Canadian Geographer, 24:5–12.

Grigalanus, T.A., Anderson, R.D., Brown, G.M., Congar, J.R., Meade, N.F. and Sorensen, E., 1986. Estimating the cost of oilspills: lessons from the Amoco Cadiz incident. Marine Resource Economics, 2(3)239–262.

Hufbauer, G.C. and Chilas, J.G., 1974. Specialisation by industrial countries: extent and consequences. In: H. Giersch (Editor), The International Division of Labour: Problems and Perspectives. Mohr, Tubingen, pp. 3–38.

Hundloe, T.J. and Parslow, J., 1988. The Crown of Thorns Risk Analysis. Report to the Great Barrier Reef Marine Park Authority. Griffith University, Nathan, Queensland.

Hundloe, T.J., Vanclay, F.M. and Carter, M., 1987. Economic and Socio-economic Impacts of the Crown of Thorns Starfish on the Great Barrier Reef. Report to the Great Barrier Reef Marine Park Authority. Griffith University, Nathan, Queensland.

IUCN, 1980. World Conservation Strategy. World Conservation Union, Gland, Switzerland.

Khan, H., 1986. Marine intensive tourism in ASEAN countries. South East Asian Economic Review, 7:175–206.

Krutilla, J.V. and Fisher, A.D., 1975. The Economics of Natural Environments: Studies in the Valuation of Commodity and Amenity Resources. John Hopkins University Press, Baltimore, for Resources for the Future.

Leibenstein, H., 1950. Bandwagon, snob and Veblen effects in the theory of consumers' demand. Quarterly Journal of Economics, 64:183–207.

McConnell, K.E., 1985. The economics of outdoor recreation. In: A.V. Kneese and J.L. Sweeney (Editors). Handbook of Natural Resource and Energy Economics, Vol.II. Elsevier Science Publishers, Amsterdam, pp. 677–722.

McConnell, K.E. and Sutinen, J.G., 1984. An analysis of congested recreation facilities. Advances in Applied Micro-Economics, 3:9–36.

Mishan, E.J., 1967. Pareto optimality and the law. Oxford Economic Papers, 19:255–287.

OECD, 1981. The Impact of Tourism on the Environment. Organisation for Economic Cooperation and Development, Paris.

Reekie, W.D., 1975. Managerial Economics. Philip Allen, Oxford.

Tisdell, C.A., 1983. Conserving living resources in Third World countries: economic and social issues. The International Journal of Environmental Studies, 22:11–24.

Tisdell, C.A., 1984. Tourism, The Environment, International Trade and Public Economics. ASEAN-Australia Economic Papers No. 6. ASEAN-Australia Joint Research Projects, Kuala Lumpur and Canberra.

Tisdell, C.A., 1987. Tourism, the environment and profit. Economic Analysis and Policy, 17:13–30.

Tisdell, C.A., 1988a. Sustaining and maximising economic gains from tourism based on natural sites: analysis with reference to the Galapagos. In: C.A. Tisdell, C.J. Aislabie and P.J. Stanton (Editors), Economics of Tourism: Case Study and Analysis. Institute of Industrial Economics, University of Newcastle, N.S.W. 2308, Australia, pp. 229–251.

Tisdell, C.A., 1988b. Measuring the costs to tourism of pollution: Analysis and concepts. In: C.A. Tisdell, C.J. Aislabie and P.J. Stanton, Economics of Tourism: Case Study and Analysis. Institute of Industrial Economics, University of Newcastle, N.S.W. 2308, Australia, pp. 253–273.

Tisdell, C.A. and Broadus, J.M., 1989. Policy issues related to the establishment and management of marine reserves. Coastal Management, 17:37–53.

Viryasiri, S. and Tisdell, C.A., 1988. Tourism and the state of the marine environment in Thailand: A case study of marine pollution in Phuket. In: C.A. Tisdell, C.J. Aislabie and P.J. Stanton (Editors), Economics of Tourism: Case Study and Analysis. Institute of Industrial Economics, University of Newcastle, N.S.W. 2308, Australia, pp. 275–286.

Chapter 11

Sustainable development and conservation

11.1 Background

Many conservationists in their quest for increased nature conservation support the goals of sustainable development and ecological sustainability and see both goals as compatible. Sustaining the Biosphere is seen to be a necessary condition for achieving sustainable development. Without sustainable development, it may be impossible to obtain political and grassroots support for conservation. A substantial group of conservationists see both goals as necessary and mutually reinforcing.

In adopting the goal of sustainable (economic) development, conservationists avoid direct confrontation with interests favouring economic growth. In the past, conservationists, on the whole, obtained a reputation for being opposed to all economic change and development. So caste in a negative role, they had little chance to influence economic growth and development decisions in a way more sensitive to environmental needs. The changed emphasis of most conservationists which began possibly with the World Conservation Strategy (IUCN, 1980) provides more scope for fruitful interaction between groups interested in economic development.

The theme of sustainable development has become of increasing policy interest since the early 1970s. Its importance was recognised at the UN Conference on the Environment and Development in Stockholm in 1972, and will be followed up by a UN conference on the same theme in Brasilia in 1992. The World Conservation Strategy (IUCN, 1980) made sustainable development its central theme. The World Commission on Environment and Development (WCED, 1987) in its report *Our Common Future* (1987) argued that global sustainable development is desirable and achievable, and that conservation and economic growth can be compatible. This United Nations' Commission, chaired by Gro Bruntdland, former Prime Minister of Norway, argued that if global sustainable development is to be achieved, account must be taken of both ecological and economic factors. It further claims that conservation goals can only be achieved in less developed countries if they experience significant economic growth and some further economic growth in more developed countries may also be necessary.

The World Institute of Development Economics Research (WIDER) of the United Nations University (Helsinki) has researched this possibility. This research will be discussed in the next chapter. The *draft* of the proposed successor to the World Conservation Strategy document (IUCN, 1980), *Caring for the World: A Strategy for Sustainability* (IUCN-UNEP-WWF, 1990), like its predecessor, emphasises the interdependence of conservation and development and the need to maintain Earth's stock of natural capital. Economic and social as well as ecological requirements for sustainability are examined in the updated proposed formulation of the World Conservation Strategy. Increasingly sustainability is being adopted as a desirable goal by policy-makers at both international and national level. But unfortunately, the concept is not always clearly defined. A variety of definitions and meanings of sustainability are possible. This in itself is not a problem. It is only a problem when the term is used loosely.

Rational pursuit of sustainability, global or otherwise, is only possible if we know what sustainability is or, more exactly, if we know what we want to sustain and in what respect. Many individuals now claim that they favour sustainability, the attainment of a sustainable society or the achievement of sustainable development. On closer examination it is often found that they want to sustain different things. Some wish to promote and sustain close-knit caring (local) communities, some want to sustain the economic welfare of future generations, some want to ensure that the human species is sustained for the longest span of time possible and others wish primarily to sustain biodiversity. These are not exactly the same goals even though the means to achieve them may well run parallel up to a point.

It is worthwhile systematically considering some of the major existing concepts of sustainability and of sustainable development. The basic concepts which it is useful to discuss are (1) the maintenance of intergenerational economic welfare (2) maintenance of existence of the human species for as long as possible (3) sustainability of production and economic systems in terms of their resilience and other properties (4) sustainability of community and (5) maintenance of biodiversity.

A hallmark of most contemporary proponents of sustainable development is their emphasis on the need to conserve natural resources and natural environments as a means towards achieving their goals. Many take the view that existing institutions, including market mechanisms, are likely in the absence of pro-conservation directives or economic incentives to conserve natural resources and environments inadequately, thereby making for non-sustainable development.

11.2 Sustaining intergenerational economic welfare

The view that current generations have on ethical responsibility to sustain the economic and environmental welfare of future economic and environmental welfare of future generations appears to be increasingly accepted. But this view has not always been accepted, particularly the view that natural resources are an inheritance held on trust by present generations for future generations. For example, the natural resource economist, Scott (1955, p. 3) was unsympathetic to this point of view.

Tietenberg (1988, p. 33) claims that 'the *sustainability criterion* suggests, that at a minimum, future generations should be left no worse off than current generations'. In broad terms, this amounts to saying that the actions of present generations in using resources should not reduce the standard of living of future generations below that of present generations. The ethical basis of this is often taken to be John Rawls' (1977) principle of justice. Given that every individual could have been born into the situation of any other, and that everyone in a hypothetical original position involving 'a veil of ignorance' would be uncertain of when and in what situation they would be born, they would it is argued opt for equality of 'income' unless inequality was to the advantage of all. Thus it would be fair or just to honour this hypothetical original contract.

However, once one adopts Rawls' principle one must not only apply it between generations but also within them for it also implies that a similar degree of equality is just between existing individuals. In particular it would seem to imply on a global scale that much larger income transfers should be made from developed to less developed nations than those taking place now or likely to take place in the foreseeable future. Indeed, we appear to have the irony at present that resource transfers from less developed nations exceed those in the opposite direction, and the developed nations are reducing their aid to the Third World.

Somewhat weaker equity rules between individuals now and in the future are also espoused. They are that the *basic* needs of all should be met because of the *chance* circumstances we all face or may face. In essence all should be assured a *minimum* standard of living, without standards of living being necessarily made equal. The World Commission on Environment and Development (1987, p. 43) states that 'sustainable development is development that meets the needs of the present without compromising the ability of future generations to meet their own needs'. The import of this statement depends upon how one interprets the term 'needs' but if it implies basic needs then this is similar to the view just outlined. The Commission goes on to say that overriding priority should be given to the concept of 'needs', in particular the essential needs of the world's poor and that full account should be taken of the influence of the state of the environment on the ability to meet present and future needs.

Pearce, Markandya and Barbier (1989, p. 2) express a similar point of view stating that 'sustainable development places emphasis on providing for the needs of the least advantaged in society ('intragenerational equity'), and a fair treatment of future generations ('intergenerational equity')'. They suggest as a general principle that '*future generations should be compensated for reductions in the endowments of resources brought about by the actions of present generations*' (Pearce, Markandya and Barbier, 1989, p. 3). Capital endowments by present generations are seen as one possible means of compensation and human capital endowment such as increases in scientific and technological knowledge are seen as particularly attractive bequests.

A number of critical observations can be made about the application of Rawls' theory of justice in this context. These include the following:

(1) Should only human beings count (as is the case in Rawlsian applications) in determining what is just? If we could have been born as any other individual could we not have been born as any other living thing, say an animal of some type? In other words, what is the appropriate universe of possibilities to consider? Could also, for example, an Australian have been born an Indian? What difference does it make to the application of Rawls' theory if one believes in reincarnation as do many Buddhists and Hindus? Given these points the Rawlsian principle of justice is not unassailable in its strict form (Tisdell, 1990b). If the possibility is accepted that a human being might have been born as any living thing this would seem to establish on the Rawlsian approach some ethical responsibility for caring for other living things.

(2) The number of individuals who will be born in the future is uncertain but it is partially under the control of present generations. This of course raises a practical difficulty for determining the size of the appropriate bequest for future generations. It also means that we face the difficulty that future population sizes are not uncontrolled variables. If we are scrupulous about observing the logic of Rawls, we should ask what are the wishes or desires of those who could have been born but were not. If any of us could have also been in that position what would we have opted for? Would we have chosen to live if we were provided with at least bare subsistence? Optimal human population policy is not effectively addressed by the approach of Rawls and of those environmental economists following his line.

(3) Rawls may overemphasise the role of chance rather than choice in our lives. Chance appears to be made dominant in his theory but arguably in our life we also have some choice, including in the amount of effort to expend on various goals. Thus his principle tends to de-emphasise reward for effort (Cf. Tisdell, 1982, pp. 416,417).

On a somewhat different point, the idea that man-made capital can be a suitable compensatory bequest for future generations is appealing to proponents of economic growth. But such capital formation may hasten environmental deterioration and may disappear itself long before the natural resources which produced it would have. Man-made physical capital is relatively impermanent whereas natural living resources such as forests and species have in normal circumstances much longer periods of longevity.

We need to be cautious about the view that man-made capital is (always) an adequate substitute for natural capital or resource stock. Unlike biological resources, it is not *naturally* reproductive and self-sustaining. Its continuing productivity generally requires continuing effort by man, and after a time its replacement by new capital. While capital in the form of knowledge (intellectual capital) is not intrinsically subject to depreciation its transmission, preservation and its retention by individuals requires investment in education and means for storing it. So its preservation is by no means automatically assured.

The view is sometimes expressed that it is justifiable to deplete natural resources if the benefits are transformed into human or man-made capital. There can be little doubt that the economic growth of many developed countries has depended on such a transformation. Without man-made accumulation of capital, it is doubtful whether developed countries could have achieved the standards of living which they now enjoy and their considerable surpluses which have been available for further capital accumulation, education and advancement of knowledge. But globally such policies hasten natural resource depletion and they may be based upon false expectations about the magnitude of continuing technological progress. It may be complacently believed that technological progress will overcome all growing natural resource constraints and environmental problems. But this is faith rather than fact (Tisdell, 1990b).

In its most naive form it assumes that science will be able to perform miracles. One needs to be dubious about the view that nothing is impossible to science as far as environmental change is concerned. No simple technological or scientific fix seems to be on the horizon for restoring the ozone layer to its original state or for quickly neutralising rising carbon dioxide levels in the atmosphere, even though science seems to have pinpointed the main causes of such environmental change.

From the point of view of sustaining income, it is definitely better to transform any gains obtained from realising natural resource stock into man-made capital rather than consume these. However, such transformation does not *necessarily* ensure higher or more sustainable income than say could be obtained by depending on the maximum yield of the natural resource stock. There is always the danger that the decision to transform living natural resource stock into man-made capital may be made without fully evaluating the benefits received from the natural resource stock, especially spillover benefits. There may also be a natural bias in favour of man-made capital because the owners of this may be able to appropriate a larger share of the gains from it than from natural resource stock.

11.3 Survival of the human species for as long as possible

A rather different view of sustainability has been proposed by economists such as Hermann Daly (1980) and Georgescu-Roegen (1971, 1976). They suggest that our basic goal should be to ensure the survival of the human species for as long as is possible – in Daly's words, as long as is compatible with God's will. These are still essentially man-centred approaches but differ from the above cases in relation to objectives (Tisdell, 1988). Daly suggests that our basic aim should be to ensure that the maximum number of people live in the maximum time span for which it is possible for the human species to survive. He suggests *in practice* that this involves zero population growth, restrictions on the rate of use of non-renewable resources and restricting consumption per head to a minimum acceptable level. In his view, this will result in a sustainable society.

Georgescu-Roegen (1976), on the other hand, while favouring restricted per capita consumption, argues that human population should be reduced to that level which can be supported by the use of renewable resources alone. This, in his view, provides the best chance for the human species to survive for as long as is possible given the inexorable working of the Law of Entropy. Thus Georgescu-Roegen has taken the concept of sustainability to an extreme.

The difference between the position of Georgescu-Roegen and Daly can be illustrated by Figure 11.1. The Doomsday scenario of the Club of Rome is also indicated for comparative purposes. The maximum possible span of existence of the human species is assumed to be until period t_n. In practice of course this is unknown. The basic Club of Rome scenario is represented by curve ABCD. After exponential growth, the system collapses at point t_1 well before the end of the maximum possible length of existence of the human species. In the case shown, the collapse is sudden and catastrophic. But of course it could be less sudden with the same end-effect, namely premature extinction of the human species.

Daly suggests that if a steady-state economic path of DEF is followed this will enable survival of the species for the longest period and ensure the maximum number of human-beings will have existed. However, Georgescu-Roegen (given that A represents the existing global population and level of economic production) believes that this is already too large to ensure that the human species can be maintained for the maximum period possible. In his view, it will not be possible to keep to this path. For example, at time t_2 adjustment may already be forced on the system and it may become obligatory to follow the broken path EJG which leads to premature extinction of the human species at time t_3. Georgescu-Roegen argues that if the human species is to survive as long as possible, the current levels of population and production must be reduced to levels which can be supported solely by the sustainable yield from renewable resources. Allowing for lags in population adjustment, a Georgescu-Roegen population/economic path might look like curve AHKJ.

An additional scenario could also be shown namely that suggested by Kahn et al., (1976). This envisages world population increasing and then stabilising automatically. Continual rises in per capita income are made possible by continuing technological progress and investment. It is a relatively optimistic scenario which projects the past experiences of the developed countries to the global scene. The ultimate solution to the world's environmental problem is seen to be more economic growth especially in developing countries in the near future. The Kahn et al., (1976) scenario suggests that no special action is required to ensure global economic and environmental sustainability. Sustainable economic development will occur 'naturally' or because of forces already present in society.

It might be noted that none of the above approaches make particular allowances for the 'rights' of other species and in that respect they are similar to the economic approach discussed in the previous section. It is, however, true that Hermann Daly (1980) suggests that Christians have some duty of care for other living things, even if this is not a major duty. Nevertheless, the approaches of Daly and Georgescu-Roegen on the whole avoid the open-endedness or fundamental indeterminacy of Rawlsian-based approaches. For example, Daly's approach is relatively clear on its population objective. Nevertheless, Daly's objective may not appeal to us all.

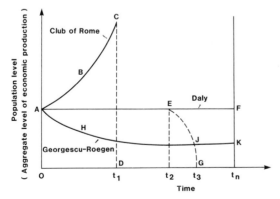

Figure 11.1. Some alternative views of the relationship between population levels, economic activity levels and the length of existence of the human species.

11.4 Issues raised by the views of Daly and Georgescu-Roegen about sustainability

The views of Daly and Georgescu-Roegen bring a number of important issues to the fore. In particular they highlight the importance of carefully distinguishing between objectives and the effectiveness of alternative means for attaining these objectives. Sustainability is not an end in itself as presumably is not the establishment of sustainable systems. Sustainability is presumably a part of some other goal and the establishment of sustainable systems is a means towards some ultimate end.

Consideration of the views of Daly and Georgescu-Roegen suggest that any one of the following might be objectives in relation to human existence:

(1) Maximise the number of people to live (at some minimum acceptable standard of living).

(2) Maximise the number of people to live (at some minimum standard of living) *subject* to the span of survival of the human species being maximised.

(3) Maximise the number of people to live but at a much higher standard of living than a minimum acceptable one.

(4) As in (3) but subject to the span of human existence being maximised.

(5) Any of the above but subject to some constraints in favour of the continuing existence of other species and/or their continued evolution.

Given any of the above objectives the question then becomes one of what is the best means to achieve it. Daly, for example, suggests that objectives (1) and (2) are likely to be achieved by zero growth of both current population and aggregate economic production. Georgescu-Roegen disagrees with this view suggesting that it will not achieve these objectives. He believes that the maximum span of human existence will only be achieved by reducing population and aggregate economic activity levels to those which can be sustained by renewable resources alone.

But if the maximum span of existence of the human species is finite, this would result in a stock of untapped non-renewable resources at the time of the extinction of the species. Little point would seem to be served in not using at least some of the stock of available non-renewable resources. Some of these resources may be subject to natural entropy even if they are not used by Man. Furthermore low levels of use of non-renewable resources are unlikely to lead to unacceptable levels of pollution since the Biosphere may be able to absorb and neutralise moderate amounts of waste. Again, the mining of non-renewable resources need not lead to an unacceptable reduction in stocks of natural renewable resources. In addition, a policy of humans relying only on sustainable yields from renewable resources may mean considerable competition between Man and other species. An economy in which there is greater reliance on the use of non-renewable resources *would* be more favourable to the survival of other species. Few species other than Man make use of *concentrations* of non-renewable resources. But *massive* reliance on use of non-renewable resources could pose a major threat to other species, e.g. via global pollution, or by providing means for over-exploiting renewable resources.

A number of further issues need to be considered. Even if one agrees that the human species should not be prematurely brought to an end by Man's own actions, it is not clear that maximising the number of humans who will live (at an acceptable income level) is necessarily a desirable objective. Some may prefer to have fewer humans at a higher standard of living or to have fewer individuals and less aggregate consumption by humans than the maximum sustainable in order to ensure greater biodiversity or survival of other species.

Figure 11.2 helps highlight some of the issues taking an extremely simplified situation. Let us suppose that any level of aggregate consumption (production) by humans on or below curve Q_3Q_3 is sustainable. The population and per capita income levels corresponding to curve Q_3Q_3 are the maximum sustainable ones. Suppose further that the maximum acceptable (or possible) income level per head is OE and that the safe minimum standard of the human population is OA. Then lines OD and EG act as constraints in the problem and the optimal situation will occur in the triangular figure BDG. The solution proposed by Daly would correspond to point G, that of Georgescu-Roegen will be below curve Q_3Q_3. If the objective is to maximise the income per head of those who live but yet ensure the

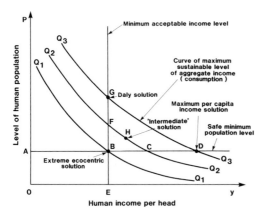

Figure 11.2. Alternative sustainable economic solutions depend on objectives which in turn depend on ethics.

sustainability of the human species, the optimum solution will correspond to point D. The human population level is only sufficient in that case to meet the safe minimum standard for survival of the human species. Intermediate positions on Q_3Q_3 are of course possible depending upon the nature of the anthropocentric preferences being expressed.

But it is possible that preferences for survival include those for sustaining biodiversity. Assume that the lower is the aggregate level of consumption by humans the greater is biodiversity. As one moves to lower Q-curves in Figure 11.2, there is an increase in the number of other species surviving and in principle this could be quantified. Those holding a very strong ecocentric view (wishing to ensure maximum biodiversity) would find the combination at B to be optimal. This implies a minimum acceptable income per capita and a human population no greater than that needed to ensure the survival of the human species. Depending upon 'ethical' preferences other possibilities also exist. For example, intermediate position such as that corresponding to H might be optimal for those who are prepared to make *some* trade-off for biodiversity and hold a more moderate view on the desirable population/income per head mix.

Of course, the problem is much more complicated than this in practice. For example, production relationships are not included in the model. In fact the achievable aggregate production level is assumed to be independent of the level of population for the sustainable possibilities under consideration. Because labour is an input in production this is unlikely to be so in practice. It may also be that increased per capita human income could up to a point be favourable to greater biodiversity. Nevertheless, the simple model highlights possible conflicts between objectives as far as sustainability and human existence are concerned.

11.5 Resilience of production and economic systems and stationarity of their attributes

Some thinkers such as Conway (1987) and Barbier (1987) have looked upon the sustainability of systems as their resilience, that is, their ability to recover when subjected to shocks. This is an interesting and useful concept which may have parallels with the concept of stability of equilibria (Tisdell, 1988). It is also discussed by Redclift (1987). As the amount of biodiversity is reduced, as variety of all types is reduced in the world and as the environment is degraded by economic processes, economic activity may become less resilient when subjected to environmental and other shocks. Thus desirable production and economic states may no longer be sustainable in the long-term given the possibilities of stresses on the system or shocks to it. Systems may become subject to jumps and irreversibilities (Tisdell, 1990a). The issues involved are worth continuing study and are of considerable relevance to modern environmental conditions.

Sustainability as the resilience of systems has already been discussed in Chapter 9 where it was pointed out that the degree of sustainability of a system or its nature may be described by a variety of attributes. This suggests that it may be desirable to develop a variety of measures or indicators of the sustainability of systems.

The systems which were discussed in Chapter 9 relied on natural mechanisms to ensure sustainability or stability. In a world of human intervention, human beings often rely on their own purposive intervention as a means to direct or ensure the sustainability of 'natural or modified' systems. The scope for human intervention depends upon the policy options available or the degree of flexibility available in the system for human influence. By conserving stocks of natural resources, it is often possible to retain flexibility or options for future action and therefore give scope for greater sustainability of systems via human intervention.

Note also that increased knowledge can be a means to greater sustainability through human intervention. It increases the *known* means of influencing systems and therefore *could* be used to make them more sustainable. But discretionary human intervention *depending upon its nature* can be a stabilising or destabilising influence on environmental systems.

The degree of stationarity of returns or benefits from a system over time is also taken as an indicator of sustainability. (See Chapters 2 and 10 for further discussion in that respect.) If, for example, two alternative economic or productive systems are being considered and if system 1 has a flow of net benefits indicated by curve ABC and system 2 that indicated by DBE, system 1 shown more sustainability than system 2 because it is stationary.

Traditionally in economics, the optimal system is chosen by comparing the net present value of the alternatives and choosing the system with the highest net present value. The higher the rate of interest used for discounting purposes the more likely is system 2 to be preferred to system 1 using this rule. As is well known, considerable debate has occurred about the appropriate (social) interest rate to apply. Some economists have even argued that a zero rate of interest is the

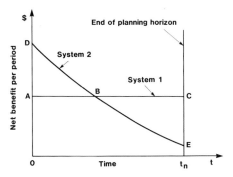

Figure 11.3. Two production or economic systems with different degrees of sustainability.

appropriate rate of interest to apply in making social choices. If the sum of the flow of benefits from system 2 exceeds that from system 1 when a zero rate of interest is used, should system 1 nevertheless be chosen because of its sustainability property? Why? To what extent is it desirable to trade-off other benefits for greater sustainability? Proponents of sustainability need to clarify their position in this respect.

11.6 Cost-benefit analysis and sustainability

The net present value method of evaluation and choice just considered is essentially the same as that adopted in cost-benefit analysis (CBA). But where CBA is being used for social choices, net benefits should be evaluated in a social context and take account of any externalities or spillovers arising from the adoption of particular systems. Yet social cost-benefit analysis (SCBA) or extended CBA is not entirely adequate as a means of social choice. It suffers from conceptual and practical limitation.

Full application of the method requires all benefits and costs to be expressed in monetary terms or, at least, all except a 'negligible part'. While there is greater scope for monetary measures than is often realised, such measurement is not always possible especially when uncertainties are great. Also estimated benefits, apart from depending on knowledge, vary with the concept and approach to their evaluation, e.g. willingness to pay versus willingness to accept compensation.

Extended CBA, which takes account of the environmental and social impacts of economic projects, can be expected to lead to superior social decisions and to greater environmental sustainability than those decisions which would be made in the absence of such considerations. Nevertheless, reliance on this technique alone for social decision-making is inadequate. Apart from the fact that its mechanical use may not be effective in settling social conflict, its partial nature may result in the influence of economic and other aggregates being overlooked or ignored. Thus, for example, with rising populations and levels of aggregate consumption, a deteriorating environmental situation can be expected even if extended CBA is widely applied. In fact, those who support its application as *the* answer to our environmental ills would seem to be guilty of a major disservice to the community by promoting such a false view.

Pearce et al. (1989, pp. 127–29) have suggested that traditional SCBA or extended CBA might have sustainability integrated into it. They propose that cost-benefit decisions be subject to a constraint or requirement that for the group of projects undertaken by an economic decision-maker 'environmental damage (i.e. natural capital depreciation) should be zero or negative'.

But a problem for this approach is how to measure natural capital depreciation. Furthermore, should the above requirement be imposed on every economic decision-maker and if so how will it be policed? If some decision-makers only undertake projects which have a positive environmental effect or which on balance add to the stock of natural resources, should they be permitted to trade their environmental 'surplus' with other economic agents whose array of projects would show an environmental deficit?

This supplemented form of extended CBA adopts the comprehensive rational approach (choice-theoretic approach) to decision-making. This rationalistic approach to sustainability and decision-making has been criticised from at least two sources: (1) by those favouring the approach of a safe minimum standard for conservation of natural resources and (2) by those urging decision-making within an evolutionary framework which recognises explicitly that individuals are bounded in their rationality.

Ciriacy-Wantrup (1968) and Bishop (1978, 1979) argue that (economic) sustainability requires the application of a safe minimum standard in the preservation of species. They reject conventional CBA approaches to environmental risk and uncertainty arguing that these fail to capture the essential nature of the uncertainties involved in environmental change (Chisholm, 1988; Tisdell, 1990c). Presumably, sustainability supplemented CBA would also need to come to grips with this issue.

Evolutionary economists recognise the essential uncertainties involved in social development and changes. Metcalfe (Metcalfe and Gibbons, 1989; Metcalfe and Boden, 1990) and Schumacher (1973) apply an evolutionary economics approach in their thought (See also Gowdy, 1983). The models of evolutionary economists tend to emphasise the value of diversity both in order to keep options open and as means of extending knowledge. Social, economic, technological and production changes are seen as being to a considerable extent the ongoing result of a large number of experiments. They are the result of knowledge obtained by trial-and-error. Such change is often the outcome of different 'experiments' conducted by different people. Evolutionary economics suggests that we cannot identify a unique optimal solution for development in advance.

Humans, in undertaking economic development, are essentially engaged in a discovery process. We may never discover *the* optimal solution but a fortiori we are unlikely to know it in advance. This has a number of policy implications, only some of which can be touched on here. For example, it suggests that constitutional structures and mechanisms need to be designed to assist the experimentation and search process, and encourage the 'appropriate' degree of diversity. Since one does not know what will be the best answer in advance, flexibility must be retained in the system so as to enable optimal adjustment to the information obtained as results unfold and extra information is obtained. It pays to retain flexibility or options in this type of world even at some cost.

The evolutionary approach may provide a more realistic view of the world than the rational comprehensive ideal. It provides an additional reason for erring in favour of conservation of living resources.

11.7 Sustainability of community

A number of writers have emphasised the importance of sustaining communities in the process of development. This was already apparent in the previous chapter when the tourism-area cycle was discussed. Sustainability of community is a complex concept favoured in particular by some 'alternative life-style' groups. For most of its proponents it implies amongst other things full participation of individuals in the social-political systems of the community, a fair distribution of income and co-operation with nature rather than domination of it (Douglass, 1984; Alauddin and Tisdell, 1988). Social structures which take power away from local communities, such as multinational corporations or large corporations with headquarters in distant places or big centralised governments, are seen as a threat to a sustainable economic order in harmony with nature (Cf. Tisdell, 1983, 1989).

In general this view tends to favour small communities, appropriate small scale technology and production units and has much in common with Gandhi's view of the appropriate economic order (Cf.Schumacher, 1973, pp. 29,30). Schumacher (1973) argues strongly in favour of small scale economic operations and small communities.

Schumacher (1973, pp. 31,32) claims that 'although even small communities are sometimes guilty of causing serious erosion, generally as a result of ignorance, this is trifling in comparison with the devastations caused by gigantic groups motivated by greed, envy and lust for power. It is moreover obvious that men organised in small units will take better care of *their* bit of land or other natural resources than anonymous companies or megalomaniac governments which pretend to themselves that the whole universe is their legitimate quarry'.

Schumacher also argues that small production units are likely to be superior from an evolutionary economic point of view and humanly more satisfying. Whether this is so could be debated. Smallness in itself does not imply variety and one can imagine some small production units involving harsh working conditions. Equally one can imagine larger units with the same unfortunate qualities.

A number of supporters of community sustainability have been critical of the application of Green Revolution technologies to agriculture in Third World countries. '.. Alternative agriculturalists and others have developed evidence that the patterns of land tenure, market structure, and government policies found in many developing countries favour large land owners at the expense of peasants in the harvest of benefits from the new seed – fertiliser innovations and this fact, they contend, is yet again destabilising to rural communities' (Douglass, 1984, pp. 19–20).

11.8 Sustaining biodiversity

Biodiversity can have economic benefits as, for example, has been pointed out in Chapters 5 and 9. The selfish economic interests of Mankind as a whole require some degree of biodiversity to be preserved. Even though we do not know the exact degree of biodiversity which is likely to be optimal, we know that biodiversity has proven valuable in the past and we can expect it to have economic value in the future. As biodiversity is reduced by effects from human economic activity, the costs of *not* sustaining the remaining degree of biodiversity may rise. As the gene pool becomes smaller, the value of each diverse living unit may become higher.

A few individuals have argued that it is necessary to save all species from extinction since the existence of each species depends upon the existence of every other. This implies that if one species is removed, all will eventually disappear in a chain reaction of extinctions. But as Randall (1986) points out, if this is so, the extinction of all species is now inevitable and the only choice might be to alter the speed or pattern of the disappearance of the various species. Clearly it would not be in the economic self-interest of Man to set in motion a force which led to the extinction of all species because *Homo sapiens* would become extinct also. However, there does not seem to be any evidence to suggest that the existence of all species is as closely interlinked as suggested by this extreme instrumentalist position. On the other hand, there is no doubt that chains of extinction of species can occur and it is not always obvious in advance just where and how far the chain of extinction will extend when a single species disappears.

There are reasons for wanting to preserve biodiversity which go beyond economic man-centred benefits. Passmore (1974), for example, points out that it is increasingly accepted that Mankind has a 'stewardship' role in relation to nature and that therefore there are ethical reasons for wanting to sustain biodiversity. Many ecologists and conservationists believe that Nature has a right to exist independently of the wishes of Mankind. Possibly Aldo Leopold is representative of this group which desires basically to sustain Nature in its diversity.

Aldo Leopold (1933, 1966) sees Man as a part of a holistic organic community in which Man has no right to exterminate a part of it. His 'land ethic' was developed in opposition to the view that Nature should be manipulated or exterminated to satisfy the narrow economic interests of Man. It might be noted that prior to adopting this philosophy, Leopold was involved in USDA campaigns to control mammalian pests for economic reasons. Possibly the land ethic will gain ground, at least in modified form. Humanity is likely to come to accept increasing responsibility for Nature, and do so not merely for man-centred ends or purposes. Even within this framework, there would be a role for economics as has already been indicated in this book.

Note that sustaining biodiversity for ethical reasons may be in *conflict* with man-centred approaches to sustainability as can be seen from Figure 11.2. Some human economic sacrifice may be necessary to sustain a very wide range of biodiversity. For example, it may be necessary to accept lower per capita standards of living or smaller levels of populations of humans than would be sustainable. While parallelism between greater biodiversity and sustainable economic development can be expected up to a point, beyond a point these goals may be in conflict.

11.9 Concluding remarks

Table 11.1 lists the different sustainability objectives which have been discussed in this chapter. It can be seen at a glance that there is a diversity of such objectives. In fact the diversity is even greater than is apparent because aims in relation to each of the broad objectives mentioned often differ. Also doubts have been expressed about the extent to which these objectives can be realised by the application of traditional rational comprehensive (or choice-theoretic) methods. So there are a variety of possible approaches to trying to achieve sustainability objectives.

Some of the early proponents of sustainability and of sustainable development have now become wary of these concepts because they feel that these concepts have become vague and debased in popular use, or because confusion has resulted from the use of multiple concepts. But to dismiss these concepts for these reasons would be premature. A multiplicity of concepts might even be regarded as a bonus provided they are defined and appropriately identified. Multiplicity of concepts provides scope for expanding knowledge in different directions.

Already, discussions of sustainability by economists have advanced our understanding of the world in several respects. Existing institutional mechanisms, including market mechanisms, for resource allocation have been found to be wanting from the point of view of economic sustainability in one or more of its forms.

Another advance closely connected with the sustainability mode of thought is the development of environmental or natural resource accounting. This accounting involves the modification of national income accounts (which were developed principally with the needs of Keynesian economics in mind) so as to provide a

TABLE 11.1
A list of different sustainability objectives

1.	Sustaining intergenerational economic welfare (of humans).
2.	Ensuring survival of the human species for as long as possible.
3.	Seeking resilience in production and economic systems and/or stationarity of their attributes.
4.	Ensuring sustainability of community.
5.	Sustaining biodiversity.

measure of sustainable income (see, for example, Pearce, Markandya and Barbier, 1989, Ch. 4), and/or to indicate national welfare more accurately, even if still crudely.

From the previous discussion it is clear that human population growth and the level of economic consumption per head are critical factors affecting the possibility of sustainable development. However, they are not the only major influences. Technological change and positive policies for environmental improvement also have a role in determining the prospects for sustainable development. These factors and the prospects for sustainable development are discussed in the next chapter.

References

Alauddin, M. and Tisdell, C., 1988. New agricultural technology and sustainable food production: Bangladesh's achievements, predicaments and prospects. In: C.A. Tisdell and P. Maitra (Editors), Technological Change, Development and the Environment: Socio-Economic Perspectives. Routledge, London, pp. 35–62.

Barbier, E.B., 1987. The concept of sustainable economic development. Environmental Conservation, 14(2):101–110.

Bishop, R.C., 1978. Endangered species and uncertainty: the economics of a safe minimum standard. American Journal of Agricultural Economics, 60:10–18.

Bishop, R.C., 1979. Endangered species and uncertainty: a reply. American Journal of Agricultural Economics, 61:376–379.

Chisholm, A.H., 1988. Sustainable resource use and development: uncertainty, irreversibility and rational choice. In: C.A. Tisdell and P. Maitra (Editors), Technological Change, Development and the Environment: Socio-Economic Perspectives. Routledge, London, pp. 188–216.

Ciriacy-Wantrup, S.V., 1978. Resource Conservation: Economics and Policies (3rd Edition). Division of Agricultural Science, University of California, Berkeley, C.A.

Conway, G.R., 1987. The perspectives of agroecosystems. Agricultural Systems, 24:95–117.

Daly, H., 1980. Economics, Ecology and Ethics: Essays Towards a Steady-state Economy. Freeman, San Francisco.

Douglass, G.K., 1984. The meanings of agricultural sustainability. In: G.K. Douglass (Editor), Agricultural Sustainability in a Changing World Order. Westview Press, Boulder, Colorado, pp. 3–99

Georgescu-Roegen, N., 1971. The Entropy Law and the Economic Process. Harvard University Press, Cambridge, Mass.

Georgescu-Roegen, N., 1976. Energy and Economic Myths: Institutional and Analytical Economic Essays. Pergamon Press, New York.

Gowdy, J.M., 1983. Biological analogies in economics: a comment. Journal of Post Keynesian Economics, 5(4):676–678.

IUCN, 1980. World Conservation Strategy. IUCN, Gland, Switzerland.

IUCN-UNEP-WWF, 1990. Caring for the world: A Strategy for Sustainability. Second draft, IUCN, Gland, Switzerland.

Kahn, H., Brown, W. and Martel, L., 1976. The Next 200 Years: A Scenario for America and the World. William Morrow, New York.

212

Metcalfe, J.S. and Boden, M., 1990. Strategy, paradigm and evolutionary change (roneod) PREST, University of Manchester. Paper presented at a workshop 'Processes of Knowledge Accumulation and the Formulation of Technology Strategy'. Zealand, Denmark, 20-23 May, 1990.

Metcalfe, J.S. and Gibbons, M., 1989. Technology, variety and organisation. In: R. Rosenbloom and R. Burgleman (Editors), Research in Technological Innovation, Management and Policy, JAI Press.

Passmore, J.A., 1974. Man's Responsibility for Nature – Ecological Problems and Western Traditions. Duckworth, London.

Pearce, D., Markandya, A., and Barbier, E.B., 1989. Blueprint for a Green Economy. Earthscan Publications, London.

Randall, A., 1986. Human preferences, economics and the preservation of species. In: B.G. Gordon (Editor), The Preservation of Species: The Value of Biological Diversity. Princeton University Press, Princeton, NJ, pp. 79–109.

Rawls, J.R., 1971. A Theory of Justice, Harvard University Press. Cambridge, Mass.

Redclift, M., 1987. Sustainable Development: Exploring the Contradictions. Methuen, London.

Schumacher, E.F., 1973. Small is Beautiful: A Study of Economics as if People Mattered. Blond and Briggs, London.

Scott, A.D., 1955. Natural Resources and the Economics of Conservation. University of Toronto Press, Toronto, Canada.

Tietenberg, T., 1988. Environmental and Natural Resource Economics, 2nd Edition. Scott, Foresman and Company, Glenview, Illinois.

Tisdell, C.A., 1982. Microeconomics of Markets. Wiley, Brisbane.

Tisdell, C.A., 1983. Conserving living resources in Third World countries. International Journal of Environmental Studies, 22:11–24.

Tisdell, C.A., 1988. Sustainable development: differing perspectives of ecologists and economists, and their relevance to LDCs. World Development, 16(3):373–384.

Tisdell, C.A., 1989. Environmental conservation: economics, ecology and ethics. Environmental Conservation, 16(2):107–112, 162.

Tisdell, C.A., 1990a. Ecological Economics and the Environmental Future. Discussion Paper in Economics No. 28, Department of Economics, University of Queensland, Australia 4072, April 1990. Revised version to be in J. Burnett and N. Polunin (Editors), Surviving with the Biosphere. Edinburgh University Press, forthcoming.

Tisdell, C.A., 1990b. Natural Resources, Growth and Development: Economics, Ecology, and Resource-Scarcity. Praeger, New York.

Tisdell, C.A., 1990c. Economics and the debate about preservation of species, crop varieties and genetic diversity. Ecological Economics, 2:77–90.

World Commission on Environment and Development, 1987. Our Common Future. Oxford University Press, Oxford.

Chapter 12

Population, development and prospects for environmental sustainability: a concluding perspective

12.1 Introduction

Our Common Future (WCED, 1987) pointed out that we live in an interdependent world in which economic, ecological, environmental, demographic, political and social issues cannot be meaningfully compartmentalised when policies and prospects for sustainable development are being considered. All these factors interact and determine the prospects for sustainable development and for environmental sustainability.

It is appropriate here to consider the prospects for environmentally sustainable development given global population projections, the economic growth aspirations of nations especially of less developed nations, the resources needed to attain these objectives and the available financing for their supply. The World Institute for Development Economics Research (WIDER) of the United Nations University at Helsinki has developed an empirically based model to address such issues (Jayawardena, 1990). This will be critically discussed and the prospects for funding a global 'sustainable development' strategy will be considered. In conclusion, some stumbling blocks at the national and international level to achieving environmental sustainability will be noted.

12.2 Global population levels, characteristics and projections

We cannot be exactly sure of the size of the world's population. But in 1990 it was around 5.3 billion having more than doubled from an estimated 2.3 billion in 1950. In the 35 years from 1990, it is still expected to increase substantially in absolute terms but its rate of growth is expected to decline. Indeed, the absolute amount of growth predicted by the United Nations is 3.2 billion, the same amount as in the previous 35 years. This will bring the world's population to 8.5 billion in 2025 if there is no special intervention or unforseen change from trends.

This United Nations' estimate (quoted by Jayawardena, 1990) is based upon the assumption of naturally declining population growth rates. The current average growth rate of global population of 1.74 per cent annually is assumed to be maintained until 2000, declining thereafter to 0.98 per cent in 2025.

World Bank (1990) estimates are rather similar. For reporting countries, world population was estimated to be 4.7 billion in 1988 and projected to rise to 5.8 billion in 2000 and then to increase to slightly over 8 billion in 2025. But these figures do not include estimates for the USSR and a few socialist and other non-reporting countries. When these are added, the 1988 figure rises to over 5 billion and, of course, all the projected figures have to be correspondingly increased to give a world estimate. When this is done the results are comparable to the UN estimates.

On the other hand, Myers et al. (1990) suggest that by 2030 the level of the world's population could be over 10 billion and that the *absolute* growth in human population in the next few decades could be greater than has seen in recent decades. The exact figures are not material. What is clear is that on either estimate a massive increase in human population can be expected in the next few decades. This will come on top of the massive global increase which has already been responsible for serious environmental degradation. For the world as a whole, the problem is likely to be even greater than in the recent past, even though slowing population growth rates provide some hope for the very long term.

As was indicated in an earlier chapter, most of this population growth will occur in today's less developed countries. At least 3 billion of the United Nations' predicted increase of 3.2 billion in world population between 1990 and 2025 is predicted to occur in present less developed countries, that is, almost 94 per cent of the total increase. Many of these countries already have a serious over population problem. Thus, indications are that this is likely to get worse in the absence of an *aggressive* population control policy. Even with an aggressive population control policy, the world's population is still expected to reach 7.6 billion 35 years hence, reaching 8 billion in 2050 (Jayawardena, 1990, p.12). Thus, even with an aggressive population control program, there is little prospect of the world achieving zero population growth before the middle of the 21st Century, and the possibility of population decrease appears to be much further off.

12.3 Environmental consequences of population growth and economics

It is difficult to see how further significant environmental damage can be avoided given these population projections. While policy actions can be taken which will ameliorate these effects and those of further economic growth, it is uncertain whether they can or will be completely counteracted. WIDER seems reasonably confident that it would be *possible* to counteract the environmental effects of such developments but is less confident that the appropriate political action will be taken. The WIDER position will be considered below.

The areas in which projected global population increase will be concentrated is environmentally significant. As pointed out above, most of the increase is expected to occur in today's less developed countries. Currently, around 80 per cent of the world's population lives in poor- and middle-income countries. By 2025, these countries are projected to contain around 90 per cent of the world's population. The global population increase will mainly occur in tropical areas - areas subject to considerable natural climatic variation. In such areas, population increase would seem more risky environmentally than in the temperate areas where most developed countries are located. While adverse environmental effects did result from the population and economic growth in today's high income countries, these environmental impacts possibly were, it can be argued, smaller than they would have been if these countries had been located in the tropics. For example, the natural degree of biodiversity in tropical areas is much greater than in the temperate zones, so one might expect greater loss of biodiversity from economic growth in the tropics compared to that in temperate areas, all other things equal.

Norman Myers, Paul Ehrlich and Anne Ehrlich (1990) have pointed out that less developed nations can be expected to become the biggest single source of global pollution within the next 40 years. This is primarily because of the considerable increase expected in their already large populations, their rising income aspirations and the likelihood that they will increasingly adopt technologies from the West (e.g. equipment using carbon-based fuel) which are globally more damaging than indigenous technologies.

Ehrlich (1989) argues that the adverse environmental impact to be expected from population increases in less developed countries is considerable because it is likely to be combined with environmentally damaging increases in consumption per head as well as new investment (capital formation) using technology more damaging to the environment than that used earlier in such countries. His ('heuristic') formula is

$$I = P.A.T$$

when I is adverse environmental impact, P is population and T represents the use of environmentally damaging technology. He argues that these factors interact in a multiplicative way, i.e. together their effects are compounded (Ehrlich, et al., 1989; Ehrlich and Ehrlich, 1990).

Myers et al. (1990, p. 5) state that this equation 'makes clear why developing nations with big populations, albeit with little economic advancement, can generate an enormous impact on the planetary ecosystem, i.e. because the P multiplier on the A and T factors is so large: consider the vast repercussions that stem from coal burning or CFC manufacture in e.g. China or India'. They go on to point out that controlling increases in greenhouse gas emissions from industrial expansion in China or India is going to be a major problem even though the agriculture of these countries can be expected to be affected seriously by the greenhouse effect. Soon the population of these two nations will comprise almost two-fifths of humanity. Myers, et al., conclude that control of greenhouse emissions cannot be achieved without extremely stringent population controls.

The Ehrlich (1989) formula is relatively crude and it is difficult to measure the technology component of it. An alternative formula might be

$$I = hP.kA.(mK_1 + nK_2)$$

where h, k, m and n are coefficients and K_1 and K_2 represent man-made capital stock which, for simplicity, has been divided in two types – K_1 which has, say, a larger adverse environmental effect than K_2 (m > n). The other symbols have the same interpretation as before. 'Development' may result in K_1 increasing at a faster rate than K_2 or at the expense of K_2. With 'economic development' it is also *possible* that the coefficients h and k trend upwards. All these developments would be environmentally adverse.

However, there is another class of expenditure or investment which should be added to the adverse environmental impact formula to provide balance. This is expenditure or investment which is environmentally beneficial or defensive. Let us represent this by D. Then the basic functional relationship

$$I = g(P_1 A, K_1, K_2, D)$$

where $\dfrac{\partial I}{\partial D} < 0.$

WIDER, in order to deal with the environmental problem of economic growth, concentrates on the scope for defensive environmental expenditures, as well as the scope for reducing population growth and technology spillover coefficients such as m and n above by purposive expenditure. Let us consider the WIDER approach (Jayawardena, 1990).

12.4 Global sustainable development objectives as formulated by WIDER

The Brundtland Report (WCED, 1987), while aware of the possible (likely) adverse environmental consequences of global economic growth, was optimistic about the possibility of finding policies to combine global aspirations for economic growth with the maintenance of global environmental quality. The World Institute for Development Economics Research (WIDER) of the United Nations University, was asked to investigate this possibility in depth.

WIDER was of the opinion that the socially necessary growth rate for GDP in the developing world during the decade beginning 1990 would be 5.5 per cent per annum, which would be an increased growth rate compared to the average growth rate experienced by these countries during 1980–89 which was 4.3 per cent. This growth rate target was felt socially necessary:

(1) to catch up on basic needs in the areas of health, education and poverty alleviation, etc.,

(2) to reduce the level of unemployment in LDCs, and

(3) to provide scope for improving the distribution of income.

However, because of *linkages* between the growth rate in the developing world and than in developed countries, an increased growth rate in the developed world is seen as necessary to accommodate the target growth rate for developing countries. WIDER suggests that a 3.5 – 4 per cent growth rate in developed countries in needed. But this is seen as only possible if there is a significant increase in investment in developed countries and this will require these countries to increase their domestic savings rates (Jayawardena, 1990, p. 23). Thus, the objective of achieving faster GDP growth rates in the less developed world will require faster growth rates in the developed world.

In addition to achieving these growth rates, WIDER assumed that it would be important to sustain the quality of the environment. For these purposes it used the estimates of the Worldwatch Institute of necessary expenditures to sustain environmental quality (Jayawardena, 1990; Brown, et al., 1988). These include estimates for raising energy efficiency, developing renewable energy, reforesting the Earth, protecting topsoil on cropland from erosion, and for means to slow population growth, e.g. through family planning services, education and health improvements and financial incentives. Over an eleven-year period these environmentally defensive measures were estimated to cost US$1.071 trillion of which US$648 billion would be needed to be spent in developing countries and US$423 billion in developed countries. Preliminary similar estimates of required expenditure for protecting the environment are also given in the draft of *Caring for the World: A Strategy for Sustainability* (IUCN-UNEP-WWF, 1990, p. 135).

Whether expenditures of the amount suggested would be sufficient to ensure that environmental quality is maintained at its current level is uncertain. For example, will the suggested expenditure on energy research achieve the increases in energy efficiency and renewable-energy development envisaged? Are the measures likely to be sufficient to preserve biodiversity?

In terms of the earlier discussion based on the extended Ehrlich formula, these measures are intended to *slow* population growth, change the technology-mix so environmental spillovers are reduced and result in positive environmental actions (and increase in D) such as treeplanting and soil erosion measures to counteract environmental degradation.

12.5 Can the sustainable development targets be achieved and are they likely to be achieved in practice?

After investigating the matter, WIDER concluded that this Earth has the resources (capacity) to achieve the sustainable development targets discussed above and WIDER indicated economic means to achieve these.

To carry out the sustainable development program, it was estimated that developing countries would require foreign savings for financing the strategy starting at US$60 billion in 1990 and rising to US$142 billion for the year 2000. The funding for this could easily be met, in WIDER's view, by the supply of funds which would be released by US defence disengagement in Europe, that is, from the 'peace dividend' as a result of improved relations between the superpowers.

Taking account of both the needs of the developing countries for economic growth, required complementary economic growth in developed countries and environmentally protective expenditures indicated above, WIDER estimates that commencing at a much lower amount in 1990 the amount of extra expenditures needed for sustainable development would rise at the outside to US$300 million annually for 2000.

In recent years, the world's defence expenditure has been around $US1 trillion annually. In 1987, for example, it was estimated to be just under $US one trillion (World Bank, 1990, p. 17). While most of that expenditure was by the NATO and Warsaw Pact countries, US$173 billion was spent by developing countries. What is clear is that this defence expenditure is several times greater than the financial expenditure estimated to be necessary for sustainable development as described above. Only a portion of defence funds would need to be diverted to satisfy the sustainable development goals outlined above. Indeed, it seems that if the developing countries were to forgo defence expenditure entirely that they would, as a whole, have sufficient funds to achieve their targets for sustainable development.

But what are the political prospects of diverting funds from defence expenditure to support sustainable development? While the accord between Western countries, the Soviet Union and China may provide hope for arms reduction and for cuts in defence expenditure, developed countries have not yet resolved to divert funds to developing countries for the purpose of attaining sustainable development. In fact, official aid to developing countries appears to be declining and, in recent years, there has been a net outflow of capital from developing countries.

Possible problems which could stand in the way of this diversion of funds from developed to less developed countries for sustainable development are:

(1) Differences of opinion about the relative contribution which should be made by the different developed countries. This involves the free-rider problem, as well as differences in opinion about the extent to which the developed countries should be responsible for the sustainable development problems being encountered by developing countries.

(2) Differences of opinion about how 'authentic' or threatening global environmental problems are and the extent to which economic developments in developing countries are likely to impact adversely on developed countries.

(3) Concerns about how such transfers will affect the relative economic and military power positions of the different nations.

In any case, a start had *not* been made at the end of 1990 on the WIDER strategy for sustainable development. A similar strategy is being proposed in the *draft* document *Caring for the World: A Strategy for Sustainability* (IUCN, UNEP, WWF, 1990) with required funding assumed to commence in 1991. However, there do not seem to be any immediate global plans to provide the necessary funding. Whether or not definite funding commitments will emerge to reflect global sustainable development as a result of the UN Conference on the Environment and Development to be held in Brasilia in 1992 remains to be seen.
While many individuals feel confident that the underdeveloped world can follow a similar development path to that experienced by developed countries, this is far from clear. There is a real risk that economic growth and population growth in the currently less developed world on the scale required for catching-up with the developed world will cause global environmental thresholds to be exceeded (e.g., those related to the greenhouse effect) or result in significant depletion of natural resources before per capita incomes in LDCs rise sufficiently to stabilise population levels. Consequently environmental barriers and natural resource depletion could thwart attempts of the Third World to make the necessary development breakthrough. The attempt *could* end in catastrophe given current predictions about the greenhouse effect for example.

12.6 Concluding remarks

The availability of economic means to address our environmental problems and to increase the likelihood of sustainable development being achieved does not mean that these measures will necessarily be adopted. Political, constitutional and other obstacles including the quest for power and the pursuit of individual selfishness may block the application of such measures.

Even though individuals may realise that collectively particular actions and collective decisions are necessary, they may, on the grounds of self interest, try to avoid being bound individually by the collective decisions. For example, *if it* were agreed that reductions in per capita consumption and income per head in developed countries are necessary for global environmental reasons, there would still be the question of how to enforce the reduction in income and share it. Voluntary restraint is unlikely to work. Would shorter hours of work be the answer? Should the available hours of work be more widely distributed so that those currently unemployed in developed countries have a greater opportunity to share in the available work? Or should the nature of work be altered so as to include more activities that are less demanding of natural resources e.g. service industries? The WIDER approach (Jayawardena, 1990) assumes that no reduction in per capita income is necessary and indeed, following the position of the Brundtland Report (WCED, 1987), accepts that rising per capita incomes in developing countries are necessary and indirectly so too are rising per capita incomes in developed countries.

Rather than shorter hours of work, some see the solution to the environmental problem as one of encouraging the growth of industries which are environmentally less damaging and more sustainable than many traditional industries. Knowledge-intensive industries and many of the service industries, such as the entertainment industries and the arts, may be of this nature, whereas heavy industries, such as steel, are not. Appropriate tax and other economic incentives could bring about such restructuring. But, to be effective globally, these measures need to be implemented globally. Otherwise, measures in one country may merely force 'dirty' industries offshore. The global impacts of dirty industries forced offshore could well be just as great as if they remained at home. Indeed, they may even have greater impact if greater pollution is tolerated offshore.

Given the growing global interdependence of countries, both economically and ecologically, we need increasingly to address issues on a global basis. While the United Nations provides a vehicle for this, it is not yet a world parliament but rather a collection of representatives of independent national states. It is not yet a satisfactory body for world governance. This would seem to require that people, rather than nations, should be represented and that existing nations forgo some of their sovereign rights. In any case, our growing global ecological interdependence must make us think more seriously about suitable structures for world government. The implementation of many global economic measures for environmental control may require such a government and effective world government may mean an end to large worldwide defence expenditures, thereby making it easier to secure funds for sustainable development.

If we cannot come to terms soon with one another about our common global environmental problems, there is little doubt that we may all reap a bitter harvest. There has been progress in addressing environmental issues since the First United Nations Conference on the Environment and Development in 1972. Nevertheless, only the first step, so to speak, has been taken. There is no global agreed strategy in place as yet for sustainable development, and political resolve has not yet emerged to embark on such a strategy and fund it adequately and resolutely. We can therefore only hope that many of the current environmental predictions, such as those about greenhouse effects, will prove to be wrong or, if this is a false hope, that a sudden change of attitude or of heart by most of humanity to international co-operation and government occurs soon.

References

Brown, L.R., et al., 1988. State of the World 1988: A Worldwatch Institute Report on Progress Towards a Sustainable Society. Norton, New York.

Ehrlich, P.R., 1989. Facing the habitability crisis. Bioscience, 39:480–482.

Ehrlich, P.R., Daily, G.C., Ehrlich, A.H., Matson, P. and Vitousek, P., 1989. Global Change and Carrying Capacity: Implications for Life on Earth. Stanford Institute for Population and Resource Studies. Stanford, California.

Ehrlich P.R. and Ehrlich, A.H., 1990. The Population Explosion. Simon and Schuster, New York.

IUCN-UNEP-WWF, 1990. Caring for the World: A Strategy for Sustainability, Second Draft. IUCN, Gland, Switzerland.

Jayawardena, L., 1990. The mission of the university in economic development and environmental preservation: management of local and regional resources in an independent world system. A Paper presented to the Ninth General Conference of the International Association of Universities, Helsinki, August, 1990. Mimeo. World Institute for Development Economics Research, United Nations University, Helsinki.

Myers, N., Ehrlich, P.R. and Ehrlich, A., 1990. The population problem: as explosive as ever? A paper presented at the Fourth International Conference on the Environmental Future: Surviving with the Biosphere, Budapest, April, 1990. To be in J. Barnett and N. Polunin (Editors), Surviving with the Biosphere, Edinburgh University Press, Edinburgh.

World Bank, 1990. World Development Report 1990. Oxford University Press, New York.

WCED (World Commission on Environment and Development), 1987. Our Common Future. Oxford University Press, New York.

Subject Index

224

232